Counseling Hispanics Through
Loss, Grief, and Bereavement

Ligia M. Houben, MA, FT, FAAGC, CPC, is a Fellow in Thanatology: Death, Dying, and Bereavement and a Fellow of the American Academy of Grief Counseling. She holds a BA in Psychology and Religious Studies from the University of Miami, an MA in Religious Studies, and Graduate Certificates in Multidisciplinary Gerontology from Florida International University and in Loss and Healing from St. Thomas University. Her work has been centered in the area of grief and loss, expanding into meaning and growth, and she is the founder of My Meaningful Life, LLC. Houben has delivered her message to audiences from corporations, educational institutions, and health care organizations and has appeared on numerous radio and television programs airing on networks such as CNN Español, NPR, NBC, and Univisión.

Ms. Houben has lectured on a variety of topics regarding life transitions, such as grief, loss, and transformation, and aging and spirituality. A pioneer in working with Hispanics and grief, Houben contributed to the creation of the first bereavement support group in her native country of Nicaragua—PUDE, an anagram for *Personas Unidas en el Dolor y la Esperanza* (People United by Grief and Hope). This group has implemented The Eleven Principles of Transformation™, a system created by Houben that addresses the emotional, spiritual, and cognitive aspects of individuals facing a transition or loss. This system was originally introduced in her self-help book *Transform Your Loss: Your Guide to Strength and Hope,* and is presented in this book, too.

Ms. Houben is an adjunct professor at Florida International University, Miami Dade College, and Kaplan University, where she teaches courses on ethics, religion, and death and dying. She offers consulting services to individuals and organizations; her private practice is based in Miami, Florida.

Counseling Hispanics Through Loss, Grief, and Bereavement

A *Guide for* Mental Health Professionals

Ligia M. Houben, MA, FT, FAAGC, CPC

SPRINGER PUBLISHING COMPANY

NEW YORK

Copyright © 2012 Springer Publishing Company, LLC All rights reserved.

No part of this publication may be reproduced, stored in a retrieval system, or transmitted in any form or by any means, electronic, mechanical, photocopying, recording, or otherwise, without the prior permission of Springer Publishing Company, LLC, or authorization through payment of the appropriate fees to the Copyright Clearance Center, Inc., 222 Rosewood Drive, Danvers, MA 01923, 978-750-8400, fax 978-646-8600, info@copyright.com or on the web at www.copyright.com.

Springer Publishing Company, LLC
11 West 42nd Street
New York, NY 10036
www.springerpub.com

Acquisitions Editor: Sheri W. Sussman
Composition: S4Carlisle Publishing Services

ISBN: 978-0-8261-2555-2
E-book ISBN: 978-0-8261-2556-9
Ancillary ISBN: 978-0-8261-9562-3

11 12 13 14 15/ 5 4 3 2 1

Transcriptions of the complete interviews excerpted in this volume are available online at springerpub.com/houben

The author and the publisher of this work have made every effort to use sources believed to be reliable to provide information that is accurate and compatible with the standards generally accepted at the time of publication. Because medical science is continually advancing, our knowledge base continues to expand. Therefore, as new information becomes available, changes in procedures become necessary. We recommend that the readers always consult current research and specific institutional policies before performing any clinical procedure. The author and publisher shall not be liable for any special, consequential, or exemplary damages resulting, in whole or in part, from the readers' use of, or reliance on, the information contained in this book. The publisher has no responsibility for the persistence or accuracy of URLs for external or third-party Internet Web sites referred to in this publication and does not guarantee that any content on such Web sites is, or will remain, accurate or appropriate.

Library of Congress Cataloging-in-Publication Data

Martinez-Houben, Ligia.
A holistic approach to counseling Hispanics through loss, grief, and bereavement : a guide for mental health professionals / Ligia M. Houben.
p.; cm.
Includes bibliographical references and index.
ISBN 978-0-8261-2555-2 (alk. paper) -- ISBN 978-0-8261-2556-9 (e-book) 1. Grief therapy. 2. Bereavement. 3. Loss (Psychology) 4. Hispanic Americans--Counseling of. I. Title.
[DNLM: 1. Counseling--methods--United States. 2. Hispanic Americans--psychology--United States. 3. Attitude to Death--ethnology--United States. 4. Cultural Characteristics--United States. 5. Cultural Competency--United States. 6. Grief--United States. WA 305 AA1]
RC455.4.L67M37 2011
155.9'37--dc23
                          2011028078

Special discounts on bulk quantities of our books are available to corporations, professional associations, pharmaceutical companies, health care organization, and other qualifying groups.

If you are interested in a custom book, including chapters from more than one of our titles, we can provide that service as well.

For details, please contact:
Special Sales Department, Springer Publishing Company, LLC
11 West 42nd Street, 15th Floor, New York, NY 10036-8002
Phone: 877-687-7476 or 212-431-4370; Fax: 212-941-7842
Email: sales@springerpub.com

Printed in the United States of America by Gasch Printing

This book is dedicated, with all my love, to the Hispanic community living in the United States and to the wonderful people who are interested in learning more about our values, traditions, and hardships as we face transitions or losses. The purpose of this book is to serve as a guide for increased awareness of the needs of diverse Hispanic groups, with the hope that it becomes easier to offer a caring and helpful hand. It is also dedicated in a special way to my daughter Dianita, so that she can learn more about her Hispanic roots.

Contents

Foreword

I was personally delighted and honored when Ligia Houben requested that I write the foreword to her book *Counseling Hispanics Through Loss, Grief, and Bereavement*. There were a few reasons that this book excited me. For my 30 years at the Graduate School at The College of New Rochelle, I have not only taught courses related to thanatology but also a regular offering on Counseling the Culturally Diverse. The goal of that course is essential to counseling—to train counselors sensitive to cultural diversity. In teaching about cultural diversity, one cannot help but bemoan the fact that there is a scarcity of resources that actually address the ways that diverse populations deal with grief and loss. Hence Houben's *Counseling Hispanics Through Loss, Grief, and Bereavement* fills a needed void.

It is especially needed for two major reasons. First, the Hispanic/Latino population is growing—now representing one of the fastest growing populations in the United States. It is national in dispersion. Virtually every community—rural, suburban, and urban, North, South, East, or West— has Hispanic/Latino communities. Second, it is a diverse community— different in many ways. As Houben is so careful to acknowledge, Hispanics come from many diverse countries that, even as they share common languages and core values, have different histories and distinct cultures. Racially, Hispanics may vary from White to Black. There are class distinctions and differences in levels of acculturation. Counselors then need to be able to assess these differences and be sensitive to the nuances implied by this diversity. Houben offers tools and insights to enable counselors to engage effectively the diversity in that community.

There also is a personal reason for my pleasure. While the surname Doka suggests that my father came from Eastern Europe—Hungary—many may be unaware that my mother's maiden name was Martín. As Houben notes, given the common Hispanic value of *familismo*, I tend to culturally identify as Hispanic. We saw my father's relatives on holidays and special occasions such as weddings. We lived amongst my mother's family. It was a rare weekend that the extended family did not come together. The family continues that heritage as my son's wife is an Alvarez. This brings another cautionary note to counselors. One should never assume the cultural identity of a client. Who would identify "Doka" with Hispanic culture?

So Houben's book is a valued resource for counselors. *Counseling Hispanics Through Loss, Grief, and Bereavement* is a book that all counselors should have on their bookshelves. Wise to the culture, Houben is sensitive to the particular issues that might arise in counseling. Two are illustrative. One value that Houben addresses is *personalismo*—or the value placed on personal relationships. The implication here is that counselors may have to self-disclose. Hispanic clients want to know not only that a counselor is competent but also who they are as individuals. Counseling can take place only in such a context.

Machismo is another oft misunderstood value. Outside of the culture, *machismo* is generally identified as an exaggerated masculinity—often with a sexual double standard. Yet, within Hispanic culture, this value has more layered meanings. There it means being a good man—however that is defined in a specific culture. To be *machismo* means that one fulfills responsibilities—being a good provider, an attentive husband, a caring father. Houben notes that this value can motivate counseling rather than being an impediment to help seeking.

In short, *Counseling Hispanics Through Loss, Grief, and Bereavement* is an extremely timely and welcome addition to the literature in thanatology. Counselors will find in it the tools, knowledge, and insights to respond to a growing and diverse Hispanic community as individuals cope with loss and grief.

Kenneth J. Doka, PhD
Professor, The College of New Rochelle
Senior Consultant, The Hospice Foundation of America

Preface

Facing a loss is never easy, no matter who you are, how old you are, or where you live. It doesn't make a difference what religion you follow or what culture or group you belong to; grief can be challenging and disorienting. It can shake you up like few other life experiences. It also prompts you to call upon all of the support and resources around you. The Hispanic/Latino population has the fastest growth in the United States (Gracia, 2008), and there has been a concomitant increased interest in its traditions, customs, and values. When one explores this culture and its members within the context of this book, one must take into consideration the many meanings of loss based on Hispanics' history (individually and cross-culturally) and the impact losses have on their lives. As a Hispanic myself, and having experienced some of the losses I discuss in this book, I feel it is my moral obligation to talk about the complex nature of loss that occurs in the lives of many Hispanics as they move to the United States.

WHY DO YOU NEED THIS BOOK, AND HOW CAN IT HELP?

Grief is not limited to particular group of individuals; loss is a universal experience. However, the way grief is expressed is greatly influenced by individual traditions and values. Despite the extensive literature on grief and loss, there is a tremendous scarcity of research on Hispanic culture and how Hispanics' traditions and values influence their grieving process and quality of life. More information is needed so that mental health professionals can effectively counsel Hispanics. This book will give readers the information they need regarding customs and mannerisms, and provide insights into the way numerous Hispanics express and process their grief.

WHAT ARE THE PREMISES OF THIS BOOK?

I am writing this book for the following individuals:

- Those who are interested in the Hispanic culture and want to expand their knowledge about the types of losses Hispanics experience when living in the United States.
- Those who work with this population and have had trouble in understanding some of their traditions, their ways of expressing emotions, or their belief system.
- Those who want to offer a better system of care to this group of people based on its needs, rather than the counselor's own.
- Those who want to embrace diversity in their practice.
- Those who want to offer clients their best support in times of grief and loss.

Taking into consideration the reality of many Hispanics, I believe the following:

- They are not aware of the many losses they may be experiencing and therefore do not look for counseling.
- They are used to relying on their family system to process grief.
- They experience a sense of alienation when compared with mainstream culture.
- They need to develop more trust in the counseling and social service systems and this can happen only if they feel valued and understood.
- They need to process their multiple losses to embrace the culture and find more meaning in their lives.

Rather than writing a textbook based solely on clinical research, I have chosen to offer a more intimate approach. The information presented, although it includes valuable information from reliable sources, is built on my personal experience with loss as a Hispanic and my clinical experience as a grief counselor and thanatologist. Case studies are included to give readers the opportunity to enter the subjective world of the grieving person and to learn the tools to be utilized to provide the best care. The cases or stories come from different sources and have been edited to some extent to make them fit the frame of this volume (transcriptions of the complete interviews from which these stories have been extracted are available as a digital appendix). Some are from my clients, others are from friends, relatives, students, or just people I talk with on the street who have shared their situation with me. I have come to realize that more and more people have a need to be heard and to share their story.

HOW THIS BOOK STARTED

For several years I have presented a seminar, "Understanding How Latinos Experience Grief and Loss," at various organizations and hospitals. In response to this seminar, many professionals working with the Hispanic population would ask me about the most salient elements embedded in this culture and how they can understand their Hispanic clients' worldview when they are facing loss and grief. Thus, the idea of writing a book about counseling grieving Hispanics emerged, and I did not hesitate to embrace such a meaningful journey. Over a decade ago, when I decided to embark on the study of thanatology, I did not realize there was such a difference between how cultures experience death and dying and other losses. Despite having lived all my childhood and adolescence in Latin America and having experienced the death of my father at the early age of 12, I never knew there were other ways of mourning or expressing grief. It was not until I took a class on death and dying at the University of Miami (in Florida), where I did my undergraduate work, that I realized that grief from such a universal experience as death can be expressed and processed in so many ways.

As Rebecca M. Cuevas de Caissie stated in her article, "Hispanic Cultural Values Family" (2009), "There are a certain set of values in the Hispanic community that sets us apart" (http://www.bellaonline.com/articles/art31982.asp). I agree with her observation because there are some common threads that are vital elements to our culture and constitute a bond among all Latinos. For this reason, having a better understanding of this culture, in combination with your empathy, skills, and desire to help as a counselor, can help make a difference in the life of a bereaved Hispanic.

When a person is not part of the mainstream society, dealing with a major loss becomes even more difficult. The ongoing effort to adjust and adapt to a different culture is challenging enough, but when such people come face to face with their loss, they may find themselves encountering new kinds of frustration and disappointment as they seek supportive and understanding help.

In addition, it is of great importance to realize that for many Hispanics the sources of strength when dealing with loss are their family and their religious beliefs. In Latin American countries, grief counseling is not common. People are generally reluctant to talk to strangers about their personal issues, especially about the death of a loved one. It is only now that persons of our culture are opening up to counseling and bereavement support groups, which can make the grieving process more manageable and meaningful. In recent times, I have regularly traveled to Nicaragua to facilitate seminars on grief and its manifestations and the value of bereavement support groups. My purpose has been to educate people on issues that have been taboo in our society. The interest in such seminars has grown exponentially, to the point that the first bereavement support group, called PUDE (*Personas Unidas en el Dolor y la Esperanza* [People United by Grief and Hope]), was born. This group formed because Orali Flores Altamirano, a bereaved mother who attended my seminar, was inspired by her love for her daughter, Albalicia, who died in a car accident. This mother's experience has shown us that grief can move us toward using unlimited resources that were likely heretofore unknown to us. The parents who created PUDE are an example of growth and transformation in dealing with loss, which is the focus of my approach to the grieving process.

THE PURPOSE OF THIS BOOK

The aim of this book is to help counselors and other helping professionals who work with Hispanics to become more skilled in understanding the perspective of this population and how to implement the tools that can help them establish and develop valuable interactions with their Hispanic clients. My main goal is to raise more awareness about the multiple losses Hispanics face, the role their values and traditions play in how they cope with these losses, and the resources available to help counselors provide the best care in a holistic manner. Because Hispanics comprise a heterogeneous population, this book provides not a strict set of rules for working with them but valuable information that can bring readers a broader understanding of what this culture is about. Keep in mind that, as human beings, we have our own history, beliefs, and values, and although these values are influenced by our cultural heritage, they are also influenced by many external and internal factors.

Although all Hispanics speak Spanish, not all of them share the same religious beliefs and traditions. People who assume that the members of this population are all the same run the risk of stereotyping. Not all Hispanics are the same. Each of us is a unique individual with our own experiences and history, and if we embrace a multicultural perspective, we can grow as human beings and as a society. As Gary R. Howard (2006) expressed it,

> Growth in multicultural awareness is possible.
> Growth in multicultural awareness is desirable.
> Multicultural growth can be observed and assessed.
> Multicultural growth can be stimulated and promoted. (p. 102)

Before a mental health practitioner can thoroughly help a grieving person, they must have some understanding of the client's worldview. In doing so, they must take into consideration the characteristics of the client's cultural heritage, social norms or mores, religious beliefs, and ways of communicating. All of these are covered in Part I of this book. One of the most valuable components of a meaningful and successful relationship between the helper and the client is the *intention* of the helper, which, according to Clara Hill and Karen M. O'Brien (1999), includes what the helper knows about the client and how he or she can integrate this knowledge to accomplish his or her goals in the helping process. People who work in the helping professions need to be aware of their own feelings and perceptions. Therefore, at the end of each chapter I have included questions that allow the reader to assimilate the information in a more natural and encompassing manner.

WHAT THIS BOOK DOES
AND DOES NOT OFFER

The majority of books about Hispanics or Latinos focus on their culture, immigration, or a sociopolitical perspective. This volume, although it takes these issues into consideration, will expand its focus to include the worldview of this group of people as they face different life transitions and explore underlying issues of grief and loss that may not necessarily be recognized at first glance. I present several theoretical concepts on grief work and how to apply them based on the history of the individual. I also introduce my approach to helping the client move beyond loss, *The Eleven Principles of Transformation*. This system, which ultimately intends to empower the bereaved to live with meaning and purpose, may be adopted by the grief counselor or any other helping professional who is able to work with the client through a certain period of time, ideally for a period of 11 weeks.

I hope that this book will be a useful and valuable resource. What this book cannot offer is a complete understanding of everything related to Hispanics and their losses. As Egan (1994) stated, "All truth about helping cannot be found in one book" (p. 15). It is impossible to include everything related to Latinos in just one volume. What I do offer is an overall picture of this diverse and multifaceted culture, with an emphasis on the most salient customs and traditions embedded within it. This view provides a useful framework that integrates the principles for helping a person facing grief, loss, and bereavement.

HOW THIS BOOK IS ORGANIZED

The book is divided into three main sections, with a variety of tools included, such as questions and exercises for the reader, interviews, and case studies. Part I covers the sociocultural aspects of Hispanic culture, including Hispanics' identity as individuals and as a culture as well as their traditions, family values, and religion. Because there is a lack of consensus on what this group prefers to be called, I also address the difference between the terms *Latino* and *Hispanic*. The more we know about a culture, the more understanding and help we can provide.

In Part II, I explore the main focus of the book, which is loss. The concept of loss is expanded so it is not limited to just the death of a loved one. Other losses prevalent in this population that are sometimes ignored, such as losses from unemployment, immigration, and illness, are examined in chapter 5. In chapter 6, I pay special attention to end-of-life issues, including funeral practices, mourning, and the impact of religion for Hispanics coping with grief.

Because Latinos encompass a group with great diversity, in chapter 10, comprising Part III, I identify the major subgroups living in the United States and examine the losses inherent within each group. Although these groups share common losses, there are sharp differences in how they deal with such losses. For example, older adult immigrants face losses that second-generation Hispanics do not face, such as the loss of their Spanish language and family traditions. I offer different suggestions regarding how helping professionals can help these individuals in a meaningful manner as they face their unique losses.

MY OWN STORY

In closing, I want to share my story as a Hispanic moving to the United States. This includes the losses I encountered and what helped me to transform my loss and change my life.

From the beginning of my life as an immigrant to the United States in 1979, I realized that the lifestyle in this country was very different from that in Nicaragua. I remember constantly wrestling with the decision to stay in Miami, Florida or move back to my home country. It was very difficult for me to adjust to a completely different environment, to learn a new language, and to embark on a more independent lifestyle than I was used to. I didn't understand at that time that I was experiencing multiple losses. Back in Nicaragua, my family had been the backbone of my life. Besides my immediate family, my aunts and uncles were very much present in my life, as were my *padrinos y madrinas* [godfathers and godmothers]. I remember that dinnertime was special for us. My father would ask us how our day had been and would give us what I call "life lessons," which have stayed with me after so many years. As a matter of fact, my *abuelita* Mamá Lola, my maternal grandmother, lived with us until she died at the age of 85. I remember we all loved and respected her. She was like a second mother to me. Many of my friends experienced similar family situations. In most cases, their elderly grandparents lived with the family, and we all enjoyed sharing time with them. I noticed that with my uprooting from Nicaragua to the United States, things that I considered part of my life were no longer there. My assumptive world had been crushed. Although I was grateful to be living in Miami, where my sisters were also living, in my mind I had the constant intention of moving back to Nicaragua. Every year I would say, "I will go back." I was not allowing myself to embrace this wonderful opportunity to expand my world and grow as a person. I was fixated with the desire to go back. I refused to accept the "loss" of my homeland. My mother perpetuated my tie with Nicaragua because she was still living there. It was not until she moved to Miami to live with us, and sold the family business founded by my father, that I realized the strongest of my ties had been severed. Eventually, with the passing of time, I did accept my reality, and my whole life changed. Even today, my bond with and love for my country are still very much present in my life, but I have also learned to embrace my adopted culture and the wonderful things it has to offer.

As I reflected on my personal experiences while writing this book, I wanted to be an instrument of awareness to counselors who may work with the Hispanic population and may not understand the depth of their sorrow as they speak nostalgically about their homeland. It is my experience that this sense of loss is prevalent among many Hispanics. Many may not be aware they are grieving for a past that is gone, a present that may be challenging, and a future that could be uncertain.

The content of this book goes beyond mere grief counseling for Hispanics. The goal is to provide strength-based tools that can enrich the lives of people in this group who are struggling to have a meaningful life in a country different from their country of origin. Many people react with disbelief when experiencing a loss, as if one shouldn't be enduring such circumstances in life. However, life has its hills and valleys. For immigrants, the valleys can be very deep and seem eternal. At times, the compassionate hand of a health care professional is what they need to come out of that place and use the inner resources they possess to face their situation, transform it, and have a better future. Hispanics who work with an empathic and culturally sensitive counselor or therapist can enter a new world of opportunities. They can start accepting themselves for who they are and feel proud of being Hispanic because accepting their ethnic identification may be a great help in promoting their personal adjustment.

AWARENESS, HOPE, AND TRANSFORMATION

My whole experience as a Hispanic going through my loss and grief has given me the opportunity to bring this message to every person who works with the bereaved and wishes to be a transformative agent in their clients' grieving process. Although in this book I include many losses experienced by the Latino community, I don't intend it to be comprehensive or present a mold into which all Hispanics must fit. A recurring theme in this book is that as individuals we are unique, and therefore our grief is unique. This book brings readers awareness of the most prominent elements of the Hispanic community, but it is not limited to those; neither does it imply that all the members of this community experience loss in the same manner.

We live in a globalized world, and because loss is a universal experience, we need to expand our awareness and open our hearts and minds to other experiences. I wrote this book with the hope of bringing some of this awareness to helping professionals who want to make a difference in the life of a Hispanic/Latino.

Transcriptions of the complete interviews excerpted in this volume are available online at springerpub.com/houben

Acknowledgments

Since the idea of this book emerged, I found the commitment to write it very compelling. It was one of those ideas that stay with you, and the more you think about it, the more you want to make it a reality. Communicating with others is essential, and knowing how to communicate the needs of a culture in times of loss can be a challenging task. It was my conviction that this challenge was an opportunity to make a difference in the lives of many Hispanics and the professionals working with this culture. It was because of this conviction that I embarked on this journey, which really made a difference in my own life. And it is because of this opportunity that I want to give special thanks to Sheri W. Sussman, executive editor of Springer Publishing, for her faith in this project, and mostly for her constant encouragement and support. She was an amazing guide and it was wonderful to work with her.

I also want to express my gratitude to the following persons who contributed to this project: Nicole Armijo for her unflagging dedication in researching and transcribing essential material for the book, Lucero Moncloa for her constant support in transcribing and organizing the interviews contained in this book, and Johnathon Pape and Hazel Hurley for their editorial assistance as I progressed through different stages of the writing process.

Special thanks go to Rev. Richard B. Gilbert, DMin, PhD, BBC, CT, for his enthusiasm and support when this book was just an idea. I also want to express my deepest gratitude to Stephen Sapp, PhD, my former professor at the University of Miami, for inspiring me to enter the rich world of thanatology. It was while sitting in his class on Death and Dying, many years ago, that I realized I wanted to embark on this meaningful journey. To all my clients who through their own stories helped me gain insight into the challenges they encounter as they face a loss. To all the wonderful persons who shared their stories and interviews, adding value to the message of the book.

From the bottom of my heart, I give thanks to my mother for being my role model of faith, hope, and strength. My heart also goes to my father because his memory has been my inspiration in helping the grieving soul. I also want to express my deepest gratitude to the members of my family and friends who throughout my writings are always present in my life. My special gratitude goes to my husband, Mario, for understanding the importance of this book and for supporting me in the process.

Finally, I want to express my heartfelt gratitude to Dr. Kenneth Doka for writing such a meaningful foreword. In sharing his personal story, he added a significant dimension to the book.

PART I

The Sociocultural Aspects of Hispanic Culture

CHAPTER 1

Counseling and Cultural Sensitivity

Counseling is a helping and caring profession, but to offer the help and care our clients need, we must value them for who they are. We live in a globalized world where people from different cultures live and interact side by side in different types of communities. Clients are diverse; however, because of a lack of education, information, or knowledge, counselors often fail to recognize and value cultures different from their own, even in the therapy setting.

When we meet a person from another culture, we may ask how this person acts, feels, or thinks. If the person looks different from us, or has an accent that is different from ours, we may wonder, "Where is he or she from?" Depending on our perceptions and biases, we may make assumptions about this person's origin or background and interpret the answer in a negative or positive manner. Furthermore, we may project the answer onto this person, who may then feel either accepted or rejected.

As a counselor or other helping professional, it is important to be aware of your cultural perspectives and biases. How do you respond when you meet a person from a different culture? More specifically, how do you work with a client who does not share your values and belongs to what is known as a racial/ethnic "minority" group?

The *multicultural perspective* evolved in the social sciences field for training mental health professionals to embrace cultural differences and incorporate a perspective that values many cultures, worldviews, and traditions (Zimmerman, 2001). With the changing demographics of many U.S. communities, multicultural counseling is essential to the process of embracing cultural differences and supporting new and effective insights into other cultures. This book can be an effective resource in understanding the importance of multicultural counseling and how best it can be applied to Hispanic/Latino clients.

CULTURALLY SENSITIVE COUNSELING

There is no pan-cultural response to grief and bereavement: People deal with their grief according to their specific cultural customs. Among Hispanics, these customs differ from country to country. According to the U.S. Census Bureau, the number of Hispanics living in the United States as of July 1, 2009, was estimated to be 48.4 million, and even though they share many values and traditions, a great diversity still exists in this population. Among Hispanics living in the United States are people from countries as diverse as Mexico, Cuba, the Dominican Republic, Nicaragua, Colombia, El Salvador, Guatemala, Chile, Perú, and the U.S. Commonwealth of Puerto Rico, among others. Many professional counselors who work with these clients are not aware of their culture-specific needs, which should be taken into account from the moment the initial assessment or first session is conducted. If we want to be agents of transformation, we need to be informed about our clients' cultures, races, ethnicities, and religious beliefs. Furthermore, we must not expect an all-purpose formula that can be used with all Hispanic clients without taking into consideration their individual histories, perspectives, and personalities.

Giger and Davidhizar (2007) developed the *transcultural assessment and intervention model* to assist with transcultural nursing care, and I have found it very useful when consulting with Hispanic clients. The model encompasses four elements—(a) communication; (b) personal space; (c) social organization; and (d) environmental control—that can influence the relationship between the counselor and the client as they address how vital it is to respect diversity and acknowledge the client's culture. The model has been adapted for working with people after a crisis and may be relevant to grief counseling with people from diverse cultures.

Communication

People communicate in both verbal and nonverbal ways. Hispanic people tend to be expressive as they talk. Sometimes they may talk loudly, but that doesn't mean they are upset. I am a Hispanic myself, and this is simply the way many of us communicate. However, some Hispanics are shy and may rarely look the counselor directly in the eyes. To them, this is a sign of respect, a topic I discuss later in this chapter. Counselors would behoove themselves to notice the differences among members of a culture.

If the client and counselor are from different cultures, this can at times be a barrier because we tend to express our feelings based on what is appropriate in our culture. I am reminded of Pablo, a Peruvian man who had lost his wife. He would hardly look at me and expressed that he felt *raro* [weird] talking to a counselor because he rarely expressed his feelings, even to his wife. Because I knew talking directly about grief or his emotions would be difficult, I asked Pablo to talk about his home country of Perú and how people there behaved after losing a loved one. He started talking about Peruvian funeral rites and how people mourned. Pablo felt that grief and funerals were completely different here in the United States. I asked him what he missed the most about his country, and after a moment of silence, he started crying. He said that what he missed the most was having his wife buried in Perú because he knew that there he would have been surrounded by family and friends.

Personal Space

The concept of personal space—how physically close one allows another person to be—differs from culture to culture. Personal space is much closer among Hispanics than among Anglos or members of some other cultures. This may cause some tension if, for example, a Hispanic client is accustomed to touching the other person when he or she is talking or would like to be hugged when feeling distraught or sad.

Social Organization

Social organization refers to the values and beliefs that are transmitted throughout a culture. These are generally learned from family, organizations, religion, or political groups inside the culture. Counselors should make note of this type of information during initial assessments of clients.

Environmental Control

Environmental control refers to the way a person takes in, or mentally processes, an event. Many Hispanics believe that things that happen to them are because of the will of God, luck, or the effect that others have on their lives. This is important for counselors to know because the less control people may perceive they have over a circumstance, the less optimistic they may feel and, consequently, the less likely they will be willing to take action.

COUNSELING GRIEVING HISPANICS

Despite the fact that grief is a universal experience, there are some cross-cultural differences that the mental health professionals must consider if they want to help alleviate their clients' suffering. Counselors need to realize that what one may find "abnormal" or "different" in one's culture may be perfectly normal in other cultures.

Dr. Alex Fiuza, a Cuban clinical psychologist who specializes in grief, explained how Hispanics cope with grief:

> Most Latinos are very private with their discussions of family illnesses and the way they deal with them. The only differences are that some keep it in their own family groups and others don't even mention it. The way to educate a Hispanic person is to help them face the fact that what happens to them as an individual can happen to anyone else, and that it's okay to grieve, cry, and to talk about it with others, that it is a normal process like eating, like sleeping, like loving. If you share with others you're not only sharing that experience but you're teaching, and that is what we want to make [the client] see. As a therapist I feel that this assistance will make it all worthwhile and will help the Hispanic person accept grief as a normal process and see the importance of sharing with others. (See the Appendix for the full interview.)

Among the most common emotional responses to grief are tears, screaming, sighing, and even cursing, although these reactions vary from culture to culture. In exploring the Hispanic culture, one also finds the need for *personalismo*, which means relationships that are warm and personal. As Hispanics experience grief, they expect health care providers to be caring, show empathy, and be respectful of their beliefs, many of which have to do with their religious and cultural traditions. They also expect health care providers to take into account the needs of the family members.

When we perceive that we are being accepted and trust the person who is offering his or her support, we feel safe enough to open up and show our vulnerability. We can express our feelings without concern about being judged, ridiculed, or rejected. We can be ourselves. This is especially true of Hispanics, who tend to expect warm, trusting responses to their situations.

In her book *Latino Families in Therapy: A Guide to Multicultural Practice* (1998), the Argentinean Celia Jae Falicov offered an interesting approach for working with Latinos, a *cultural generalist* framework that helps both the client and the therapist to bring with them their own perspectives, which she called *cultural maps* (p. 18). Each person carries a "map" that represents his or her perception of reality; however, as the saying goes, "The map is not the territory." We may see a map and understand that it depicts the layout of a city, but it is not actually the city itself. The same concept applies to the cultural maps that the counselor and client bring to the session. Each person's map comprises his or her set of beliefs based on that individual's culture and life experience. Even though I am Hispanic, I never assume that my perspective is the same as a Hispanic client. For example, if a client says, "I am not a happy person," I would ask the client to describe a happy person to me, or if a client says, "I have been grieving for a long time," I ask, "What is a long time for you?"

One of the reasons that Hispanics may be reluctant to seek therapy is the fear that the counselor won't be sensitive to their needs; indeed, most counselor training programs in the United States are based on a European American model (Smith & Montilla, 2006). Smith (2004) asserted that many Hispanics consider counseling a stigma or as something that doesn't resonate with them. Although I agree with this at a certain level, I also believe that attitudes have changed in recent times. Many of my clients are Hispanics, and although they do not always know what to expect in counseling, they are willing to explore the possibility of getting outside help.

Something common to bereaved Hispanic clients is the familial hierarchal rule of *respeto*, or "respect," which can play a vital role in the grieving process. One of the reasons Hispanic individuals may seek outside help is that they do not want to be a burden to their family, so they want to feel better. Another reason is that in the presence of their family members they pretend to be strong, when in reality they feel a tremendous pain in their hearts.

Each Hispanic/Latino person displays unique responses and engages in unique practices regarding his or her loss. I have witnessed these differences when I conduct training workshops on how to establish bereavement support groups. The participants are from different countries, and although they share their traditions regarding bereavement and mourning, the diversity is huge. It is virtually impossible for one to know all of these customs, even among the various Hispanic groups.

As the world becomes more and more a global society, certain cultures are influenced by other cultures, and this is true of counseling too. Even in Latin American countries, where counseling was once unheard of, counseling is accepted by many people today because it has been accepted in other Hispanic countries and cultures. When I travel to my native country of Nicaragua, I have the opportunity to see this shift in perception about talking to "a stranger." This is very interesting for me because I remember that when my father died, 39 years ago, counseling was not common in Nicaragua. If you had suggested then that someone see a psychologist, they would have responded "*¡Yo no estoy loco!*" [I am not crazy!]. Emotional support was offered by the family *puerta cerrada, por el que dirán* [behind closed doors because of what people would say]. Now, things have changed, and it is frequently the case that Hispanics are going to therapy and are more willing to share their family matters. However, I find it vital when working with Latinos to explain what counseling is and what to expect in the counseling session.

I met one of my clients, Lily, a Nicaraguan in her 50s, at a workshop I conducted on Alzheimer's and spirituality. Lily was the caregiver of an elderly woman and felt an immediate connection with me when she learned I was also from Nicaragua. She asked for my business card to make an appointment with me. When she came to see me, she was ecstatic, saying, "*¡Que felicidad que sos Nica!*" [What a joy that you are a Nica (a diminutive of Nicaraguan)!]. I, too, felt the connection, and although I do not think a Latino need necessarily be counseled only by another Latino, I believe that, for some people, the fact that one shares the same language and values can make a difference in building the therapeutic alliance. As Lily stated, she felt at home: "*Con vos me siento como que estuviera en Nicaragua*" [When I am with you I feel I am in Nicaragua].

Falicov (1998) considered it irrelevant whether the therapist is Hispanic and offered the following observation:

> Good therapists have always explored individual complexity with various degrees of sensitivity to cultural and social factors in their clients' lives. I don't believe, however, that there is a Latino therapy or a Latino way of doing therapy or that only Latinos can adequately treat Latinos. (p. 6)

On the other hand, Adriana, a Colombian marriage and family therapist whom I interviewed, has a different opinion regarding the relationship between the client and counselor if they belong to the same culture:

> I think it makes a difference if they are both Latinos and especially if they're both from the same country, because the client manifests this. For example, they may say, "How nice that you're also Colombian." It's like you're matching, you're identifying with the client and that motivates the client. They may be open . . . to change. They feel like there is an understanding there. When the person doesn't feel understood they're more resistant to change. (See Appendix for full interview.)

From her own cultural perspective, Adriana advised how a counselor can approach a Latino client:

> I would say not to rush to find the problem; take some time with the client. Try to find out more about the client's life, their culture, what country they're from, if what you know from the news holds any validity. That initial chitchat is so important for Latinos. They feel valued if you know about their culture. There is already a wall placed just knowing that you are from two different cultures, and the client will most likely not be receptive. The Anglo therapist must be sure that they have their Latino client engaged, motivated, and ready for change. (See Appendix for full interview.)

In writing this book, I have performed a balancing act between generalizing as to how Latinos experience grief and offering a background on the uniqueness of this ethnic group in relation to its members' values and mores. The idea is not to present a collective identity that overlooks each client's individual qualities but to increase the reader's awareness of salient commonalities among these people.

Santiago-Rivera, Arrendondo, and Gallardo-Cooper (2002) offered the following Latino-specific competencies that can provide counselors with insightful guidelines when working with Hispanics:

- *Awareness.* Culturally skilled counselors are aware of competency-based models and guidelines relevant to working with clients in general and with Latinos specifically.
- *Knowledge.* Culturally skilled counselors have knowledge about the historical and political contexts for the development of multicultural

and culture-specific competencies and guidelines in the fields of counseling and psychology. Culturally skilled counselors are able to describe Latino-specific models and frameworks that can serve as reference points when working with Latino clients.

- *Skills.* Culturally skilled counselors are able to conceptualize the dimensions of personal identity model for working with individuals from different Latino groups. Culturally skilled counselors can identify specific [multicultural counseling competencies] and guidelines that can be resources for their work with Latino clients and institutions that serve them. (p. 4)

Santiago-Rivera et al. (2002) also used the following model, which includes different dimensions that counselors can use when assessing clients. I find it helpful when working with Latinos because it is holistic in its approach and can provide insightful information.

Dimensions of Personality Identity

"A" Dimensions
    Age
    Cultural ethnicity
    Gender
    Language
    Physical disability
    Race
    Sexual orientation
    Social class
"B" Dimensions
    Educational background
    Geographic location
    Income
    Marital status
    Religion
    Work experience
    Citizenship status
    Military experience
    Hobbies/recreational interests
"C" Dimensions
    Historical moments/eras

SPECIAL ISSUES TO CONSIDER WHEN COUNSELING HISPANICS

Grief changes the way we experience the world. It can turn a sunny day into the darkest night and turn our world inside out. One of the most crucial needs of bereaved individuals is companionship and comfort during their mourning.

Lack of Communication and/or a Language Barrier

Good communication is essential between a counselor and the client. When sociocultural differences, such as language, culture, and social status, exist, difficulties may arise. Clients who perceive many differences may be cautious about trusting the counselor, which can interrupt the development of a good therapeutic relationship. Hispanics who do not have a good command of the English language will likely have difficulty expressing their feelings in an appropriate manner. It is very difficult for a person to share "intimate and personal matters that are emotion laden with subtle cultural nuances . . . [that] are more readily expressed in one's first language" (Smith, 2004, p. 170). Furthermore, as Aponte, Rivers, and Wohl (1995) asserted,

> Some individuals who seek treatment and services may speak a language or dialect that differs from that of the clinician or service provider. These differences may lead to confusion, frustration, and an inappropriate diagnosis. In addition, the lack of professionals who are a part of the individual's ethnic culture may result in an unwillingness to seek or accept services. (p. 256)

Hence, when language is a challenge, it is best that counselors who are not proficient in Spanish be willing and be able to refer clients to a Hispanic colleague. If a client cannot adequately express his or her grief to a counselor when he or she has experienced a loss, how can he or she possibly process that grief? We naturally express our grief in our native language; I can attest to that. If we need to search for words that can describe how we feel, we may lose the connection with our self and consequently deviate from the whole experience of grieving. There are some words that Hispanics use that cannot be translated to another language, and if clients feel that they are not communicating to the counselor what they want to express, the flow of the counseling is interrupted. Attention becomes focused on the language itself instead of the content. Furthermore, many

Latinos feel embarrassed to speak English because of their accent, and they may be too preoccupied with how their words sound instead of focusing on openly expressing their grief or concerns. As a person whose native language is Spanish, I have found myself in situations where I haven't been able to use a specific English word to express what I want to convey, and it is truly a frustrating situation.

Biased Interpretations of Rituals and Traditions

Our culture is the background from which we interpret the behavior and worldviews of others—specifically cultures with customs that differ from our own. To give an example, Brammer (2004) posed the following question: "[What] would you think of a Latina who believed the ghost of her [m]other spoke to her regarding the inappropriateness of her pending marriage?" (p. 9). Brammer suggested that if this were considered a hallucination, then there would be more Hispanic women suffering from schizophrenia than are reported because such paranormal experiences are common among them. Most non-Hispanic counselors are likely to be skeptical about such a "strange" occurrence on the part of their client and possibly dismiss it.

Although many Hispanics may use alternative resources when experiencing emotional distress, in recent times more and more have been accepting counseling more readily. This is owing to increased education regarding the benefits of counseling and the greater availability of psychological services. For example, more than 60% of my clients are Hispanics. Nevertheless, many Hispanics reject traditional Western medicine, including mental health services, and at times adopt what is simply known as "folk medicine." A classic example is when many bad things happen to a person with no apparent reason. A Hispanic might say "*Te echaron mal de ojo*" [You have evil's eye], or at times "*Necesitas una limpieza*" [You need a cleansing; this means visiting a *curandero*, a folk medicine healer]. I discuss healing with folk medicine or nontraditional practices and the effect they may have on the therapeutic relationship in more detail in chapter 4.

Cultural Differences in Physical Social Distance

Among most Hispanics, the physical social distance between people is less than that of other groups in North America. It is our custom to greet a person with a kiss and/or a hug, touch each other's arm or hand, and feel comfortable with proximate distance. Adriana, the therapist I interviewed, commented on how these gestures are not well received by North Americans at her place of work:

> As you know, many times [we] greet each other with a kiss, something that isn't done in the Anglo culture. This way of making physical contact with someone is the norm with us, but may not be in different settings here. For instance, you would not greet a client this way, but among friends you would. If you did this with a client, the first word out of someone's mouth [might] be "harassment." I think people start to fear, even the Anglo American feels fear that he/she may have compromised their job or broken the law somehow (by doing this). Anglos tend to be more "by the book," and strict with their laws and customs, including keeping social distance.

I agree with Adriana's assertion. When I receive Hispanic clients, they expect I greet them with either a hug or a kiss. They feel welcome and *en casa* [at home].

Lack of, or Inadequate, Multicultural Training for Counselors

According to Sue and Sue (2003), many mental health professionals' multicultural training is inadequate. The focus of counseling is primarily from a White perspective and is generally not supportive of racial/ethnic minority groups, including awareness of their religion, culture, ethnicity, or economics. This can perpetuate, or even produce, stereotypes in individuals who are training to be mental health professionals. Sue and Sue recommended that mental health professionals have "educational experiences that generate sensitivity and appreciation of the history, current needs, strengths, and resources of minority communities" (p. 51). Although for three decades many mental health professionals have acknowledged their limitations regarding the best type of therapy (e.g., person centered, cognitive behavioral) to use with culturally diverse clients, there is still no consensus on which therapy works the best.

A challenge that counselors may encounter is when their clients exhibit values that differ from their own but may have a close relationship with their culture as the following case, told by a non-Hispanic counselor, reveals:

> Brenda arrived at therapy with her eye covered with a patch. Carolyn, an Anglo American therapist, asked her what happened. Being an advocate of women's rights, Carolyn feared the worst—that Brenda had been hit by that *machista* of a husband. Unfortunately, she was right. Pablo had come to the house drunk, and Brenda didn't have dinner ready, so he hit her out of anger.

Brenda quietly took her children and left for her mother's house. When she told her mother she wanted to leave Pablo, her mother told her "*Ésta es tu cruz*" [This is your cross]. Brenda then remembered that her mother was a submissive woman who never had [words] with her husband; therefore, she expected the same from her daughter. Confused, angry, and scared, Brenda went back home, where Pablo was already sleeping. Brenda ended up staying with her abusive husband, feeling depressed and desperate.

Brenda shared with her therapist that she wanted to leave her husband but didn't want to disappoint her mother. Also, she was afraid of *el que dirán* [what would people say] if she got divorced. Carolyn felt like telling her client to leave her husband immediately and argued against [Brenda's] concern for her mother, but then remembered the value Hispanics place on family and respect for elders. After Brenda left, [Carolyn] continued to reflect on which approach to use with her and decided she would try to empower her first, based on her strengths, so that she could become more assertive and able to communicate in an open manner with her mother and stand up for her rights. What Carolyn didn't know was that Brenda didn't have *los papeles* [legal documents] to live in the United States, so basically she depended on her husband to support her.

Brenda's story is the experience of many Hispanic women, and demeaning situations such as hers often contribute to their loss of self-esteem and hope. However, mental health professionals should not assume that simply because a client is Hispanic he or she will behave in a certain manner—that would be stereotyping. I believe the best approach is to be present as a counselor and to be careful with your body language and facial expressions because oftentimes we may say more with our nonverbal communication than with our words.

THE COUNSELOR'S APPROACH

Therapists who want to establish an effective bond with their clients can use social influence to their benefit. The theory of social influence, developed by Strong (1969), includes the following three dimensions: (a) attraction; (b) trustworthiness; and (c) expertise/competence. Each of these dimensions, applied to counseling, can enhance the relationship between the counselor and client. Brammer (2004) described these elements as follows:

- *Attraction.* This goes beyond physical attractiveness to include finding something appealing in the other person. It encompasses the ability not only to establish a feeling of familiarity but also to correctly perceive the client's nature without prejudice but instead with warmth. Attraction, by definition, is the power that draws two entities to one another.

- *Trustworthiness.* Besides believing that the person will keep the information confidential, trustworthiness also implies a feeling of safety produced by the knowledge that this relationship won't cause them any harm. A counselor who is regarded as trustworthy by the client will permit deeper feelings of trust to blossom and provide a greater ability for the client to open up because the client will not perceive imminent danger to himself or herself.
- *Expertise/competence.* Expert/competent counselors are able to effectively and impart their training and professionalism to help their clients.

Although all these dimensions are fundamental to the counselor–client relationship, they may have a different interpretation when working with clients from other cultures. The most important seems to be trustworthiness. A counselor must have sufficient knowledge of issues concerning members of racial/ethnic minority groups, and sufficient experience working with them, as well as an awareness of issues specific to various cultures. I suggest that counselors who work with a specific cultural group become educated about the various elements of that culture, including its history and the social issues the members of this group face, such as employment, housing, and/or immigration.

Counseling is a process in which interpersonal interaction as well as communication and social influence occurs (Sue & Sue, 2003). For a good communication, the messages sent and received by the counselor and client should be exchanged with accuracy; otherwise, this could prevent the development of an effective therapeutic relationship as well as inhibit trust and rapport. The therapist should also encourage clients to take time for inner reflection so that they can act based on their self-exploration.

Because of the discrimination or prejudice that many members of racial/ethnic minority groups experience, some clients may be defensive if a counselor implies that what happens to them is their responsibility. Often our behavior is the result of our treatment by others; as Thomas (2000) observed: "Frequently people's failure to enjoy optimal development is the result of their being treated in prejudicial ways by others" (p. 15). This may be the case, for example, when a Hispanic client is suffering from loss of self-esteem (discussed in chapter 5). Clients experiencing low self-esteem, who perceive that there is some prejudice or bias against them because of their ethnicity, can be even more frustrated and upset. Our clients have their own world-views and unique frames of reference. An empathic counselor tries to understand their clients' experience if they want to enter those worldviews.

Nonverbal communication differs from culture to culture. For example, a conflict may arise between an Anglo American therapist working with a Hispanic client who does not look the therapist in the eye. The counselor may assume that the client is hiding something, when in actuality, out of *respeto* [respect] for authority (the counselor), the Hispanic client may avoid direct eye contact. Because *respeto* is a virtue that is distinctive in Hispanic cultures, I think it is necessary for the counselor to have an accurate understanding of what it means:

> *Respeto* is more than the tone of social relations, it is the relation of one person to another, child to parent, student to teacher, citizen to police officer, worker to boss, and neighbor to neighbor. Ideally, *respeto* does not operate in only one direction; ideally *respeto* serves as a brake on the driving individualism of Anglo society and makes a person more familial, more communal in his orientation. (Shorris, 1992, p. 106)

QUALITIES OF A SENSITIVE COUNSELOR

When conducting grief counseling with culturally diverse persons, counselors should listen attentively and quietly, make sincere eye contact, project acceptance of the clients, and help the clients identify and express their emotions. It is best to avoid saying to clients that you know how they feel and what they are going through. It is a better idea to use open-ended statements such as "I hear that you. . . ." Mental health professionals need to be aware of their clients' values so that they will be alert to cues that will reveal what is most important to a particular client. I believe that the best thing you can do as a counselor is to be present in both body and spirit and to be aware of how you express your responses to issues that may sound alien or unacceptable to your values or beliefs. Be careful with your body language and facial expressions.

Helping the Client to Have Hope

When we face a loss or a difficult transition in our lives, we need inspiration to keep going, which can be ignited by hope. Ronna Jevne, in her foreword to Cutcliffe's book *The Inspiration of Hope in Bereavement Counseling* (2004), expressed the immense value of integrating hope into the counseling setting. Counselors should conduct their assessments of how they find themselves integrating hope and positive psychology into their work with clients. Keep in mind, as Jevne stated, that "not only do we assess the hope and hopelessness of our clients but they indeed are assessing whether we are hopeful enough to be useful to them" (p. 10). The more I work with clients, the more I realize how counselors tend to project their expectations onto them. If one is not hopeful regarding a particular client's situation, he or she will perceive this, and this can impair the therapeutic relationship and the outcome of therapy.

There are several questions counselors can pose to themselves: How do my views of hope influence my practice? How does my practice influence my views of hope? How culturally bound am I in terms of my perceptions of hope? (Jevne, 2004, p. 10). This last question has a strong relationship to being culturally sensitive and being sure that your own cultural parameters do not interfere with your clients' worldviews.

Showing Compassion

In recent times, the concept of integrating compassion into the therapeutic alliance has been brought to counselors' awareness. This has to do with how counselors relate to their clients, especially at the beginning of therapy, including the emotions the counselor conveys and how effective he or she is in showing empathy for the client. Because as counselors we want our clients to feel safe and cared for, we need a better understanding of compassion. Gilbert (2005) emphasized that being compassionate makes us "open to the suffering of self and others, in a non-defensive and non-judgmental way" (p. 1). When we are compassionate toward others we visualize ourselves in their place and respond to their pain and suffering in a more caring manner. In working with clients—both Hispanics and non-Hispanics—I have come to realize that this is the most valuable skill that we as counselors can possess.

Before a therapeutic alliance can be developed, the counselor must establish a connection with the client, and a compassionate counselor will be able to provide a sense of safety for the client so that the client will have the desire to work with the counselor and establish a meaningful bond. In addition to specific techniques or therapeutic tools, showing genuine care and compassion toward clients can make an enormous difference in their lives. Therapists who are able to collaborate with their clients and are able to show compassion, empathy, can provide more hope to clients than most formal or sophisticated psychological interventions. (Greenberg, Elliot & Pos, 2007).

Offering Empathy

Empathy is a value that is highly recommended when working with clients who belong to a different culture, but at times it can be challenging to express because there may be few shared qualities between the client and the therapist. Therefore, it is fundamental that the counselor "transpose[s] [him or herself] into another, rather than [intrude] upon one's own feelings, and in this way achieve a more complete understanding of culturally varied predispositions, personal constructs, and experience" (Jones, 1985, p. 178). Egan (1994) stated that empathic counselors should be able to do the following:

- *Build the relationship.* Counselors who are able to get inside the worldviews of their clients demonstrate respect, and this by itself helps build a therapeutic bond.
- *Stimulate self-exploration.* Clients who perceive that they are understood will feel inspired to continue exploring their inner self, which is one of the vital elements for the progression of the therapeutic relationship.
- *Check understandings.* Empathic counselors are open with clients and make sure clients understand what they mean.
- *Provide support.* Clients feel understood if the counselor lets them know whether he or she can get into their frame of reference.
- *Lubricate communication.* Empathy facilitates the dialogue and thus smooth communication between the counselor and client.
- *Focus attention.* This is a valuable skill that enables the counselor and client to focus on core issues, or what is important to the counseling session.
- *Restrain the helper.* Empathic counselors know that helping is not about giving advice but about motivating clients to take action.
- *Pave the way.* Empathy lays the groundwork for eventually working with clients to begin addressing issues that are more challenging and helping them set goals for themselves so they can move into action and growth.

Among the best ways I have found to show empathy is to consciously listen to my clients without judgment and to keep my internal dialogue and self out of the way. According to O'Connor and Lages (2004, p. 72), coun-selors need to pay attention to the three roadblocks to conscious listening:

1. *Internal dialogue.* Counselors should avoid having an inner conversa-tion with themselves instead of listening to the client, including hav-ing an internal dialogue about what the client is saying.
2. *Muscle tension.* To be fully present, we need to be relaxed. In the case of working with clients from another culture, we may tense up, wor-ried that we might show bias, or realizing we do not really know much about their values and/or traditions. Tensing up does not help with establishing rapport. If you find you are getting tense, take a deep breath and relax. Actually, you could do this with your client at the same time, which could give you both a sense of relief and connection.
3. *A focused stare.* When gazing at your clients, it is better to soften the way you look at them. Do not always look at them directly in the eye (some Hispanics feel uncomfortable with staring, because they may find this disrespectful); instead, expand your vision to other visual fields.

Furthermore, to provide the best care, the counselor should be aware of any of his or her own emotions, biases, or conflicts and develop self-awareness regarding race and ethnicity. Do you overgeneralize? Have you had a negative experience with any Hispanic that may influence your rela-tionship with your client? Do you have a strong affiliation with a particular ethnicity or culture? This is considered as *countertransference,* and it could negatively influence your perception of the client, preventing a successful therapy outcome.

Hays (2001) believes that to develop self-awareness therapists need to do some personal work that includes certain exercises, as in the ADDRESSING approach comprising the following elements: Age-related is-sues, Disability, Religion, Ethnic identity, Socioeconomic status, Indigenous heritage, National identity, and Gender-related information (p. 6).

With the ADDRESSING approach, counselors can evaluate their knowledge and awareness of each component. Hays (2001) also advised using this framework when assessing clients, to "avoid making inaccu-rate generalizations on the basis of a client's physical appearance, language abilities, and/or family name" (p. 6). The ADDRESSING framework can provide a counselor with greater awareness of his or her history. I con-sider the last two guidelines (i.e., national identity and gender-related information) to be fundamental to helping clients resolve loss-related grief issues and to empower them when confronting a crisis.

As we have seen, with the large variety of cultures in the United States, therapists are expected to be aware of the values and traditions of a number of ethnic groups. This book was born to facilitate this task; however, my purpose in writing it was not to give counselors all the information pertaining to Hispanics. That will be impossible, for three reasons: (a) space limitation does not allow me to integrate all the aspects of this very diverse culture; (b) Hispanics are a heterogeneous group comprising a variety of subgroups, each with its values and traditions; and (c) although I am a Hispanic, I don't know everything about my culture. Furthermore, I don't know all the differences among the various Hispanic groups. I can write only on the basis of my personal experience as a Hispanic counselor, born in Nicaragua, who works with people going through losses and life transitions.

THE COUNSELOR AS A TRANSFORMATIVE AGENT

Wainrib and Bloch (1998) advocated encouraging clients to move away from the perspective of being a victim to one of becoming an empowered individual. They favored an approach that focuses on the clients' strengths instead of just their difficulties or weaknesses so that they, like the mythic phoenix that rose from its ashes, can be resurrected to a new life. I embrace this philosophy because it resonates with my own. Mental health professionals working with clients who are facing a loss can act as transformative agents in guiding and supporting them through the grieving process and helping them find meaning in life again.

One of the most powerful ways we can guide and support our clients through their grief is simply by being a healing presence. It is our choice to create this for our clients and ourselves. As transformative agents, we also engage in our own process of transformation:

> To create [a] healing presence, we fine tune our inner experience to the inner state of the other person. We transform ourselves in response to the basic needs of the person we are trying to heal and to help. Ultimately, we find within ourselves the psychological and spiritual resources required to nourish and empower the other human being . . . [a] [h]ealing presence is a

way of being that by its very nature tends to reassure and encourage people, to lend them moral and spiritual strength, to provide confidence that they can overcome suffering and continue to grow. (Breggin, 1997, pp. 5–6)

If we feel the depth of our clients' grief, we will be able to connect with them at a profound level and accompany them on their journey of spiritual and personal growth. Until we sense deeply how people are feeling inside, we cannot be agents of healing and transformation.

HELPFUL SUGGESTIONS

- Be mindful of the fact that you might experience countertransference based on your cultural or ethnic affiliation. The more aware you are of your ethnicity and how this influences the way you see other cultures or ethnic groups, the better service you will provide your clients.
- Develop your listening skills and be present. If you do not agree with some of the issues or concerns your Hispanic clients share with you, try to keep your values and opinions to yourself. If you confront clients or disregard traditions that have been passed from generation to generation, they will not feel they are in a safe place, and you may risk them not returning to therapy or finding another counselor who accepts them for who they are.
- Be more than a counselor: Be a transformative agent in the lives of your clients. Be the springboard they need to help them go through the grief they are experiencing and become the unique persons they are.

PERSONAL REFLECTIONS FOR THE COUNSELOR

- Are you aware of some of the traditions and values of your Hispanic clients?
- Are you able to enter your clients' worldviews and integrate different modalities besides the traditional mental health approach?
- Do you believe that your Hispanic clients have strengths that, despite their losses and difficulties, they could use in their growing process?

CHAPTER 2

Exploring a Culture: Hispanics and Their Heritage

Before exploring the uniqueness of the Hispanic culture and discussing how to counsel Hispanics in their grief and loss, we need to have an appreciation of what constitutes a culture. According to Eliot (1948), in his classic treatise *Notes Towards the Definition of Culture*, the "culture of the group or class is dependent upon the culture of the whole society to which that group or class belongs" (p. 21). Mishan (2005) added the following:

> Culture means the total body of tradition borne by a society and transmitted from generation to generation. It thus refers to the norms, values, and standards by which people act, and it includes the ways distinctive in each society of ordering the world and rendering it intelligible. (p. 45)

Culture is generally passed from generation to generation and helps to shape our experience as human beings. In essence, it comprises a set of values, traditions, norms, and beliefs shared by a group of people that influences the way they see and understand life. These norms, values, and so on also influence how individuals and families behave and grieve.

In reference to the U.S. Hispanic community, DeSpelder and Strickland (2007) asserted that Latinos are considered a *subculture* because they "share a distinctive identity and lifestyle within a larger society . . . [and] . . . a distinctive language" (p. 76); however, regarding Hispanics as a single subculture with one set of values and beliefs seems an oversimplification. In actuality, the Hispanic population represents a diverse blend of ethnicities and traditions. This community encompasses people from more than 17 Spanish-speaking countries (Rallying Points, 2002). The story of Hispanics in the United States is a complex one of diversity, acculturation, values, traditions, family, religion, fears, and hopes. Although some people may simply assume that all people who speak Spanish are of the same culture, and thus Hispanic, the reality is that they are not the same. There are natural differences among Spanish-speaking people comprising a diverse group encompassing many countries, as far apart as Cuba and Argentina.

Although Spanish is the first language of most Hispanics, there are differences in language and dialects among the people of these countries. For example, in Nicaragua, Argentina, and El Salvador (to mention a few), the pronoun *vos* [you] is used, whereas Cubans, Peruvians, and Venezuelans use the familiar pronoun *tú*. In addition, within each country different dialects are spoken in different provinces. As Sonia Martinez, director of patient relations at the University of Miami (Florida) hospital, stated, "In Cuba we even have 'Chinese Cubans,' 'African Cubans,' . . . and we all speak different dialects."

Ideally, neither the Hispanic population nor any other population should be labeled; instead, the members should be embraced as who they really are: human beings with particular needs and desires. I want to emphasize that my attempt to explain the difference between the terms *Latino* and *Hispanic* is not done with the intention of stereotyping this group of people or to focus on the differences; however, because the purpose of this book is to serve as a reference manual on the most salient aspects of the Spanish-speaking population, I do explore the meaning of both terms and explain why I decided to use the term Hispanic in this context.

HISPANIC OR *LATINO/A*: EXPLORING THE DIFFERENCE

In determining whether there is a difference between the terms Hispanic and Latino/a, it is important to become familiar with the feelings and associations each term triggers among this cultural group in the United States today, keeping in mind that not all of these individuals are immigrants. Does one broad term best fit a community of people from countries as diverse as Mexico, Puerto Rico, Cuba, Nicaragua, El Salvador, the Dominican Republic, Venezuela, and other Latin American countries? Is there in fact a difference between the two terms? With which term do the people of a particular community identify better? Some people may receive the term Hispanic well, whereas others may take offense at being addressed by this term. Personally, I have always been comfortable with either term. For me, it is the same whether I am called a Latina, Hispanic, or Nicaraguan, although others in the community feel differently.

This debate over nomenclature has recently triggered several articles and position papers on the issue. Angelo Falcon, a senior policy executive for the Puerto Rican Legal and Education Fund, stated, "I think the debate reflects the flux this community is in right now" (quoted in Fears, 2003, p. A01). According to Cafferty and Engstrom (2002),

> The term Hispanic is used to describe people in the United States who are descended or have migrated from countries in which Spanish is spoken. Because the term is rooted in the use of language rather than in race, Hispanic is a term that encompasses White, Black, and mestizo/mulatto. (p. xvii)

Mestizaje is a Spanish word for "the racial and cultural mixing of European, American Indian, and Africa[n] blood in Latin American and Latino people," and it is associated with "mixture, hybridity, transculturation, and racial miscegenation" (Stavans, 2005, p. 112). The term *mestizo* often led both Hispanic leaders and other Americans to refer to Hispanics as a "brown race" (Cafferty & Engstrom, 2002, p. xvii). Therefore, many Anglos believe the myth that all Latinos are dark-skinned. For example, in a virtual chat room I found the following question very representative of how many Anglos think about Latinos: "I have a friend who has blue eyes and has blond hair. He says he is Latino but I am not sure I should believe him. How can I find out?" This is a misconception: Many Latinos, besides the traditionally brown-skinned mestizos, can and do have blond hair, blue eyes, red hair, fair skin, and so on.

The term Hispanic was originally derived from *Hispano*, or Spanish. The word was first given prominence as a racial category when it was added to the U.S. census questionnaire in 1970 (Stavans, 2007), although Congress had previously authorized President Lyndon B. Johnson to proclaim National Hispanic Heritage Week in September 1968 (U.S. Census Bureau, 2006). This term was used to clearly and specifically define the group of people who spoke the Spanish language. Stavans (2007), a specialist in Latin American studies, explained that the term Latino:

> [E]merged in the late twentieth century to describe the richly heterogeneous minority comprising people from different parts of what had been the Spanish Empire, an area that once spread from Florida and

Puerto Rico to the archipelago of the Philippines and from California to the Argentine Pampas. (p. 1)

However, as I interviewed people from Peru, Cuba, Nicaragua, Argentina, Mexico, Colombia, El Salvador and the Dominican Republic, invariably all of them refused the use of either Hispanic or Latino. They indicated that they lose their identity when being placed under such an umbrella term and thus prefer to be addressed by the name of their country of origin (e.g., Cuban American, Argentinean, Nicaraguan). Vázquez (2004) agreed, asserting that "the one thing most Hispanics/Latinos agree on is that they prefer to be called by their immediate ethnic group [name]" (p. 1). To others, however, Latino is the preferred word. Many feel a sense of pride connected with this term. Of course, the word Latino did not even exist 50 years ago. However, by the year 2050, "Nearly 100 million people will be able to trace their ancestry to the Spanish-speaking, Latin American, and Caribbean worlds. From 1990 to 2000, the Latino population grew by 58%" (Suárez-Orozco & Paez, 2002, p. 2).

Suárez-Orozco and Paez (2002) chose to use Latino over Hispanic "because the vast majority of Latinos in the United States come from Latin America," and Hispanic is a term "that emphasizes the population's link to Hispania or Spain" (p. 4). They contended that the term Hispanic is used only in the United States, but I disagree with them based on my personal research. I have found that Latino is also used in Latin America. This is very important to take into account because although Latino is considered by some to be insulting when used in the United States, as it labels them as a "minority," people in Latin American countries are more comfortable with the term. My visit to Lima, Perú, to attend the Latin American Congress for Palliative Care in March 2008 confirmed this. After my presentation, when I asked the participants which term they preferred—Hispanic or Latino—they unanimously responded, "Latino" because Hispanic is nonexistent in Latin America. Obviously they do not need a special label there to indicate that they speak the Spanish language.

Another reason I use the term Hispanic is that not every Latino speaks the Spanish language, which, according to Fox (1997), is a way of bonding all Hispanics because it connects us all. He says that the language is a source of pride and unity. After weighing these considerations and opinions, I decided that Hispanic was the more appropriate term of reference for the title of this book because the purpose is to raise awareness about the Spanish-speaking population living in the United States.

However, I want to reemphasize that the most important factor is to regard people in this community with the greatest respect for who they are as individuals and to address them personally by their preferred term. It is my sincere hope never to offend anyone, and even though the term Hispanic is part of the title of this book, as I continue my analysis and discussion I use, when needed, the terms Latino and Hispanic interchangeably.

CHARACTERISTICS OF HISPANICS/LATINOS

Because Hispanics come from many different countries, we cannot assume that they all have the same traits, education level, or religion. As Barnett (2004) suggested, "One . . . can't make assumptions about the income or educational level of South Americans living in North America . . . some are quite wealthy, well traveled, and highly educated" (p. 17). This applies to the rest of Latinos from Central America, Mexico, or the Caribbean. Gracia (2008) reminded us:

> Not all Latinos speak the same language, are of the same race, hold the same religious beliefs, belong to the same political party, live in the same territory, display the same cultural traits, enjoy the same economic status, have the same degree of education, share the same social class, or come from the same genetic line. (p. 99)

As we can see, settling on a Hispanic/Latino identity is not easy; however, some common characteristics form the foundation of the cultural group about which I have written this book.

The purpose of this book is to establish a frame of reference through the exploration of the most salient values and traditions of Hispanics/Latinos as they face losses. As Rosenblatt (2007) observed,

> If we want to understand and help people we cannot make the assumption that they are like us or like people from our own culture(s) or that they grieve and mourn the way a textbook or a theory says people do or should. We also should not stereotype people based on our understanding of their culture . . . we have to understand and respect cultural differences in the emotionality of bereavement . . . we have to be open to the complexity, diversity, and changing qualities of how people within a culture deal with loss. (p. 118)

ACCULTURATION AND ASSIMILATION OF HISPANICS

To most effectively serve Hispanic people in the health and human services fields, it is important to understand acculturation and assimilation from their point of view. *Acculturation* occurs when people from one cultural group acquire and integrate into their own lives the behaviors and beliefs of another culture. *Assimilation*, according to Korzenny (1999), is the process of replacing one's first culture with a second culture. In the case of Hispanics living in the United States, many factors influence their acculturation and/or assimilation. What follows is quote from a Latina who came to the United States at an early age and was easily assimilated into the "American way":

> My mother insists I speak Spanish at home, but I prefer to speak in English. All my friends speak English. Furthermore, I prefer to watch TV in English because I don't like the *novelas* [soap operas]. I asked my mom to understand me but she insists I need to behave like a Latina. Next year I will be 15 years old and my family is planning a huge party because I will be a *quinceañera* [equivalent to a sweet 16]. In my country of origin, Nicaragua, we celebrate *los quince* [age 15] as a grand event where I dance with my father a waltz and everybody watches. I am supposed to wear this fancy pink dress, but I am more comfortable in plain clothes. I don't want to participate in this celebration. We don't live in Nicaragua; we live in Miami.

On the other hand, the following account shows how one Latino has kept his Hispanic roots while acculturating to the United States:

> I consider myself more American than Latino. I was born in Cuba but came to Miami when I was three years old and am used to the customs of the United States. Still, [because] Spanish [is] my mother tongue, I have made the effort to speak it every time I can, especially because I want to be able to communicate with *mis abuelos* [my grandparents] since they arrived from Cuba when they were in their seventies and they never learnt the English language.

These processes of acculturation and assimilation could evolve to the point of forming new societies, as different cultures merge and influence each other (Sam & Berry, 2006). Moreover, within the assimilation process is the adoption of practices and attitudes as well as modifications of the language and use of words that are characteristic of the other culture.

For example, we may find Hispanics saying *printear* (a word derived from printer) instead of using the Spanish word *imprimir*, or speaking the word *chatear* (a word derived from chat) instead of saying *conversar*. Actually, some Hispanics speak what is known as *Spanglish*, a combination of words in Spanish and English. As Cafferty and Engstrom (2002) claimed, the "assimilation of successive generations of immigrants into American society also means assimilation into speaking the English language" (p. 69). In chapter 5, I explore in more detail the concept of language and loss and its implications for a person's sense of identity.

For some time, the metaphor of America as a melting pot has applied to the assimilation of immigrants living in the United States, but in reality this concept no longer applies because members of each immigrant group do not, or need not, completely disconnect from their homeland and native culture to fit into or function in the mainstream American culture. This is possible because of today's means of high-speed communication and the greater ease of traveling back to one's country of origin. With the advent of these means of globalization, the whole process of acculturation and assimilation has become somewhat less necessary. For many Hispanics, this may translate to living in the United States yet keeping much of their cultural identity. Assimilation may have a different implication now and, according to Marcelo Suárez-Orozco (2002), it should be reevaluated.

Although differences exist within the Hispanic community, there is also a great deal of commonality: "Regardless of the country of origin, or how long a family has been in the United States, though, there are culturally based attitudes and behaviors that unite them" (Rallying Points, 2002, p. 1). For example, Hispanic culture stresses the importance of family and relationships. Even though a vast majority of the Hispanic cultural groups living in the United States have kept most of their unique traditions, most share similar family values, such as respect for elders and the protection of all family members. For the Hispanic culture, the matter of *la familia* [family] is sacred. In chapter 3, I elaborate on the concept of *familism* and the principles that Hispanics highly value.

In addition to being familiar with the concepts of acculturation and assimilation, mental health professionals should be able to recognize the differences within the heterogeneous Hispanic community itself. Some Hispanic families have been in the United States for generations; others are newly arrived immigrants (Rallying Points, 2002). Adapting to a new society can be challenging. Most Hispanics tend to preserve the traditions and mores of their country of origin very closely.

A question posed by psychologists concerning acculturation is, "How do people born and raised in one society manage to live in another society that is culturally different from the one they are used to?" (Sam & Berry, 2006, p. 3). People who must adjust to a new society may either retain their same behaviors and cultural customs or adapt to their new situation and cultural environment. This latter possibility, complex in itself, involves a variety of psychological processes, such as "social learning, stress and coping, identity, resilience, mental illness, conflict and many others" (Sam & Berry, 2006, p. 4). To these psychological processes I will add the sense of loss that occurs as the person realizes that he or she no longer belongs to the familiar and known environment. This sense of loss is expressed in grief, which may prevent the individual from becoming acculturated within the adopted culture and from living a functional and fulfilling life.

The difficulty of acculturation when one has not fully reconciled the loss of one's homeland is made personal through the experience of Juan Antonio:

> I was born in Caracas, Venezuela's capital, which used to be an affluent and prosperous city in South America. My family belonged to the upper class and had Italian origins. My parents provided us a stable life, filled with family and religious values. I remember that every Sunday we shared time as a family, going to church and then having lunch at the club. We had a good life. My father worked for the *petrolera* [oil company], and my mother stayed at home, which was typical at those times. Men worked and provided for the family. I had a life of abundance, filled with parties, visits to the club, and constant traveling to the United States. I didn't have to worry until I was 18 years old and the situation in my country got unbearable. My family sold what they could and moved to Miami (Florida). Because my father had stocks in companies that were confiscated by the government we had to leave the country with [only] enough money to buy a small house and start a new life. The change was shocking. I had to realize things wouldn't be the same in Miami. I moved to a nice neighborhood where many Venezuelans live with the hope of keeping a "piece" of my homeland. In this neighborhood many businesses are Venezuelan, we eat Venezuelan food and read the Venezuelan newspaper. Still, I live with a sense of loss and nostalgia.

The following helpful questions may give you an idea of your clients' level of acculturation and the culture with which they identify the most:

- Do you consider yourself a Hispanic or a Latino/a?
- Are you proud of your culture?
- Where were you born?
- How long have you been living in the United States?
- How do you like to be referred to? (e.g., as a Cuban, Argentinean, South American)
- Do you miss your homeland?
- What do you miss most about your homeland?
- Are most of your friends from your homeland?
- Do you share time with people from other nationalities?
- Do you enjoy living in the United States?
- What do you like the most about the United States?
- What do you like the least?
- Have you been able to adapt to the lifestyle here?
- If not, what do you find to be the most difficult aspect of this lifestyle?
- Do you feel you will never adapt to the lifestyle of the United States?

Health care professionals seeking to assist Hispanics in dealing with losses need to be aware of the specific backgrounds of the individuals with whom they are interacting. Although individuals from subcultures mainly adapt to the main culture, they tend to keep their values and traditions as they process their grief at the loss of their homeland (DeSpelder & Strickland, 2007). However, even when people share the same culture, they may cope with losses and process grief differently. The following questions may be useful when assessing such customs:

- What is it like when someone in your family dies?
- How do you mourn death in your country?
- Do you hold any rituals or ceremonies surrounding the dying person?

Mental health counselors and those in other helping professions also need to be aware of the important role of religion in all aspects of the lives of Hispanics, including how they face loss. According to a study conducted by researchers at Ohio State University, "In the Hispanic world, religion has traditionally played a significant role in daily activity" (Clutter & Nieto, n.d., http://ohioline.osu.edu/hyg-fact/5000/5237.html, accessed 2011).

Another study of Hispanics and faith revealed that 68% are Catholic, 15% are born-again or evangelical Protestants, 5% are mainline Protestants, 3% are identified as "other Christian," and 8% are secular (Goodstein, 2007).

The role of religion is evident in how Hispanics speak of what happens to their loved ones who have died. Among Hispanics as well as people of other cultures it is very common to use euphemisms as a way of softening the fact that a person has died. Phrases such as *Está con Dios* [He/she is with God] and *Se fue al cielo* [He/she departed to heaven] are common. In chapter 3, I discuss in more detail how religion shapes Hispanics' responses to loss, including the concept of *milagros* [miracles], which at times interferes with decisions concerning end-of-life issues.

DIFFERENCES WITHIN CULTURAL GROUPS

Although more than 17 Hispanic groups are living in the United States, because of space limitations I have chosen to focus on the following groups, which represent the majority of U.S. Hispanics: Mexican Americans, Cuban Americans, Puerto Ricans, Dominican Americans, Central Americans, and South Americans. I have also based my selection on Cafferty and Engstrom's (2002) approach, that is, not including Spaniards from Spain, or Brazilians or Portuguese (both groups speak Portuguese). My focus is on Hispanics who speak Spanish and live in the United States.

Mexican Americans

Mexicans represent more than 61% of the Hispanics living in the United States; 58% of them live in the Western states (Sullivan, 2002). According to the U.S. Census American Community Survey and estimates by the Pew Hispanic Center, the Mexican immigrant adult population of the United States totaled 10.4 million in June 2007 (Inter-American Development Bank [IADB] 2007). According to Lochhead (2006), almost 10% of the 107 million people who make up the population of Mexico live in the United States. She further stated that one of every seven Mexican workers migrates to the United States. According to Lochhead, this wave of Mexican immigrants to the United States started in 1982, and because of the economic boom increased rapidly in the 1990s. Furthermore, "Today [the population] has reached record dimensions" (p. 1).

Cuban Americans

The immigration of Cubans to the United States started after the Spanish American War in 1898, but it was in the 1960s, after Cuban dictator Fidel Castro rose to power, that a rapid exodus occurred, especially from Cuba to Florida, mainly to Miami (Menard, 2004, p. 8). By 1960, thousands of Cubans who had emigrated banded together in one area of Miami and became known as "Little Havana." On visiting this sector of the city, a person may not even feel that he or she is in the United States. The atmosphere is Latin, the music is Latin, the food is Latin, and the language is Spanish. It is like being transported to a Latin country. It is this bonding and identification that makes this area of the city so nostalgic and powerful to Cuban Americans and other Hispanics. When Cubans celebrate their annual carnival, *El Carnaval de La Calle Ocho* [The Carnival of the Eighth Street], thousands of Latinos—including Nicaraguans, Venezuelans, Peruvians, Colombians, Dominicans, and Cubans—join together as one community, one identity. People dance in the streets to the Latin music, and for one day, the feeling of being in one's country brings many immigrants a sense of belonging.

After the Cubans established themselves in Miami, people here in the United States still had very little knowledge of Cuban life and traditions. The knowledge about this culture was so scant that in 1986 Florida International University offered an evening course called "Cuban Miami: A Guide for Non-Cubans" (Didion, 1987, p. 55), to educate "Anglos" (Hispanics' name for Americans) about this immigrant group that fled a disruptive revolution in their country. Furthermore, Didion (1987) observed the following:

> Anglos did not on the whole understand that assimilation would be considered by most Cubans a doubtful goal at best. Nor did many Anglos understand that living in Florida was still at the deepest level construed by Cubans as a temporary condition, an accepted political option shaped by the continuing dream. (p. 57)

The case of Cuban immigrants as well as some Latin American immigrants is unique because of their being *in exilio* [exile], an issue I explore in chapter 9.

It is of the utmost importance to emphasize that the city of Miami has been, for many Hispanic immigrants, a gateway to the United States.

The majority of its residents, 50.9%, according to those registered in 2000, is of foreign extraction. In 2000, Miami was considered, after Los Angeles, the U.S. city with the most Hispanics, with a total population of 1,291,737 Spanish-speaking people. According to Stavans (2005), Miami's population is nearly 80% "minority" (p. 142).

Puerto Ricans

There are almost 3.2 million Puerto Ricans—12.1% of the U.S. Hispanic population—living in the United States. A large majority, 69%, live in the northeastern United States, where the term *Puertorrequeño* is commonly used (Sullivan, 2002), although they are also known as *boricuas*. The case of Puerto Rico is unique in that, because the country was colonized by Spain, they share its culture and language, but the island became a U.S. territory after the Spanish American War in 1898 (Lew, 2005). Cuadrado and Lieberman (2002), in *Traditional Family Values and Substance Abuse*, concluded the following based on a survey of 1,100 Puerto Ricans living in the New York City area:

> Puerto Ricans, unlike other Hispanic groups that have come to the United States, are American citizens from birth; however, almost half the respondents do not identify themselves as Americans, and slightly over one third identify themselves as both Puerto Ricans and Americans. It appears that although Puerto Ricans have the status of U.S. citizenship, their identity as an American may be weaker than that of other so-called hyphenated Americans. (p. 34)

There is also a dilemma regarding the use of the term Hispanic to refer to people from Puerto Rico. As Schutte (2000) observed about Latina women in "Negotiating Latina Identities," there are different ways to name a Latina independently if her homeland is inside or outside of the United States, as is in the case of Puerto Ricans. Schutte posed the following questions: "Is it the case that *puertoriqueña* would reference one with respect to the island culture or its diaspora, whereas 'Latina[,]' used to refer to the same person, would make her a minority of Latin origin in the United States?" and "What are the social expectations accompanying one term or another?" (p. 69). Actually, Schutte found this issue with "one's homeland heritage and one's minority condition [to be] a source of conflict or tension" (p. 69).

Central Americans

Central America, an isthmus connecting North and South America, comprises seven countries: (a) Belize, (b) Guatemala, (c) El Salvador, (d) Honduras, (e) Nicaragua, (f) Costa Rica, and (g) Panama. According to the U.S. Census American Community Survey and estimates by Bendixen and Associates, there were 2.5 million Central American adult immigrants in the United States in June 2007 (IADB, 2007).

From my personal experience, many Americans living in the United States are not aware of the existence of Central America. Although I am Nicaraguan, many people assume I am from South America. However, for an immigrant such as myself, it is meaningful when a person from another culture has some notion of my country of origin. Many Central Americans prefer to be associated with their original country and culture rather than broadly identified as Central American. Although Central Americans have cultural differences, especially between Hispanic and indigenous people, there are significant similarities among the people and cultures in that region (Kemp & Rasbridge, 2004).

My focus with Central American clients is on Nicaragua and El Salvador because their civil wars in the 1970s and 1980s account for a large number of immigrants in the United States.[1] Let's be aware that post-traumatic stress disorder caused by wartime experiences, and its consequences, often arise in counseling.

South Americans

South America is a continent that comprises 12 countries: (a) Argentina, (b) Bolivia, (c) Brazil, (d) Chile, (e) Colombia, (f) Ecuador, (g) Guyana, (h) Paraguay, (i) Peru, (j) Suriname, (k) Uruguay, and (l) Venezuela. With the exception of Brazil and Guyana, and some indigenous languages, such as Quechua (Torero, 1983), the official language in these countries is Spanish. In general, people from South America prefer to be associated with their country and culture of origin—Brazilian, Peruvian, Colombian, and so on—instead of being identified simply as South Americans. From the 1960s to the present, the number of South American immigrants to the United States has grown dramatically, because of different circumstances,

---

[1] See Miranda and Wood (1992), *The Civil War in Nicaragua: Inside the Sandinistas*, and Wood (2003), *Insurgent Collective Action and Civil War in El Salvador* for details on the political struggle and war that caused many Nicaraguans and El Salvadorans to flee their countries.

among them "serious political and economic problems, including repressive military dictatorships, bloody insurgencies and a severe debt crisis that rocked the region at the end of the 1980s" (Barnett 2004, p. 20). For example, immigrants from Colombia have "fled political violence and economic turmoil" (Brinkley-Rogers, 2001), and Venezuelans have felt impelled to leave their homeland because of "political and economic unrest" (Abbady, 2002). Another fact that is of utmost importance in Colombia and Venezuela is personal safety. It is quite common to hear stories of people being kidnapped from their homes and either killed or tortured by their kidnappers for political reasons or for the purposes of obtaining a ransom. Because of their unbearable situations, many Colombians and Venezuelans have sought haven and freedom in the United States.

HELPFUL SUGGESTIONS

- Be aware of the difference between Hispanic and Latino and how these labels do not exist in Latino America. The Hispanic person prefers to be identified with their country of origin.
- Don't assume that because your Hispanic client has lived in the United States for several years he or she is already acculturated. Ask them if they have adapted to the new lifestyle of if they continue totally immersed in their culture. You can ask the language they speak at home, the food they eat, and/or the TV shows they watch.
- If you are not sure about something in relation to your client's culture, ask. As members of another culture we feel pleased and grateful to talk about our traditions and customs if you ask us to, because it shows that you care.

PERSONAL REFLECTIONS FOR THE COUNSELOR

- Do you feel comfortable working with people who come from a culture that is different from yours?
- Are you sensitive to culturally different ways of thinking or behaving?
- Are you able to assist, in a nonjudgmental fashion, a person of another culture who is going through grief?

CHAPTER 3

Sociocultural Perspectives on Hispanics

It is important to be aware of the values and the most salient elements of the cultural traditions of Hispanics in order to understand how they experience and express grief. Some recent studies have shown that a relationship exists between a culture and the way grief and bereavement are expressed, whereas other studies have not found a connection. It is essential for culturally sensitive counselors to know the values and norms of different cultures and to understand how they influence the grief experience (Bougere, 2008). It is through this knowledge and understanding that we can comprehend the impact of a loss on our clients and thus know how to offer them the best help. In this chapter, I explore the role of the family and discuss certain Hispanic values that the counselors should be aware of so that they can effectively help Hispanic clients cope with their crisis or loss. I also explore two issues prevalent among Hispanics that in many cases can bring a sense of despair and grief: (a) domestic violence and (b) *machismo* (a strong sense of masculinity).

Mental health professionals need to understand that there is not a single prototype of a Hispanic family living in the United States. The diversity of this population is the same as in the different Latin American countries. The members of each group bring their mores, traditions, accents, and religious beliefs to the United States. According to Flores and Carey (2000), therapists need to be more "culturally resonant" and aware of the following:

> Client's country of origin, present location, social contexts, and economic needs . . . [because] . . . acculturation produces great

changes over time and for each new generation of Hispanics born in the United States. The differences in first-, second-, and third-generation Hispanic families are . . . manifested [at] behavioral, emotional, and cognitive levels. (p. x)

As you work with this population, it is imperative to be aware that some of them are wealthy, and others face poverty; some live in large cities or the capital, others in rural areas; many are immigrants from various Latin American countries, and many are citizens of the United States. To establish a rapport that is based on trust and respect, culturally sensitive counselors consider these factors in their therapy relationships.

HISPANIC IDENTITY, VALUES, AND TRADITIONS

In the following discussion of Hispanics' values and traditions, the variables involved should be kept in mind: "No culture is so homogeneous that a certain set of beliefs or behaviors can accurately be said to apply to all members of the culture" (Welland & Ribner, 2008, p. 51). Most Hispanics have a value system that they consider important in their lives. These systems comprise personal and cultural values and, according to Stavans (2005), can be traditional, modern, or transitional. Stavans considers the values to be reflections of the way we feel. He asserted that we can idealize our values or enact them. The term *idealized values* refers to the cultural scripts of how we think things "should" be; for example, "Among Latinos the idealized family is characterized by interdependence, solidarity, cooperation, respect and hierarchically-based rules and roles" (Stavans, 2005, p. 168). *Enacted values* refer to the way these are played out in real life.

Although idealized family values are present in Hispanic culture, many Hispanics might have been influenced by other cultural values inherent in the United States. Some may have a conflict between being interdependent on their families and independent, as 20-year-old Rafael explained:

When I turned 18, I felt I was ready to leave home and move with my friends to an apartment. It is what most of my male friends do here in the United States, but when I shared my plans with my mom, she almost had a fit! She expects me to live at home until I get married . . . I don't intend to get married until I am 30! How can I explain to her we are not living in El Salvador anymore?

Such conflict is often observed by therapists working with families who have experienced a loss of their traditions and need to learn to adapt to a new culture. Maintaining their family values while living in a different kind of society can be challenging for Hispanics, but culturally sensitive counselors can facilitate their adaptation with specific tools to help them reframe their perspective. In subsequent chapters, when I introduce counseling cases, I present various techniques that can assist counselors in helping their clients identify their sources of grief and deal with them in a meaningful manner.

The following questions may be appropriate when assessing the sociocultural environment of a Hispanic client:

- Which are the most salient values and traditions of your family of origin?
- Do you live according to these values?
- What challenges do you face in the United States as a Latino?
- Do you think there is a difference between you and the Hispanics from countries different from yours?
- Do you think Hispanics risk losing their identity and/or self-esteem living in a new country?
- What will help you to feel valued?

Familismo

For Latinos, familism, or *familismo*, is the value of maintaining interdependence among the members of the family. It places the needs of the family as a unit over the needs of the individual. This value is very common among Hispanics and entails having a commitment, responsibility, and obligation to the members of the family (Figueredo, 2002). For example, the roles of the father and mother are very specific. In general, the father is considered the head of the family and is highly respected. He can be, at times, feared by his children. If a loss happens in the family, the father will expect his son(s), even if a little boy, not to cry but to behave like a man. Whereas, the mother is the nurturer, and she usually acts as a mediator between the children and the father. In traditional families, the woman is supposed to conform to what her husband says and mandates. Honor and pride are vital in traditional families.

Another prominent value in *familismo* is interdependence, which is a way of showing solidarity, collaboration, and support within the Hispanic family. Because the family usually extends beyond the parents and children, this support can be of almost inestimable value in times of grief. Mental health professionals should be aware of this dynamic and be more open to the inclusion of other persons, including close friends or fictive relatives who are back in the clients' home country, who may be referred to as, for example, *Tío Juan* [Uncle Juan]. An excerpt from *The Hispanic Way* (Noble & Lacasa, 1991) shows the strength of such strong family ties:

> The term *familia* goes beyond the nuclear family. It usually means the extended family . . . and may consist of father, mother, younger children, older children, and their spouses and children, grandparents, aunts, uncles, and cousin, and in an outer circle, *padrinos* [godparents] and *compadres* [godfather or godmother of one's child; father/mother of one's godchild]. Family ties are very strong. (p. 41)

Hispanics do not believe in individuality within the family. Collectivism is part of the culture. For example, Carolina, a 32-year-old native of the Dominican Republic, explained a conflict between her job and her family:

> I am really proud to be the manager of a clothing store. It gives me new responsibilities, and I feel valued. Still, my schedule is always changing, and that represents a conflict with having dinner with my family on Saturdays. My sisters are upset with me because I have broken a family tradition, especially now that our mother is an elderly woman. I don't want to cause more problems; therefore, I think I will resign.

A counselor conscious of the value of interdependence among Hispanics, when working with a patient such as Carolina, will be very careful not to make her feel that she is making the wrong decision but will help her make a choice congruent with her values that is to her benefit.

Most Hispanic adult children live with their parents until they get married. Although they value their independence, they value their family structure more, in contrast to the Anglo culture, which "values independence, freedom, privacy, and the Protestant work ethic" (Montalban-Anderssen, 1998).

Family Values

When a member of a Hispanic family has a problem, it becomes a family problem. It is common for other family members to give advice, get involved, and provide a lot of support. Hispanics usually resist looking for external help, such as grief counseling or a support group. They consider problems to be private and believe that *las cosas de la casa se quedan en la casa* [private matters stay at home]. This expected behavior may be a source of difficulty for a person who wants or needs professional help. Hispanics may feel inhibited about openly sharing their issues, especially when another family member, such as the father, may be involved. Maria, a woman from El Salvador, shared her discomfort about speaking about members of her family when she went to therapy for the first time:

> I felt really uncomfortable talking about my problems because I didn't want to involve my family. I felt like I was betraying them, especially if I talked about my dad. And I am not the only one. My sister felt the same.

The issue of privacy in the Hispanic culture can be a source of a client's resistance to opening up, so the therapist needs to be very careful not to appear too demanding or intrusive. In chapter 7, I will explore different ways of connecting with the patient and establishing a trusting relationship.

Social support for Hispanics, especially family support, has a great buffering effect for many of the issues the members of this group may face, including mental health challenges. This conclusion received empirical support from a study of 850 Hispanics living in Miami–Dade County, Florida, regarding acculturation and mental health (Rivera, 2007). However, as Rebecca M. Cuevas de Caissie (2009) stated, it is important to notice that although there are some values inherent to most Hispanics, one cannot and should not generalize and expect all of them to hold these values. The following is her definition of one of Hispanics' most important values:

> I think there [is] a certain set of values in the Hispanic community that sets us apart. . . . Family by far is the most valued part of any Hispanic's life. . . . Beginning with growing up as a young Hispanic, we do not look forward to the life ahead of us with thoughts of ourselves outside the family. We are not independent of the family unit. . . . Everything you go through as you are growing up is shared with some member of the family. Children grow up hanging out with their brothers, sisters, and cousins as friends. . . . I would have to say [the most important value] . . . is family. They are your hopes, dreams, support, strength, cheerleaders. Family loves you when no one else will. When all has failed you as a Hispanic, family will never fail you. They give you roots, identity, acceptance, devotion, promise, passion, drive and life. Yes, family is life. (http://www.bellaonline.com/articles/art31982.asp p. 1)

Hispanics find diverse ways of relating to others. Among friends and acquaintances, there is much camaraderie and physical expression, such as kisses and hugs, which are commonly exchanged. However, when dealing with strangers, the treatment is more formal and distant:

> Spanish speakers tend toward formality in their treatment of one another. A firm handshake is a common practice between people as greeting and for leave-taking. . . . The Spanish language provides forms of formal and non-formal address (different use of *usted* vs. *tu* for the pronoun "you," polite and familiar commands, the use of titles of respect before people's first names such as Don or Doña [for example Don Pedro or Doña Rosita]). (Clutter & Nieto, n.d., http:// ohioline.osu.edu/hyg-fact/5000/5237.html)

Addressing a person with a certain pronoun or title shows respect and is of great significance among Hispanics. For example, the counselor may expect to be addressed as *Don* or *Doña*, and the client will expect the same form of address in return, especially if he or she is older than the person addressing him or her. Many Hispanics find it disrespectful to address a person older than them by his or her first name, as is often the custom in the United States. Even if the person has a close relationship with the elder, it is preferable to use a means of formal address. In Argentina, Nicaragua, and El Salvador, we use the pronoun *vos* instead of *tu* [you] when we refer to a person in a familiar way. Otherwise, as stated above, we all use the more formal version, *usted*, to show respect for authority, when we have just met the person, or when we are talking to a person older than us. However, it is customary and common among Hispanics to use the name in a diminutive form when addressing a person in a caring manner, especially if the son or daughter has the same name as the parent. For example, Peter Jr. will be *Pedrito*.

The Role of Grandmothers in the Hispanic Family

Elders are respected members of the community in certain cultures, and many of them live with their grown-up children and grandchildren (Kemp & Rasbridge, 2004). The role of Hispanic grandparents, especially that of the grandmother, or *abuelita*, has a great effect on the lives of the grandchildren. Cherlin and Furstenberg (1992) analyzed different cultures in their study of compensation for grandchildren's care. They concluded that black grandparents were more likely than white grandparents to take on "parent-like" roles with their grandchildren, therefore not expecting any payment or compensation for their care and they speculated that the same is true of Hispanic grandparents. I would add that, for Hispanics, taking care of grandchildren is in itself more rewarding than receiving compensation for it. Helping to take care of family members is part of our culture.

Grandparents are vital members of the extended family in Hispanic cultures. I remember that in my country (Nicaragua), my *abuelita* lived with us until she died. She was respected and cared for. Even my close friends called her "Mama Lola." The role of *abuelitas* has evolved over the years because of increased mobilization, cultural influences, and migration. It is essential that therapists who work with Hispanic clients be aware of the bond they will likely have with their grandparents and know that they may experience intense grief when grandparents pass away. In many cases, grandmothers are the ones who actually raise the grandchildren; therefore they also become the children's *mamita* (mommy).

In addition to the questions presented earlier in this chapter, you can ask your clients the following questions to get a better idea of the family dynamics and how family members relate to each other:

- Do you live with your father and/or your mother?
- Who makes the most important decisions in the house?
- How is your relationship with your father? With your mother?
- In your family, do men have more power than women?
- Do you share your problems with your family? With your friends?
- Do you feel comfortable sharing family matters with others?

Communication Among Hispanics

Members of other cultures often consider Hispanics to be very emotional, which may be owing to the fact that Hispanics are very open when expressing positive or negative emotions (Carillo, 1982). It is common among Hispanics to talk louder than Anglos and make gestures as they communicate thoughts and feelings. This can be misinterpreted by people in other cultures as being rude or ill-mannered. Hispanics may raise their voices to make a point or simply out of excitement, even though they are not angry or upset. Several of them may talk at the same time and engage in a vivid conversation, interrupting the conversation of people nearby. This can be disruptive in public places such as hospitals, where more subtle behavior is expected. Sonia, who works in patient relations for a hospital, commented to me that in the emergency room one may find many relatives of the patient (Hispanic), all talking at the same time and expecting to remain with the patient all the time, even while the patient is being treated in the emergency room.

Gracia, in *Latinos in America: Philosophy and Social Identity* (2008), explored the issue of identity in a comprehensive and exhaustive manner. Space limitations prevent me from exploring here all the variables involved in defining a person's identity as Gracia proposed, but I do want to include his "Four Basic Questions About Identity," which counselors should take into account when working with Hispanics:

1. How do identities function?
2. How do identities arise?
3. How do identities endure?
4. What does having an identity entail?

The way Gracia (2008) explored each of these questions resonates with how many Latinos, including myself, feel about our identities. For example, I am Nicaraguan, but I am also Hispanic, Latina, and/or Latin American. Many of my clients and friends are Latinos, but they do not want to be labeled because they are more than just a "Latino." They live in the United States, but they continue listening to Latin music, eating the foods of their home country, and paying attention to the news from their home country. Does that mean they have two different identities? I have come to realize that our essence, our most fundamental idea of "self," cannot change simply through transplantation to another country. Some people adapt to the recently acquired identity, but others remain isolated, longing for their "lost" identity. A sensitive counselor will take this into consideration as the client elaborates his or her history of losses. The blurring of lines between identities can occur also in cases of war, immigration, or a natural disaster, when people may come together as a group and then develop a common identity.

Consider the case of Carlos Fernando, a Venezuelan whose parents were Italian and who now lives in Miami. He considers himself Italian–Venezuelan, but because he has blond hair and green eyes some people talk to him in English and do not consider him Latino. He once shared the following with me:

> I am tired of people being surprised of my physical appearance. They think that because I am not "brown" I am not Latino. But that is who I am. What's more, people think I belong to the Venezuelans living

in Weston (a city in Florida where many Venezuelans live), so I have been confined to a new group of people.

The way Carlos feels is common among many immigrants; as Gracia (2008) affirmed, our identities are not fixed but flexible. This concept of the impermanence of identities was introduced to the field of psychology by Erikson (1963, 1968) and is highly connected to our relation to others and to our personal history (Gutmann, 1996).

As Hispanics establish their identities in the United States, they will have to deal with negative comments about what is expected of them. For example, some schoolteachers may ask, "Why should [Mexican students] take college prep classes if they are just going to be field workers and maids?" (Carbajal & Medina, 2008, p. 52). The negative implications of such questions may have a great impact on the self-esteem and self-confidence of Hispanic students, influencing the choices they make in life. Counselors should remember that at times, people do not use words to express this attitude; the body language can communicate how one feels toward others. They should be aware of the value of nonverbal communication when working with clients of other cultures, especially when counseling Hispanics.

Common Stereotypes About Hispanics

In the United States, people often tend to generalize their conception of a group of people based on the actions or behaviors of a few. This is known as *stereotyping*, and it can be very damaging because it can result in discrimination or prejudice toward a group and/or an individual. Most stereotypes, including ones about Hispanics, are inaccurate or misleading, giving rise to damaging misconceptions. Sullivan (2002), in her essay "A Demographic Portrait," identified certain stereotypes about Hispanics. I consider the following two to be most relevant to the topic at hand.

Stereotype 1: Hispanics Are Primarily a Rural People

Because at the beginning of the 20th century, as Chavez (1991) observed, many Hispanics worked on farms, many still consider them to be rural people:

> Stereotypes of Latin immigrants persist. Many people continue to think of them as peasants who come north seeking jobs in agriculture. The stereotype is probably a holdover from the era of the Bracero Program (a U.S. government program that started in 1942 and

ended in 1960), which brought some 350,000 Mexican men a year to work as contract laborers in agriculture during the 1950s. . . . But the stereotype of the Latino farm worker is at best an anachronism. Not only do most immigrants today work in urban areas, but most lived in towns and cities before coming to the United States. (p. 123)

Stereotype 2: Hispanics Do Not Value Education

Sullivan (2002) observed that:

[Although many Hispanics have a] relatively low level of educational attainment . . . [this] does not indicate . . . that Hispanic families do not value education. . . . It is more probable that the availability of educational opportunity plays a crucial role. (p. 14)

This can be one of the most damaging stereotypes because a Hispanic may suffer from discrimination based on this assumption. In fact, in Latin America the level of education in the school system is very advanced, and many Hispanics living in the United States attain high levels of education, accomplishing great success in their professional lives. In *Building the Latino Future* (Carbajal & Medina, 2008) one can read the stories of

dozens of men and women who, despite humble beginnings, meager resources, and limited opportunities, beat the odds and rose to become leaders in their professions . . . over the last two decades, Latinos have risen to places of prominence in every walk of life in the United States. (back cover)

Misconceptions regarding Hispanics' view of education can have negative consequences for the self-worth and self-esteem of this population, especially because success among Hispanics is at times masked, as Chavez (1991) affirmed: "The success of middle-class Hispanics is an untold—and misunderstood—story perhaps least appreciated by Hispanic advocates whose interest is in promoting the view that Latinos cannot make it in this society" (p. 101). The case of Maria Josefina, a cleaning lady I interviewed, illustrates how debilitating to one's self-esteem it can be not to be able to pursue an education because of an inability to speak the language or a lack of financial support:

I am cleaning houses now. It is not that I find it embarrassing but I know that if I would speak the language I could be working in an office. *Los Americanos* [the Americans] think that we want to be cleaning houses because it is easy or because we are illegal. I am not illegal! I came from Honduras 8 years ago and have my papers, but wasn't able to study because I came with my two young children and had to work. Now I am studying English and signed up to become a medical assistant.

The language barrier remains one of the greatest hindrances to Hispanics' pursuit of higher education, and it is directly related to the many challenges this community faces, such as high unemployment, a skyrocketing high school dropout rate, widespread opposition to immigration reform, and crowded communities (Fears, 2003, p. A01).

Hispanics need to feel proud deep in their hearts about who they are and to rely on their culture and tradition to bring meaning and sense to any circumstance or situation they face: "Cultural meaning systems may be better conceived as a set of tools individuals have available to use in different situations according to their identity dynamics and situational relevance" (Benet-Martinez, Leu, Lee, & Morris, 2002, p. 512).

Celebrations and Holidays

Hispanics very much enjoy celebrating holidays surrounded by family and friends, and many of them nostalgically remember the manner in which specific celebrations or traditions were conducted in their country of origin. It is not uncommon to hear "Do you remember when . . ." or "In [country of origin] it was different." These comments express the Hispanic person's loss as he or she adapts to different ways of celebrating holidays in their adopted country. However, most of them have kept their traditions. Among the most celebrated of holidays are *Los Quince*, Mother's Day, and Christmas, which I describe briefly in the following sections.

Los Quince

For Hispanics, to celebrate *Los Quince*, or the 15th birthday of a girl (the equivalent of a sweet sixteen celebration) is an occasion of joy, extensive planning, and celebration. It is a festivity and families of all social levels do their best to give it to their daughters. This event is a rite of passage, or a coming of age. To be a *quinceañera* is an event highly anticipated by many Hispanic teenage girls and their parents (Menard, 2004). In most cases, the girl dresses in a long pink dress and dances the first song, generally a waltz, with her father. If the father has died, many *quinceañeras* dance with their older brother, a cousin, or an uncle. Many girls whose fathers are deceased refuse to celebrate *Los Quince* because of the intense pain they experience with the absence, as in the case of one of my clients, Marcela, who was not even able to talk about her recent birthday. Because I noticed she was reluctant to talk, I suggested she write a letter to her deceased father telling him how she had missed him the day she turned 15 and how much she would have loved to dance the waltz with him. The following week, Marcela brought the letter. She was quiet and in a very soft manner she extended the letter to me. She asked, "Will you read it, or do you want me to read it?" I asked her what she preferred. She chose to read the letter, and it was a very powerful moment for her. She could express to her father all the grief she had been holding in her heart for months. Marcela felt relieved and shared the experience with her mother.

However, with their acculturation, many young Hispanic women in the United States prefer to celebrate becoming "sweet sixteen" instead of *Los Quince*. Nevertheless, *Los Quince* is a unique event that unites the whole family, from the grandparents to the aunts, uncles, *compadres* and *comadres*, who have all been very much present in the life of the girl since she was baptized. At times the godparents are considered responsible for the upbringing of their *ahijado* or *ahijada* (godson or goddaughter) if the parents die.

Mother's Day (*El Día de las Madres*)

Although the Hispanic family seems to revolve around the father or a patriarchal structure, the mother has great influence on different issues, including medical care. Even though *machismo*, or a strong masculinity, is predominant in Hispanic families, the mother figure is of vital importance in this culture:

> Latino devotion to motherhood is clear and evident from the veneration of the Virgin Mary; [and] the extravagant celebrations that surround Mother's Day, or [El] *Día de las Madres*; and the fact that many Latinos living in the United States celebrate it twice in one month. (Menard, 2004, p. 47)

In the Nicaraguan community, we celebrate Mother's Day on May 30 as well as on the second Sunday in May, as is the custom in the United States. This is an example of acculturation to American traditions while keeping those of one's country of origin. In Mexico, the celebration of Mother's Day is so important that it is a national holiday (Menard, 2004). For a

Hispanic, being away from one's mother on *El Día de las Madres* is a source of grief, as Josefina, a client from Honduras, indicated:

> I call my mom every week because I miss her a lot, but this year I won't be able to go to Mexico because I don't have money to travel. I feel very sad because it is not the same being away from her. She will be disappointed because I won't be with her. How can I explain to her? I am afraid something [will happen] to her if I don't go.

As we see from Josefina's words, she has a variety of feelings. Besides being sad, she is experiencing guilt because she won't be able to visit her mother on *El Día de las Madres*; at the same time, she experiences fear that something may happen to her mother and anticipated guilt that it would be her fault as an absent daughter.

Christmas

Christmas is very important for Hispanics, who celebrate it on Christmas Eve, also called *Nochebuena* or *El 24*. Although many Hispanics have adopted the typical American menu (turkey, stuffing, mashed potatoes), most prefer to also include some of their traditional holiday foods, which may differ from country to country. For example, Mexicans celebrate with tamales, Nicaraguans with hen or turkey, and Cubans with pork. As a way of passing on their traditions, some of the food served on this holiday generally reflects the country of origin, as Jesse Moreno, the owner of a Mexican tamales store, put it: "[Eating tamales is] a tradition that means a lot to us. The main reason I'm doing this . . . isn't for the money, it's for my sons. I want them to know this tradition" (cited in Menard, 2004, p. 185).

Mourning

Mourning customs among Hispanics have been conventional until recent years, probably changing because of acculturation. Although chapter 7 is dedicated to a discussion of death, dying, and bereavement, here I introduce some of the most vital elements of Hispanic mourning customs. Traditionally, the mourner wears black, black and white, or dark colors for the funeral as well as for a length of time after the loved one's death. The length of the mourning period, which generally is from a month to a year, varies according to the bereaved individual's relationship with the deceased, but during this time the bereaved are expected to abstain from social activities, such as going to a party or spending time with friends in a social setting. It is a sign of *respeto* [respect] to wait for a certain amount of time to pass before resuming normal activity. Most Hispanics are Catholic and thus have many religious rituals related to death and dying, such as celebrating a Mass for the soul of the deceased or praying the rosary. Relatives and close friends are a source of comfort and constantly accompany the bereaved. Their presence makes a big difference in our bereavement. As Hispanics have moved to the United States, they have given up some of these customs, to the bewilderment of the elderly members of the family, who are used to their traditional values and customs and expect certain behaviors in times of mourning. Although many younger and second-generation Hispanics have abandoned traditional mourning customs, certain behaviors are still expected during the time of bereavement. For instance, people comment when a widow wears a color other than black immediately after the death of her spouse; or they may use this dress code because it is expected in society and they care about what people will say. However, the mourning customs are not the same now. In my recent visits to my home country of Nicaragua I have noticed how the majority of people have shortened the mourning period and embraced more modern approaches. One of the changes, as I shared in the Preface with the story of *Personas Unidas En El Dolor y La Esperanza* [People United by Grief and Hope], is the embracing of bereavement support groups, something that was unheard of earlier. This shows the transition from depending only on family for support in times of grief to a willingness to share one's grief with strangers who also have experienced a loss.

How Latinos Conduct Business

Many Hispanic businesses are run by a father, a son, or an uncle. Today, there are more women entrepreneurs; therefore one may find a Hispanic mother and daughter working together in a business venture. Many of these ventures are small commercial shops called *bodegas* and import/export businesses with the country of origin. Now, however, they are expanding into more sophisticated areas, such as advertising, flower shops, or home health care. Because of their family ties, it is common for Hispanics/Latinos to welcome a new member of the family to work in the business, especially if that person has just arrived in the United States and needs a job. Clarita, a Cuban American woman, expressed her joy about her uncle being reunited with her family in Miami after 50 years:

> Uncle Roberto is so happy to be here. Everybody came to see him and everybody is offering their houses for him to stay. He is happy that even at 70 years of age, he already has a job at my other uncle's *bodega*.

In *The Hispanic Way* (1991), Noble and Lacasa observed that Latinos conduct business "on a personal and sociable level . . . [and how] this can be surprising and somewhat disconcerting to someone from another culture who is used to a very direct, straightforward, fairly fast-moving way of conducting business" (p. 13). This is one cultural custom that may provoke nostalgia and require adjustment among Hispanics as they try to assimilate into mainstream American culture.

Traditional cultural values may have a positive effect on the undesirable behaviors of some members of this cultural group, including substance abuse. In their book *Traditional Family Values and Substance Abuse*, Cuadrado and Lieberman (2002) discussed a study of traditionalism and alcohol/substance abuse, conducted with 1,084 Puerto Ricans living in the New York area, which showed the significance of traditionalism:

> Adherence to a more traditionalist view of one's culture has the socially desired consequence of inhibiting the emergence of deviant behaviors such as alcohol and other forms of substance abuse . . . the traditional values discussed in this volume are family values; the values that help define the roles of husband and wife toward each other and the raising of children on a day-to-day basis. (p. 2)

Patriarchal Family System

It is the male who, as the head of the family, has the last word on making decisions. As I mentioned at the beginning of this chapter, some decisions involve all members of the family but, in general, the person who represents the family system is the father or the oldest male of the family. For men who come from Latin America, letting go of their patriarchal behavior is at times challenging because it is all that they have known. It has been part of their culture to provide for and take care of the women in their lives, which is considered *ser un hombre* [to be a man].

Many Hispanics face the challenge that their adolescents, caught between two cultures, find that unquestioning obedience to the father can undermine their attempts to fit in with their peers in the United States. It is not uncommon to hear expressions among second-generation Latinas, such as the following:

> My mom insists that a friend should come with me when I go out with my boyfriend. She doesn't understand that life here is different . . . she always refers to the chaperones in Cuba. I don't want to be "different" among my friends.

Marianismo

Latin American women have been portrayed as submissive to an extent, but Asunción Lavrin (1978) intended to create a new perspective of *marianismo*—veneration of women for traits such as purity and moral strength—through a collection of essays that "tried to revise the stereotype of the Latin woman as a passive element in society by emphasizing the role of women as doers or agents" (p. 5). This intention is in contrast to the idealization of the Hispanic woman, according to the following:

> In Hispanic folk culture, *marianismo* is a characterization of the ideal personality of women. Across the literature on the subject, this ideal woman is emotional, kind, instinctive, whimsical, docile, compliant, vulnerable, and unassertive. She has a higher status in the community if she has children. The roots of *marianismo* reside in Roman Catholic theology. . . . Therefore, *marianismo* alludes to the expectation that the ideal wife and mother is required to be immaculate and spiritually superior to men. This translates into a kind of sex-based role behavior in which the ideal woman is expected to suffer without complaining, and to place the needs of her husband and children before her own wishes and desires. (Enos & Southern, 1996, p. 200)

Machismo

Scholarly literature, soap operas, everyday language, and even stereotypes have tried to represent and define *machismo*, but despite the fact that *machismo* has been identified with Hispanic culture, it is really just another word for "the masculine force, which to one degree or another drives all masculine behavior" (Andrade, 1992, p. 34). Certain characteristics of *machismo*, such as violence and aggressiveness, have been ascribed to Mexican men; however, according to Abalos (2002), these men can redefine themselves in the roles they have in their families and society. Moreover, many psychologists and researchers are expanding this unilateral view to one that differentiates the *macho*, which focuses on dominance, and the *caballero* [gentleman], which focuses on emotional connectedness:

> Within the field of psychology and sociology, the growing trend is toward a more bidimensional assessment of machismo . . . [researchers have] hypothesized that there are really two separate constructs

underlying machismo, one positive construct and one negative construct. (Arciniega, Anderson, Tovar-Blank, & Tracey, 2008, p. 20)

Although *machismo* is considered a Latino male trait, and to some extent still exists in traditional families, today the roles of Hispanic men and women have been challenged and changed. Many women are active members of the community, at times earning more money than their spouse. Men, on the other hand, have learned to be more communicative and to share important decisions with their spouse, including financial and work decisions. All these changes have to do with acculturation and globalization and can be observed in all areas of society, even in the way women are portrayed in popular *novelas* [soap operas]. In Latin America the term *machismo* is identified with the power exercised by the men in the family, but this is not true in all families. In *Muy Macho: Latino Men Confront Their Manhood* (Gonzalez, 1996), *machismo* is explored as 16 men share their experiences and break the culture of silence that seems to have predominantly characterized the development of this identity. Their stories may be of great interest for counselors who work with the male Hispanic population. In one of the essays in *Muy Macho*, Rudolfo Anaya described what being macho means:

> The word macho has one of the shortest definitions in the Spanish language dictionary, and yet the cult of macho behavior (machismo or the macho image) is as ambiguous and misunderstood as any aspect of Hispanic/Latino culture. To be macho is to be male, that's simple, [it] is essentially a learned behavior; as such it is a conditioned behavior. We males learn to act "manly" from other males around us; the "macho" that preceded us was learned from the cultures from which it evolved. (p. 59)

If one pays close attention to this description, one can see the tremendous impact of role modeling. This role modeling can change as men move to another culture and are exposed to different kinds of behavior. However, in families where *machismo* exists, men treat their women with superiority or just continue the tradition of their fathers and grandfathers. Some of these men abuse their wives physically or emotionally, or engage in extramarital relationships, which are sources of grief and loss.

Because the structure of the Hispanic family has been patriarchal and is characterized by male dominance, mental health professional who work with Hispanic women should empower them so that they can feel strong enough to be part of mainstream society (Mayo & Resnick, 1996).

Not all Latinos are "macho men," however. Therefore, therapists who work with this population need to be able to "appreciate contemporary Latino males and transcend the myths concerning their 'macho mystique'" (Flores & Carey, 2000, p. vii).

Domestic Violence

Domestic violence is experienced by women of all cultures (although men also can be victims), but among Hispanic women it can be quite prevalent. Although I feel it is necessary to clarify that intimate partner violence (IPV) is not confined to the Hispanic culture (Carrillo & Tello, 2008), it is a known fact that race and culture matter in this regard. For example, Carrillo and Tello asserted that the "historical roots of colonization have contributed significantly to the learning of violence as an accepted form of power, control and learned oppression" (p. xvii). Sandra, a woman dedicated to work with abused women, made the following observation:

> I mostly help women who are not economically established in this country. . . . Many of these women [from] Nicaragua, Honduras, Guatemala, El Salvador, Mexico, Colombia, Chile, Ecuador, have been abused. You mostly see a lot from Central America. That's the majority, the most abused. By being in this country alone without any identity, they lose their self-esteem. When you lose your identity you tend to lose the value of a woman you have. You forget the values you gained in your own country . . . these women find themselves in a tough economic situation. I knew this woman who I love very much, who never told me she was abused. I came to her one day but she was frightened and denied it. But she is a woman that God helped because at that moment her son came to say hello and asked me to help them. The man had hit the child as well.
>
> I talked and talked to her and explained to her that this was not the place for her. She called me 6 months later. I told her "Mariana, I haven't heard from you in a long time. I just want to know you are okay and that the Lord loves you very much. I have prayed for you

every day." She told me that she had suffered lots of injuries and she finally called the cops and filed a report.

The devastating prevalence of domestic violence, which affects the physical, emotional, and spiritual life of a woman, and even the lives of her children, is one of the most difficult problems facing the Hispanic community today. However, to understand the patriarchal structure of Hispanic culture, especially as related to *machismo*, counselors would benefit greatly from the information offered by *Mujeres Latinas en Acción* (www.mujereslatinasenaccion .org), an organization that was established in Chicago in 1973 and offers diverse programs for Hispanic women, including an extensive program on domestic violence. According to this group, some deeply held cultural beliefs held by Hispanic women inhibit them from reporting domestic violence:

> A strong sense of culture keeps Latinas from "betraying" long-standing values. Those who step outside of these norms shame not only themselves but also their parents, grandparents, etc. . . . . A batterer who is a U.S. citizen may manipulate and control his immigrant wife by threatening to have her deported if she complains about his violence. He may coerce her to stay with the empty promise of filing her residency papers. In Mexico, a law called *abandono de hogar* (to leave one's home) punishes women who leave their homes, even to flee violence. (http://www.mujereslatinasenaccion.org/Latinas%20 &%20DV.html)

There is an obvious correlation between keeping traditional Hispanic values or religious beliefs—that is, "keeping up with appearances" to avoid gossip—and maintaining the role of a victim because of lack of socioeconomic resources. When treating persons suffering from domestic violence, the counselor needs to address such issues as codependency, low self-esteem, and fear.

Furthermore, Hispanics may avoid reporting domestic violence or mistreatment because of the belief that IPV is private and should not be shared with others. Moreover, they may experience

> feelings of shame, guilt, loyalty to their partners, and fear. Latina immigrant women, principally because of social or economic pressures, lack of legal residence status, language and cultural barriers, isolation and mothering responsibilities, find it extremely difficult and unsafe to report the abuse and seek help. (Carrillo & Tello, 2008, p. 72)

Organizations and interventions have been developed to help Hispanic men cope with the prevalence and danger of domestic violence. For instance, intervention models, such as *Hombres Nobles* [Noble Men], have been developed to provide Hispanic men with useful tools to become *hombres de palabra* [men of their word] (Carrillo & Tello, 2008, p. 77). Many of these models, such as *Hombres Contra la Violencia in Nicaragua* [Men Against Violence in Nicaragua] and *Colectivo de Hombres por Relaciones Igualitarias* [Group of Men for Equal Relationships in Mexico], have developed in different Hispanic countries. The purpose of these organizations is to work with men to take responsibility for their behavior and promote safe communities so that domestic violence does not occur (Carrillo & Tello, 2008).

These questions may be helpful when working with Hispanic women facing the issue of domestic violence:

- Do you have the support of your family of origin?
- Are you religious?
- Do you know of any community resources?
- Are you fluent in English? If not, do you feel this is an obstacle?
- What other roles, besides being a wife, do you have?
- Do you rely on your husband for "the papers" (i.e., legal immigration documents)?
- Do you feel competent to raise your children by yourself?

Another technique that could be of great value is to ask your client to narrate her story under different perspectives. One could be told from her own perspective from inside the story, another from the perspective of an observer (e.g., third person, as a storyteller), and finally she could narrate a story of her in the future, living a different life.

Although I have explored how prevalent IPV is among Hispanic women, studies indicate that the rate in Hispanic cultures is not significantly higher than the rates in other cultures. The National Violence Against Women survey, conducted in 2000 by the National Institute of Justice, showed that 53.2% of Latina women and 51.8% of non-Latina women reported having been physically assaulted "either by an adult caregiver when they were children or by their partners" (Welland & Ribner, 2008). It is important for the counselor or therapist to consider this fact when working with this population. Although these incidents may be enough reason for a Hispanic woman to terminate a relationship or leave her spouse, many variables may prevent these women from acting. In addition to the factors mentioned earlier is the fact that immigrant men threaten to take their wives to authorities so they can be deported to their country of origin. Sandra, the woman who works with abused women, made the following comment:

> You have those women [whose] loneliness allows [them to] get trapped into being with men who promise them the American dream and end up used, abused, traumatized. They are scared, panicked that [Immigration and Naturalization Services] will take them. This is where we step in. If you ask them, they blame themselves. When God steps into their lives, they begin to see, they see it is a process.

Because many Hispanic women who are victims of IPV are facing similar situations, counselors can offer their understanding and assistance in empowering these women to better their lives and simultaneously provide them with the resources necessary to change their personal situation. Counselors can also work with men in helping them understand they do not need to perpetuate a cultural or family tradition and that they posses the necessary resources to live a fulfilling family life without being controlling or abusive.

HELPFUL SUGGESTIONS

- Respect different values and traditions. At times this is not easy, especially if these are not in congruence with your own. If this poses a challenge to you as a counselor, it is better to refer. You will be doing your client a favor and will be loyal to your own values.
- When in doubt, ask. If you are not sure about something in relation to the culture, ask the necessary questions. As members of our Hispanic culture we feel pleased and grateful to talk about our traditions and customs because it shows that you care as a counselor.
- Treat each person as the unique individual that he or she is. Do not consider all Hispanics to be the same. We share a language, values, and traditions, but not all of us are the same. Each of us brings our own history, upbringing, and expectations to counseling.

PERSONAL REFLECTIONS FOR THE COUNSELOR

- Do you find domestic violence a difficult issue to work with?
- Are you sensitive to different ways of thinking or behaving?
- Are you able to assist a person going through grief in a nonjudgmental fashion?

CHAPTER 4

Religion and Spirituality

Counseling professionals are increasingly aware of spiritual health as they assess their clients because this dimension is a vital component of mental health. In their essay "Spirituality and Death: A Transformation Into New Life," Von Dras and White (2006) explored the connection between the spiritual and the psychological and how individuals' spiritual beliefs influence the way they view and experience death, which is one of the greatest sources of grief. The terms *religion* and *spirituality* are sometimes used interchangeably, and in this chapter I explore the difference between them and the role they play in the lives of Hispanic people as they experience grief and loss.

DEFINING RELIGION AND SPIRITUALITY

Spirituality has to do with the relationship we have with something greater than ourselves, the transcendent, and involves finding meaning and purpose in our lives, a sense of connectedness and peacefulness (Koenig, 2008; Sulmasy, 2002). Generally, religion embodies specific doctrines that are maintained by a social institution, in contrast to spirituality, which denotes the subjective experience a person has of the sacred. I teach a class on world religions at a university, and my students frequently ask about the difference between spirituality and religion. I emphasize the fact that one can be spiritual without being religious. Furthermore, spirituality is what the person experiences internally, whereas religion has to do with external events, such as behaviors and rituals.

RELIGION AND HEALTH

According to Koenig and Cohen (2002), religious beliefs have since the beginning of civilization influenced how people deal with their health and how they use healing practices. Among the practices people have used are "healing rituals, prayers, incantations, or religious pilgrimages" (p. 11). Although, as these authors observed, the effect of religious beliefs on mental health or social support was not really explored until the second half of the 20th century, they discovered more than 850 studies that had examined "the relationship between religious belief or practice and mental health or social functioning" (p. 12). Studies have shown that there is a positive relationship between religious practice and health, including mental health. Dr. Harold Koenig, a pioneer in the field of religion and well-being, coedited, with Michael E. McCullough and David B. Larson, *Handbook of Religion and Health* (2001). The research in this exceptional book is extensive and includes more than 1,000 cases that—according to Koenig, McCullough, and Larson—suggest that religion influences physical and mental health. This work is unique in its structure and content; its reports on health measures range from physical ailments to psychological disturbances. It illustrates the many ways people deal with issues such as illness, loneliness, and death. Koenig and Cohen stated that most studies of religion show a correlation between religious involvement and well-being, hope, and adaptation to bereavement among other positive factors. Research also shows that many people resort to religion when attempting to find meaning in trying situations, such as when coping with serious illnesses (Becker, 2009).

Pargament (1997) reminded us that we all go through different kinds of transitions in life, from family quarrels to illnesses and death and that it is through these times that many people find a source of hope and meaning in religion. Thus, as therapists we need to be aware of our clients' religious beliefs. When I conduct an intake interview with new clients I ask them about their religious beliefs, and I like to integrate those beliefs into therapy in a way that brings meaning to the clients. Moreover, as Badillo (2006) stated, religion is prevalent among immigrants, including the Hispanics, because it helps to preserve traditions that originated in their homeland. For example,

> Many self-described Chicano artists have improvised and revived the Mesoamerican *Día de los Muertos* (the Day of the Dead) tradition, and several predominantly Mexican parishes in the Archdiocese of Los Angeles have incorporated it into their liturgical calendar. (Badillo, 2006, p. 188)

Many Hispanics depend heavily on their religious faith to cope with adversity, whether that adversity has to do with physical health problems or emotional problems. If we want to treat our clients in a holistic manner, part of our assessment of their situation should include their religion and spirituality. The American College of Physicians offered a short assessment containing the following questions (Sims, 2007):

- Is faith (religion, spirituality) important to you in this illness?
- Has faith (religion, spirituality) been important to you at other times in your life?
- Do you have someone to talk to about religious matters?
- Would you like to explore religious matters with someone?

The idea behind such questions as part of an intake assessment is that the counselor communicates to the client that he or she is interested in treating the client as a whole person, which could have a positive impact on the counselor–client relationship. In fact, I developed a "Spiritual Inventory" that the client can fill out during this first assessment. The information gained from this questionnaire can give the counselor insight into the client's religious beliefs.

Spiritual Inventory

1. Do you have any spiritual needs?
2. Do you believe in a higher power/God?
3. Where do you find connectedness?
4. Do you feel connected to others?
5. Do you believe we have a soul?
6. How important is forgiveness to you?
7. What brings you hope?
8. Do you engage in a religious/spiritual practice that brings you closer to a higher being/God?
9. Do you set a time aside every day to devote to your religious/spiritual practice?
10. Do you find comfort in praying?
11. Do you prefer to pray alone or in a group?
12. Some people integrate meditation into their spiritual practices. Do you meditate?
13. Do you enjoy nature?
14. What is your concept of God?
15. What do you think happens after one dies?

continued

continued

16. Do you think we are "more than a body"?
17. What specific people are important in your life?
18. Have you had a spiritual/religious leader?
19. Are you fulfilled with your life?
20. Do you feel your spirituality gives you a purpose in life?
21. How important is it in your life to attend a religious service?
22. How can you describe suffering?
23. Do you like children?
24. Do you enjoy music?
25. How do you express your feelings?
26. Do you like to be hugged?
27. Are you angry with somebody?
28. Do you find spirituality to be a source of strength or hope? If not, mention what your sources of hope and strength are.
29. What are your thoughts about the future?
30. When do you feel most peaceful?

Smith (2006, p. 8) offered two wonderful tools that could also be included in such an assessment. The first is to ask the client the following questions to discover what gives him or her strength and peace:

Concerning strength:

1. What is strength for you?
2. Where can you go to get it?
3. Who gives it to you?
4. How can you get more?

Concerning peace:

1. What is peace for you?
2. Where can you go to get it?
3. Who gives it to you?
4. How can you get more?

I have found this tool very helpful for the insight it yields with my Hispanic clients, and it has helped me confirm that, in addition to their family, religion provides both strength and peace to many of them.

The second means of spiritual assessment that Smith (2006) found helpful is what he called "My Meaningful Symbols," a process that can be extremely valuable to a counselor who is hoping to get an idea of what is important to the client. In this process, the client is asked to bring in objects such as pictures, letters, and/or books that mean a lot for him or her. Some of the objects that Smith said clients might bring include the following:

- one or more books
- one or more photographs
- religious objects
- a letter or letters, or other personal documents
- a record, CD, or tape

When using this tool, the counselor should pay careful attention to religious symbols. For example, if one of the books selected by the client is the New Testament or the Torah, one may surmise the religious tradition of this person. If among the meaningful objects the client chooses a rosary, this suggests that the person is Catholic and likely devoted to the Virgin Mary. Observing the client's choices helps the counselor have meaningful conversations with the client so that the counselor knows what is important to him or her.

In recent times, the impact of the integration of body, mind, and spirit has been more readily embraced by Western society than it was previously. This integration can be seen in the proliferation of meditation centers and yoga classes. Cecilia L. W. Chan, Si Yuan Professor of Health and Social Work at the University of Hong Kong, who is a pioneer in the Eastern integration of body–mind–spirit, uses this approach when working with the bereaved. I had the opportunity to attend one of her workshops in April 2009 at the conference of the Association for Death Education and Counseling in Dallas, Texas, where she talked about her holistic model— which she uses to work with bereaved clients—and engaged the participants in activities integrating the body, mind, and spirit. These techniques are contained in the book *Integrative Body–Mind–Spirit Social Work: An Empirically Based Approach to Assessment and Treatment* (2009) that Chan coauthored with Lee, Ng, and Leung.

Idler et al. (2009) also observed that meditation and prayer may help reduce stress, to the same degree as repentance and forgiveness. Counselors can embrace these practices without cultural boundaries and incorporate them into their work with Hispanic clients. I have used body–mind–spirit integration extensively with my Hispanic clients, with wonderful results;

however, I have found that it is important to emphasize the benefits of using prayer and meditation to the clients and to accompany them during their first experiences of it. Later, they can learn to use it by themselves, with a script or a recording.

To help clients enhance the meditation experience when they are alone, I suggest they create a sacred space in their homes where they can meditate. For example, they can designate a corner of a room as their "sacred space." It is important they find this place soothing and peaceful. The following questions can help clients create their sacred spaces:

- What's your favorite color?
- What is your favorite fabric?
- As you pray or meditate, do you prefer to sit or kneel?
- What is your favorite time of the day?
- Do you enjoy listening to music? The sound of bells?
- Do you like the smell of incense?
- Do you enjoy candles? Flowers?

As the clients and I gather all this information, I give them ideas on how to set up the sacred space, including where they can find candles, fabrics, and so on. It is like giving them a spiritual plan of action. Some of my clients have even shared with me pictures of how their sacred space looks.

An example of a sacred space is the domestic altar often used by religious persons. Most of the women in my study on devotion to the Virgin Mary (Martinez-Houben, 2004) had a domestic altar where they would have the statue of the Virgin Mary, flowers, and candles.

Body–mind–spirit integration through meditation is at times questioned by religious persons who consider prayer to be the best source of hope; however, both practices can complement each other, depending on the desired outcome. Alex, a Cuban American and a devout Christian, shared with me how we can differentiate both practices. As he observed, he experienced a powerful spiritual transformation after the death of his son, and believes that both kinds of rituals, prayer and meditation, helped him tremendously in his process. He defined them as follows:

> When I pray to God I say all my requests to God. I am in awe [of] Him. When I am in pain I talk to him as a father and a friend. He has been extremely compassionate with me. When I meditate I do it listening for an answer. I have patience, discipline, and quiet the mind.

Although Idler et al. (2009) primarily focused on the impact of religion/ spirituality on health, both meditation and prayer can be used to help alleviate people's grief. Many researchers have stated that, for meditation and prayer to be effective, the person must acknowledge the role that religion/spirituality has as a motivating force for behaving a certain way, instead of focusing on the behavior itself. To apply this principle to grief, the individual would rely on religion/spirituality as a source of hope, instead of focusing on the outcome. It is also essential to understand that hope provides an element of optimism that has been proven an important resource for coping with challenges or crises we encounter in life:

> While attempting to more carefully and operationally define spiritual optimism, there also seemed to be value in considering the growing recognition among researchers of the importance of distinguishing optimism from other positive psychological constructs, such as self-efficacy and hope. According to Magaletta and Oliver (1999), the three constructs are similar in that they are all determinants of behavior and focus on expectancies and individual goals or outcomes. Optimism is the general expectancy that one will experience positive outcomes in life. Self-efficacy more specifically relates to an individual's belief that he or she is able to effectively accomplish tasks or behaviors that result in desirable outcomes. Hope involves both the belief in one's ability to successfully meet goals (agency) and belief in one's capacity to generate routes for meeting these goals (pathways). (Bassett et al., 2008, p. 7)

HISPANICS AND CATHOLICISM/PROTESTANTISM

Roman Catholicism is the predominant religion among Hispanics living in the United States, representing the denomination of 68% of this population (Pew Forum on Religion & Public Life, 2007). In recent times, however, many Latinos have moved from Catholic to Protestant churches (Hernandez, Peña, Davis, & Station, 2005). At the National Summit of Hispanic Religious Leaders, held at Duke University in October 2003, as many as 33 spiritual leaders from various denominations discussed different issues concerning Latino theology, including social services, lack of theological education, and diversity among Hispanics. The following excerpt indicates this diversity:

> The Latino population is far from monolithic in its demographic and religious profile . . . While a majority of Hispanic Protestants are

U.S.-born, a majority of Catholics are foreign-born. Seventy-four percent of Protestants, but only 63% of Catholics are U.S. citizens. Significant differences exist between Catholic and non-Catholic Hispanics in terms of significant religious differences among Hispanics of various national origins. The number of Mexican Americans who identify themselves as Catholics ranges between 77 and 87%, Cuban Americans between 66 and 80%, and Puerto Ricans between 65 and 70%. (Hernandez et al., 2005, p. 19)

There are also generational differences in religion among Hispanic Americans: "Approximately 74% of first-generation, 66% of second-generation, and 59% of third-generation [are Catholic]" (Hernandez et al., 2005, p. 19).

Because Hispanics are having a great influence on how the Catholic Church is changing, owing to their increasing population and the manner in which they practice their religion, the Pew Hispanic Center and the Pew Forum on Religion and Public Life conducted a collaborative study called "Changing Faiths: Latinos and the Transformation of American Religion" (2007), which consisted of more than 4,600 interviews of Hispanics/Latinos. The results of this study show the influence this group is having on the Catholic Church:

> Hispanics are transforming the nation's religious landscape, especially the Catholic Church, not only because of their growing numbers but also because they are practicing a distinctive form of Christianity. Religious expressions associated with the pentecostal [sic] and charismatic movements are a key attribute of worship for Hispanics in all the major religious traditions—far more so than among non-Latinos. Moreover, the growth of the Hispanic population is leading to the emergence of Latino-oriented churches across the country. (p. 4)

From the Pew report (Pew Forum on Religion & Public Life, 2007) we can also see that among Hispanics there are differences in how members of this group identify their religion. This has to do with their demographic characteristics, beginning with nativity:

> In the Hispanic foreign-born population, for example, 74% of adults identify as Catholic, compared with 58% of the native born. Hence, the demographic composition of religious congregations also differs. While about two-thirds (68%) of Hispanic Catholics are foreign

born, just a bit more than half (55%) of Latino evangelicals are immigrants. Given the differences in nativity, it is not surprising that Latino Catholics are less likely to speak English and tend to be less educated and poorer than Hispanics of other religious traditions. Religious affiliation also varies somewhat by country of origin. For example, the share of Catholics among Latinos who trace their ancestry to Mexico is larger than among those of Puerto Rican origin, a group with a higher percentage of evangelicals. (p. 8)

In addition, in trying to attract more Hispanics to Protestantism some Protestant ministers are bringing Catholic religious symbols into their churches, such as hanging a picture of Our Lady of Guadalupe, who is "a very important figure in Mexican Catholicism and history . . . Even if Protestants do not share devotion to Our Lady of Guadalupe, they can build on the spirit of this figure" (Rogers & de Souza, 2003, p. 9; I discuss Our Lady of Guadalupe and her significance to Hispanics later in this chapter). Protestants are also including other Roman Catholic customs, such as keeping holy water at the entrance door of the church so that people can use it to make the sign of the cross (Rogers & de Souza, 2003).

Some Catholic Hispanics tend to believe that change is possible only if they pray to saints or the Virgin Mary for intercession. It is not uncommon to hear a Latino mother say, "If only you prayed harder to the Virgin you could have gotten that job. . . . You need to believe in miracles." Although having faith can be a powerful means of helping one process grief, it can prevent a person from taking responsibility and making things happen himself or herself. Latinos need to feel they are able to transform any loss or situation they are facing.

Rogers and de Souza (2003) believed that ministers need to be aware of the situations endured by their congregation and their needs; therefore they conducted a study in which many preachers shared their points of view regarding the characteristics of the Hispanic population living in the United States. These preachers said they believe that Hispanics "are shaped by experience and religion" (p. 1) and that clergy, in particular those who are not Hispanic, should adjust the content of their sermons when preaching to this community. Among the most salient themes of interest are social justice and instilling a sense of hope because of the many hardships Hispanics face that may produce a sense of helplessness. Counselors who keep in mind the challenges many Latinos face can expand their understanding of how much hope is necessary to inspire this group to have faith in *un mañana* [a tomorrow], especially if they have left their homeland looking for a better future.

Keep in mind that Hispanics comprise almost one-third of all Catholics in the United States and that the way they practice their religion may promote changes in mainstream religious institutions. Many Hispanic Catholics consider themselves charismatic and believe they have experienced renewal through "divine healing and direct revelations from God" (Pew Forum on Religion & Public Life, 2007, p. 4). A recent study that examined Latino preferences regarding clergy and religious services revealed that two-thirds of Hispanics, including those who speak English and those who are native-born, prefer Latino clergy and services that are conducted in Spanish (Pantoja, 2005). This preference is motivating many seminarians to study Spanish (Davis, 2005). Hispanic theologian Virgilio Elizondo exemplifies the religiosity of Mexicans:

> I was born in the Mexican tradition of Christianity that is held by two icons or main figures: Jesus of Nazareth, who suffers for us on the cross and accompanies us in our struggles; and Our Lady of Guadalupe, who majestically reigns in the temple of our heart and offers to us all her love, defense and protection. (Elizondo, 2007, p. 1, translated from the Spanish)

Devotion to the Virgin Mary

When I completed my master's degree in religious studies, I wrote my thesis on "Devotion to the Virgin Mary and Nicaraguan Women," which eventually became the book *La Virgen María y la Mujer Nicaragüense: Historia y Tradición* (Martínez-Houben, 2004). This study was qualitative as well as quantitative. To quantify the prevalence of my participants' devotion to the Virgin Mary, I asked, "Are you devoted to the Virgin?" The vast majority, that is, 96%, responded affirmatively, and 84% added that that their devotion to her was based on their personal faith and not because it was a tradition or an inherited faith. Faith, as stated by Fowler (1981), is deeper than religion itself because it is a personal way to respond to the transcendent. My results are supported by those of Ramsey and Blieszner (2000), who found that faith was one of the major factors for older persons in helping them cope and even transforming a stressful situation into a transcendental experience. For the women in my study, the belief that Mary would hear their prayers enabled them to cope with problems and losses. When I visited some of these women at their homes or prayed the rosary with them I witnessed their faith and devotion. Many women shared that, without the Virgin, they would have never been able to deal with so many losses and transitions.

These are the words of Susana, a 78-year old widow:

> Every morning at 4:30 a.m. I pray the rosary to the Virgin. I love her . . . I pray to be happy and to be able to live every day to praise her. Since my husband died I have become closer to the Virgin and I know she listens to my prayers. (Translated from the Spanish)

The following tables also show the influence the devotion to the Virgin Mary had on the 125 women I studied for my master's research (Martínez-Houben, 2004).

When you have prayed to Mary, how do you usually feel?

Emotion	Frequency	Percentage	Valid percentage	Cumulative percentage
Happy	47	37.6	37.6	37.6
Relieved	23	18.4	18.4	56.0
Heard	35	28.0	28.0	84.0
More calm	20	16.0	16.0	100.0
Total	125	100.0	100.0	

When you feel nervous or sad, what do you do?

Activity	Frequency	Percentage	Valid percentage	Cumulative percentage
Go for a walk	3	2.4	2.4	2.4
Talk about it	11	8.8	8.8	11.2
Pray to the Virgin	106	84.8	84.8	96.0
Ignore it	5	4.0	4.0	100.0
Total	125	100.0	100.0	

Do you think you are more resilient in life because of your devotion to the Virgin Mary?

Response	Frequency	Percentage	Valid percentage	Cumulative percentage
Yes	117	93.6	93.6	93.6
No	5	4.0	4.0	97.6
N/A	3	2.4	2.4	100.0
Total	125	100.0	100.0	

The presence of the Virgin Mary is so vital among Catholics that for many to touch the feet of her image may be more powerful than any liturgy (Rogers & de Souza, 2003). Medina (2009) considers Our Lady of Guadalupe (one of many forms of the Virgin Mary and the patron saint of Mexico) to be "a key religious symbol for understanding the faith of the Catholic Latino/a people" (p. 5), which would be particularly special among Mexican Americans.

One of the most prominent symbols of the Catholic faith is the devotion among Mexicans to *Nuestra Señora de Guadalupe* [Our Lady of Guadalupe], also called *La Virgen de Guadalupe*. This devotion was born after the Virgin Mary appeared to the Indian Juan Diego in Mexico in 1531 (Poole, 1995). The account of Mary's appearance to Juan Diego was written in the Nahuatl language and was orally transmitted generation after generation before it was accepted by the Catholic Church, which canonized him as Saint Juan Diego (Sandoval, 2006). In Texas, for example, this popular devotional figure has indigenous elements; for example, among "the San Antonio Tejanos/as, their popular religious celebrations served as a demand for resisting efforts by others to determine their identity" (Barton, 2006, p. 19).

Devotion to the Our Lady of Guadalupe is prevalent among Mexicans living in the United States but has been transmitted to other generations of Mexicans through rituals and *promesas* [promises], which are common practices among immigrants. An example would be "to publicly enter a sacred place on one's knees to demonstrate a sacrifice" (Hagan, 2008, p. 166). For example, in the case of Luisa, who was suffering from cancer, her mother made *la promesa* of taking her to the shrine of Our Lady of Guadalupe in Mexico City, Mexico, to be healed. Cases such as this are plentiful, and similar promises may be made to a person who is facing health problems or having difficulty getting a job.

Heidi, a young Mexican woman, shares her devotion to Our Lady of Guadalupe:

> *Las Mañanitas* [is] a celebration we Mexicans do for *La Virgen de Guadalupe*. It is on December 12th, which is the day we celebrate her apparition in Mexico. I invited a *gringa* [non-Mexican] friend who is the stereotype of what we would call *gringa Americana*—blond with blue eyes. She came with me to the celebration to be part of our tradition. A mariachi (band) was also invited as well as the chorus from the church. People started coming at 4:00 a.m. and it's a whole-day

event. People sing to Our Lady of Guadalupe's image. Some people go to work later on; some stay the whole day. In Mexico, people start celebrating the night before. It is customary to go walking in *una procesión* [a procession], making offerings such as baskets with bread; some girls are dressed as *niñas huare* [indigenous women from Michuacán, near where the apparition occurred]. They leave offerings at the altar.

Cubans, on the other hand, consider *La Vírgen de La Caridad del Cobre* [Our Lady of Charity] their patroness:

> A small sign in Spanish—*Ermita de la Caridad*—announces the location of a shrine in Miami (Florida) that rests on Biscayne Bay just south of the downtown skyscrapers. The conical shrine is dedicated to the patroness of Cuba, Our Lady of Charity. It is the sacred center of the Cuban Catholic community in exile. . . . By the 1990s, it had become the sixth largest Catholic pilgrimage site in the United States. (Tweed, 1997, p. 3)

Another avocation of the Virgin Mary is *La Virgen de Suyapa* [The Virgin of Suyapa] in Honduras. Lourdes shared how they celebrated the festivity:

> In February we celebrate *La Virgen de Suyapa*; she is the patron of Honduras. I used to go with my family to a Catholic church outside New York. They had the statue of the Virgin of Suyapa and they retold the story of the apparition to Alejandro Colindres, an indigenous [Honduran], in 1747. The Virgin appeared to him in a mountain and in Honduras people have a great devotion for her.

Other Religious Rituals and Customs

For Hispanics, religion is not only a faith but is also a means to form an identity and to participate in activities that keep the essence of the traditions of their homeland, maintaining stability and cohesion in the family and providing hope when facing personal crisis or losses. Some of these losses, as we have observed, can be socioeconomic and personal. The role of *abuelitas* [grandmothers] is also an essential tradition among Catholic Hispanics because the grandmothers and mothers pass on their religious beliefs, such as Marian devotion, from generation to generation. They teach their children to pray the rosary and say their evening prayers.

One of the most popular prayers that children say at night for protection of their guardian angel is *"Angel de la Guarda, dulce compañía, no me desampares ni de noche ni de día. No me dejes solo que me perdería"* [My Guardian Angel, sweet company, forsake me not night and day. Do not leave me alone because I would get lost]. My mother taught me this prayer when I was a child, and I taught it to my daughter. It is part of our Catholic religious tradition. Counselors who work with Hispanic clients should be aware of these traditional prayers because such knowledge can give them a better understanding of how important these rituals are for this community.

The primary ritual that provides much hope and peace to Catholics is the holy Mass, and people who cannot attend Mass have the opportunity to hear it on the radio or watch it on television. The well-known Spanish-speaking radio station popular with Hispanics, known as *Radio Paz*, from Pax Catholic Communications Net, airs Mass everyday at 1:00 p.m. EST. It is a service that many people listen to daily because it is a way of unifying Hispanics. The Radio Paz Mass, which is celebrated in Spanish, is generally broadcast from Miami, and at times it is transmitted to other Latin American countries, giving Latinos a sense of unity in their Catholic faith. The message of Radio Paz focuses on uniting all Hispanics in faith: Colombians, Cubans, Nicaraguans, Venezuelans, and people from other Latino countries can listen. Sometimes the station also airs Mass from a Latin country so that there seem to be no barriers that separate the various Latino communities. I have had the opportunity to listen to this Mass and share with other women, including my elderly mother. The solace and hope this service brings to Catholics are very real. Radio Paz also advertises social services for Hispanic communities and offers programs related to faith and hope.

THE POWER OF PRAYER

The need to pray, or to make some kind of supplication to a god or gods, seems to be ingrained in human nature and is very important to many Hispanics. Historically, people of some cultures have danced at times of drought with the hope that their efforts would bring rain. Some people may consider this action or ritual a kind of prayer; some may even consider the answer to it a miracle. Indigenous people believed (and still believe) that when they perform such rituals, the gods will listen and answer. In *Prayer, Faith and Healing: Cure Your Body, Heal Your Mind, and Restore Your*

Soul (1999), Caine, and Kaufman reflected on how, in the past, prayer and miracles played a special role in people's lives:

> Once upon a time, we believed in miracles—spiritual miracles. When we were ill, injured, or afflicted with any sort of course—emotional, interpersonal, financial, legal—we made appeals to God. We turned to our spiritual guides—our holy men, our priestly purveyors of prayer therapies. We recited prayers prescribed by the church. We turned to healers, medicine men, saints, and the somehow spiritually charged symbols of faith: icons, statues, pictures, and medals. We looked for signs that prayers, faith, religion, belief, and God could heal us. And we found them. Often, they worked wondrously. (p. xiii)

Caine and Kaufman (1999) further stated that although science was the first means by which we dealt with illness, expecting a cure through a pill or operation, one cannot deny the connection between prayer and health, which they said has been proven in more than 200 studies. Faith helps us in all the dimensions of our lives. It influences our outlook for the future, our expectations, and our physical, mental, and spiritual well-being.

In my master's degree study on Nicaraguan women and their devotion to the Virgin Mary (Martinez-Houben, 2004), I used different questionnaires to measure the frequency of their prayers. More than 55% of the women, with a mean age of 65.83 prayed daily; 28.8%, with a mean age of 67.08 prayed two or more times a day; 12%, with a mean age of 63.80 prayed as they felt the necessity; and 3.2%, with a mean age of 68.25 prayed weekly. Only one participant, age 64, reported not praying at all (Martinez-Houben, 2004).

Based on these results and my work as a grief counselor, I have found prayer to be a valuable resource for people. It can be done individually or with others. Many people attend prayer circles or groups, or they may choose to read the Bible or do other spiritual reading. Any of these activities may help them in their time of need. For people who are religious, just engaging in the act of praying when one is facing a transition, crisis, or loss can make a difference in the perceived outcome. However, many people do not agree with the efficacy of prayer, thinking it will give people who are in a devastating situation false hope. This argument may have some validity, but I don't agree. Do we not place our hope in every action we take to get better? We go to a doctor, take medicine, undergo surgery, or seek other treatment because we hope to get better or be cured. If we have psychological issues to resolve, we go to counseling or psychotherapy, expecting to feel better with the help of a psychologist or counselor. As Dossey (1996) said, prayer is like medicine: We are not sure it will work; we just try it and hope it does. We pray with faith, hoping that something good will happen. Hispanics, like persons of other cultures, pray for many reasons, but if a counselor doesn't understand the power of prayer and minimizes its value for his or her clients, the clients may feel invalidated or, worse, they may even think the counselor is trivializing their beliefs because they belong to another culture.

According to Dossey (1996), although prayer may not work all the time, the holistic benefits show that it is generally effective. When a person faces a loss or crisis, one of the most difficult things to do is to accept the situation or what has happened; this is the first step in the healing process. Prayer seems to help in that acceptance. Josefina, a Catholic Nicaraguan woman who prays the rosary every day, after the death of her child said to me, "In the midst of my pain, I know God had other plans for my child. He is now in a better place. ¡Que se haga la voluntad de Dios!" [It is God's will].

On the other hand, people who are very religious may have a problem accepting that they are experiencing anger at God if they think He did not answer their prayers. They may resist praying or going to Mass and may be hesitant to share this anger with their family. Because is it not easy to experience these feelings, many people may face a faith crisis, wondering whether God exists and, if He does, why He didn't hear their prayers. In cases such as this a sensitive mental health practitioner can be of great assistance in giving the client the opportunity to express his or her emotions and work through them. More details on techniques for working with emotions are offered in chapter 9.

Even if expressing this anger may be uncomfortable for religious people, Dr. Van Duivendyk (quoted in Caine & Kaufman, 1999) stated that one dialogues with God as one expresses it: "The anger itself, the frustration itself, are expressions of faith in God. You don't express anger toward someone you don't believe exists" (p. 351).

Religion plays an essential role in many Hispanics' life transitions, so "health care providers should educate themselves in the basic beliefs of the different religions and on how they may affect their patients' medical care" (Kamel, Mouton, & McKee, 2002, p. 282). For example, many times secular activities, such as the launching of a business or moving to a new home, may begin with a Mass or blessing by a priest. For example, a home blessing may be a sign of future happiness for the family. At times people may be surprised if a new home isn't blessed or concerned if it is not, as in the case of Carla, a Peruvian woman who had just bought her new home:

> After many sacrifices, I was able to buy a new home in a very nice neighborhood and I wanted to celebrate the occasion with family and close friends. To my surprise, in the middle of the party an aunt pulled me aside and asked, "When is the priest coming?" To which I responded, "No priest is coming; it is only us." To my dismay she started making the sign of the cross, saying, "I hope nothing happens to you in this house! How is it possible you are not having it blessed!"

POPULAR RELIGION

Another element of great value to Hispanics, which has a strong influence on how they perceive their relationship with the Virgin Mary, the saints, and rituals, is *popular religion* that encompasses activities that may or may not be officially sanctioned by the Roman Catholic Church. According to Goizueta (2004), Catholic practices, mainly popular religious ones, can bring back Catholic traditions to the United States that have been lost over time. He believes that the integration of such symbolic Catholic traditions could play an important role in how American Catholicism could revive vital aspects of "our common Catholic heritage" (p. 255).

Among Hispanics, in addition to the domestic altars found in many homes, it also is common to have altars in public places, which is an element of popular religion. Badillo (2006) observed that the tradition of public altars is kept by many Hispanics: "Near downtown Los Angeles [in] La Placita Square, following evening [M]ass, the clergy lead a procession through Olvera Street, blessing altars constructed in businesses and restaurants" (p. 188). This practice can also be observed in Miami among the Nicaraguan community. As one visits businesses on Flagler Street, for example, one finds altars with the image of the Immaculate Conception, especially at the celebration of *La Purisima*, a Nicaraguan festivity on behalf of the Virgin Mary. The presence of religious objects and rituals is very prominent among Hispanics, as Badillo (2006) explained:

> East Los Angeles parishes construct *ofrendas* [offerings] in their worship space. Latinos in the United States retain a religious emphasis on family, children, and immediate community. Home *altarcitos* [altars] create sacred space for prayer. Such forms of religious expression have

been transplanted to suburbs where a *rezadora* [a praying woman or a leader of prayer] may offer religious guidance at weddings, baptisms, and *quinceañeras* [a girl's celebration of turning fifteen, similar to a sweet sixteen party] and adorn front and back yards. . . . Some aspects of rural and small-town Catholicism have gained international appeal, such as the *ermitas*, or shrines, long neglected by the institutional church, which have become centers of devotion in the town of San Juan in the lower Rio Grande Valley of Texas. (p. 188)

Furthermore, these rituals provide a special help to mourners because they bring hope and unity to the worshipers. Elena, a Guatemalan woman who lost her husband when she was 24, shared with me that getting together with other worshipers every Sunday in church has been a source of solace and hope.

To give readers a better understanding of what popular religion is I have included the definition given by the Fourth General Conference of the Latin American Episcopate: "A privileged expression of the inculturation of the faith. It involves not only religious expressions but also the values, criteria, behaviors and attitudes that spring from Catholic dogma and constitute the wisdom of our people, shaping their cultural matrix" (Hennelly, 1993, cited in Empereur, 2005, p. 13).

An example of popular religion will be devotion to the Virgin Mary that can include elements that are spontaneous in nature and are not included in the official teachings of the church. Rodriguez (1994, cited in Martinez-Houben, 2004) considers these elements spontaneous "in that the people celebrate because they want to and not because they have been mandated by the official hierarchy, in this case the Roman Catholic tradition" (p. 60).

One of the main values of popular religion is its ability to unite people and establish a special bond among them. Popular devotion or popular Catholicism, as in public celebrations for Our Lady of Guadalupe, is what has helped this group of people find meaning and hope in times of crisis. As a counselor, it is important to be open to these religious practices, especially if they are alien to your concept of religion because they make sense to Hispanics. If clients tell you they are praying to the statue of the Virgin Mary or another saint, and celebrating feasts on their behalf, it is because they find these celebrations meaningful for their faith. Furthermore, some even believe that if they don't carry on these rituals, something bad may happen to them.

Many people, including Hispanics, believe in miracles, which can bring an element of hope to a difficult life situation. Miracles are accepted and expected among Hispanics when they have sick relatives, are going through difficulties or transitions, or when a change is needed in their home. Men and women pray for a miracle and often, in return, promise to do something for receiving one. Mourning can be a powerful experience, and during this time the person yearns for something to change for the better. He or she expects a miracle. In the words of social activist and self-styled theologian William Stringfellow,

> A miracle in healing is not the conjuring of some magic, nor a disruption in the created order, or something supernatural. Rather, healing exemplifies the redemption of fallen creation, the restoration of the created order, the return to the usual, the normative, the natural. (cited in Kauffman, 2008, p. 70)

Moreover, Goizueta (2004) noted that Hispanics express their faith through symbols and rituals. Many rituals have been maintained in Latino communities in the United States, such as La Purísima, mentioned earlier in this chapter: "At its best, Latino/a popular Catholicism offers us a fundamentally sacramental, organic worldview that affirms an ultimate interconnectedness—ontological, if you will. Latino/a Catholicism reminds us that one indeed is not alone" (p. 268).

Lee (2008) found a similarity between traditional Christian practices and popular religion because both are interculturally oriented. Furthermore, he considers that the Latina/Popular Religion has the possibility of shaping communities if they become more ecumenical. Recognizing their religious practices can have a direct effect on Latino clients because they would feel validated and recognized for their traditions.

Popular religion offers a nearly 500-year history of resilience, adaptability, and continued vibrancy made possible by the ingenuity of the people themselves. Despite its lack of philosophical and theological moorings, U.S. Hispanic popular religion offers valuable strategies and insights (Lee, 2008, p. 5). According to Pineda-Madrid (2006),

> It is through popular Catholic practices that most U.S. Latinos/as become Catholic and sustain their Catholicism. When in the midst of life's struggles, Latino/a Catholics will turn to popular religious practices and in the process negotiate their Catholic identity and lay claim to it anew. (p. 208)

HISPANICS AND TRADITIONAL/FOLK RELIGIONS

The Rev. Sosa (1999), in his book *Sectas, Cultos y Sincretismos* [*Sects, Cults, and Syncretisms*] offers an objective and a profound study of the Hispanic experience regarding different religious and spiritual movements that includes *Santería, espiritismo,* and *curanderismo*:

> *Espiritismo* and *Santería* continue to involve Hispanic and non-Hispanic believers in a ritualistic and symbolic world where God's presence manifests Himself through the immediate response He provides through an intermediary (spirits or *orishas*) in order to assure an immediate solution for any crisis. (p. 151)

Because these belief systems, in addition to mainstream religions, are often endorsed among Hispanics, in this section I explore three traditional folk systems of healing: (a) *Santería*, (b) *espiritismo*, and (c) *curanderismo*. They are also known as "ethnomedical systems . . . [and each of them] . . . synthesizes beliefs and practices derived from the separate colonial histories of the three ethnic communities with which they are associated" (Trusty et al., 2002, p. 287). Because of space constraints, I briefly present each belief and the value it has for many Hispanics living in the United States.

Santería

Santería is a religious tradition that originated in Africa and was brought to Cuba by the Yoruban slaves who were imported to the island in the late 1700s and early 1800s. It is a syncretic religion that combines elements from the Yoruba cult with elements from Catholicism. For example, the deities of *Santería* are often identified with the saints of the Catholic church (Gonzalez-Wippler, 1989).

    Santería spread to different regions of America under different names or traditions. In Cuba, for example, it is commonly known as *Santería*, but it can also be recognized as "*Lukumi* (or *Lucumí*) *Regla de Ochoa*, Yoruba Traditional Religion or Orisha" (Clark, 2007, p. 2). *Santería* was first introduced to the United States in 1960 after the Cuban revolution. The second *Santería* expansion took place when the Marielitos escaped Cuba in 1980 and arrived in the United States. It is estimated that, between the United States and Latin American countries, more than 100 million people practice *Santería* today. Still, this tradition is secretive in nature, and many of the rituals are private and performed at home (Clark, 2007). The name derives from the word *santos* [saints] and is also known as "the way of the saints" (De la Torre, 2004, p. xi). To understand Latino religiosity and spirituality one needs to be aware of the prevalence of *Santería* among many Hispanics living in the United States and the influence it has psychologically and spiritually. Many Hispanics prefer to go to a session with a *santero* [a male healer] or *santera* [a female healer] than to a psychotherapist. With the purpose of presenting a real experience of what *Santería* is, I interviewed Pedro, a *santero* for 22 years, who was able to share with me some aspects of this religion. As he said, this religion is highly secretive, and some information cannot be divulged. These are his words in response to my question of why he decided to become a *santero*:

> First of all, my ancestors . . . are from the province of Matanza, a province in Cuba where many Africans from western Africa settled to live, and they were descendants of the African tribes Yoruba and Oyo. . . . In the sixteenth and into the seventeenth century, they introduced these Africans into the island for farming purposes, and they brought their dialects, their cultures, [and] their social structure with them, and since they were slaves and didn't have the same rights as whites of the time, they came up with the idea of adapting themselves and their religion with Catholicism. . . . In those times, they had colors and *santos*, like *Hermana Mercedes*, who was dressed in all white, like *Santa Bárbara*, a Spanish saint dressed in red, and so on. When the Spaniards and their monks and priests would tell them this is such and such a saint, the Africans would say, yes, this is *Obatalá* to us, and when they would tell the slaves, this is Santa Barbara, the slaves would reply, yes, that's *Changó*. So they would mix things up and start introducing [these things] into the Catholic religion. . . . They were allowed during weekends to practice their Yoruban religion in a controlled environment. That's why they had to reduce and mystify certain aspects of their religion. For example, a ritual that would normally take seven days in Africa would not be able to be performed in seven days since they had to work all week as slaves, and then they would go to sleep in their quarters. So those rituals would be performed in two or three days in order to keep their religion alive. That was the beginning of the adaptation of the Africans in Cuba, with the Spanish regime of the time. The Yoruba religion is now known as *Lucumi*, as adopted in Cuba. . . . It has been suggested that in some cases the intervention of a *santero* in therapy or the use of *curandero* [a traditional healer] as part of healing may work well with certain Hispanics.

Gonzalez-Wippler (1989) also affirmed the importance and value of these beliefs: "Social workers, psychologists, and psychiatrists are also beginning to realize that the Santero's magic and spiritual practice are of great therapeutic value in the treatment of mental illness and social displacement among Hispanics" (p. 288).

In addition to the strongly held beliefs of those practicing popular religions, many Catholics believe that a person has an eternal protector known as a guardian angel. From the time they are young, Hispanic children pray to their guardian angel to protect them from evil. This belief has a strong correlation with the notion of an *eleda* in *Santería*, which is believed to be a

> guardian spirit [and] is the protector god of the individual; others claim that it is a spiritual force in the individual; and still others believe that it is the spirit of a dead person who protects the individual. Some have no familiarity with the term, *eleda*, and they speak, instead, of their "Guardian angel" or "Angels" when they refer to their protector spirits. (Cros Sandoval, 2006, p. 90)

A counselor working with a grieving client who persists in believing that his *eleda* is protecting him as he suffers cannot evaluate the situation based only on his or her own perspective. The counselor needs to recognize and acknowledge the client's belief system so that he or she can understand the strong effect these beliefs may have on how the client processes grief.

There are often many misconceptions about *Santería*, even within the Hispanic community. In May 2009 I taught a class on world religions at a local college, and one of my students did an excellent study on *Santería*. When he presented it to the class, he explained that before his project he had many misconceptions regarding this religion, especially because of its reputation in regard to animal sacrifice. But he said that he discovered how rich in traditions and rituals this religion was and the vital role it has among many Cubans living in the United States, in his case Miami.

Santería often employs a religious system known as *orisha worship*, also known as *Osha* or *La Regla Lucumi*, which is the result of "the syncretism of African religion and Catholicism" (Nuñez, 2006, p. 11). In his study of Santeria, Borges-Díaz (2009) explained this practice:

> Cuban Yoruba Santería is based upon the worship of spirits called *orishas* or *santos* because they have more control over human affairs.

Each believer in the Yoruba/Afro-Cuban Santería faith has their own orisha that protects and supports them throughout their lifespan. As a result of this concealed practice that combines a mixture of the Roman Catholic religion and Yoruban beliefs, a new type of religion was formed that is known as Cuban-Santería. (p. 5)

There are many ways that people integrate Catholic and *Santería* beliefs when coping with losses. Many find that the *santos* give them strength, and others protect them against "the evil eye." Some Hispanics use other tools, such as Tarot cards and other means of foretelling the future, to help them cope with loss. Consider the case of Jackie, a 57-year-old Cuban woman who has looked for answers since she was a teenager. She has had the Tarot cards read and "thrown the *caracoles*" [seashell divination], a process also known as *Diloggun*. These seashells have a shape with an opening on one side, through which, according to *Santería*, the *orishas* speak to the *santero* and deliver the message (Gonzalez-Wippler, 1989). Jackie shared with me her experience of the loss of a loved one:

> I have a glass of water with perfume for each of my loved ones who have died. I do that to elevate their spirit. I also have a candle for Santa Bárbara and San Lázaro so they can give me strength. I have gone through a lot in life and people tell me I am a very strong woman. I suppose this has helped me.

Espiritismo

Espiritismo, as stated by Fr. Sosa (1999), is a syncretism of Catholicism and indigenous Caribbean elements. It also has great influence from the esoteric school of thought of the French (Kardec, 1987, p. 23). The core belief is that the spirits of the dead can communicate with living people through an intermediary or medium (Kardec, 1987, p. 86). According to professor of psychology Mario E. Nuñez-Molina, "*Espiritismo* (Spiritism) is one of these indigenous healing systems that is used by a significant number of Puerto Ricans as an alternative to the professional health system" (2001, p. 2). I interviewed Manuel, a man well versed in *espiritismo*, who explained more about its use and practice:

> We all have different experiences with this, whether you are Mexican, Dominican or from any island. Don't forget, those of us from the islands

were introduced to that way of life through the African culture early on. I am Puerto Rican and that's a very common thing to practice, *Espiritismo*. My mother was what you might call a *curandera* [folk healer]. She would go to that house and gather a few leaves and would make you a tea or take a leaf and you would be healed! People would come from all over the island to see her. She dabbled in that along with the herbs. She was also a spiritualist. What I mean is that a spirit would come upon her and speak through her.

Moreover, as Bernal and Gutierrez (1988, cited in Trusty, Looby, & Sandhu, 2002) stated, *espiritismo* is "primarily associated with Puerto Ricans [but] is also practiced in the Oriente region of Cuba" (p. 287). Puerto Ricans have a strong belief in the power of *espiritismo* and its healing rituals. Other studies suggest that it is even more accepted than traditional religious practice because it is ingrained in their tradition and expectations as a culture:

> *Espiritismo* (spiritism) is a widespread religious practice among Puerto Ricans in Puerto Rico and Puerto Ricans in the United States . . . it combines pre-Columbian, African, Catholic and European spiritual–religious practices into one system to fulfill the spiritual needs as well as the psychocultural needs of the Puerto Rican people. (Harwood, 1987, cited in Torres Rivera, 2005, p. 1)

However, studies concerning folk healing practices have generally focused more on American Indians than on Latinos, and "The use of *espiritismo* has been identified as an alternative treatment approach when working with Puerto Ricans in mental health settings" (Harwood, 1987, cited in Torres Rivera, 2005, p. 1). Therefore, it is urgent that counselors be more aware of this alternative healing modality to understand its effect on this group of people because, according to Manuel, *espiritismo* is for many Hispanics "a way of life."

According to the belief in *espiritismo*, the spiritual world (which is inhabited by spirits) and the material world are connected. In the spiritual world, according to Nuñez-Molina (2001), there are different kinds of spirits related to a person's moral development and the extent of their attachment to the material world. In *espiritismo* there are the ignorants, who are at the lowest level, and the *espíritus de luz* [spirits of light] that have evolved and who protect humans from the ignorant spirits (Nuñez-Molina, 2001, p. 3). For Puerto Ricans, the essential practice of *espiritismo* is the spiritist meeting, and the way these meetings are set up is similar:

Usually there is a long cloth-covered table which is occupied by the group leader, the *Presidente*, and the various mediums. On the table there may be a goblet of water, flowers, cigars, statues of different Catholic saints, incense and other paraphernalia. Generally, the room is adorned with pictures of Christ and the Virgin Mary along with other religious personalities. (Nuñez-Molina, 2001, p. 6)

Nuñez-Molina (2001) also indicated that the session, or *seánce*, starts with a reading of *The Gospel According to Spiritism*, which contains "the Spiritists' view and explanation of the New Testament as brought to us by the Spirit and codified by Allan Kardec" (*The Gospel According to Spiritism*, 1987, p. vii).

In my experience while working with Hispanics of different cultures I have found *espiritismo* to be a way of continuing the connection with the deceased. Javier, a 63-year-old Puerto Rican man, shared his story:

When *mami* died we were all devastated. She was the head of the family because my father left us when we were very young. My mother was diagnosed with cancer in the brain and three months [later] died. We were very sad and needed to talk to her and see she was OK. One day my sister Raquel called me to let me know about a woman who did séances. I immediately told her to make an appointment and that same evening we all three went to see the medium. The experience was spooky because the woman got transformed as the spirit possessed her, but she told us my mother sent us the message that she was in a happy place and to continue being a close family. We felt her presence in the room and cried and hugged each other. Since that day I have the conviction she is fine and looks after us.

Curanderismo

Curanderismo, a Mexican American folk healing practice, is an important health resource for Mexican Americans living in the Lower Rio Grande Valley of Texas and other places. The terms *curanderismo* and *curandero* come from the Spanish verb *curar* [to heal]. In their book *Curanderismo: Mexican American Folk Healing* (1997), Trotter and Chavira stated the following:

Loosely, the word *curandero* could be applied to anyone who claims to have some skill in the healing arts. . . . [but] for Mexican

Americans a *curandero* represents a healer who is part of a historically and culturally important system of health care. (p. 1)

Curanderos are considered healers and use preparations from herbs and other plants and flowers to treat their clients. Some clinicians consider folk medicine to be superstition or magic. They may not understand if a patient comes to them complaining of a *mal de ojo* [evil eye], when something or someone has inflicted evil on them, like a curse. So, how can counselors help a client who is complaining about such an outcome, which is based on his or her belief system? I would suggest acknowledging the client's worldview and not dismissing his or her beliefs because this could make the client not want to return to therapy. You may want to ask the client to tell you a little more about his or her beliefs and what they represent in the healing process.

As Avila and Parker (2000) stated, most people who go to a *curandero* are Hispanic or Anglo women who have already had experience with this sort of treatment. Among Hispanics of Mexican ancestry, 18.3% believe in spiritual practices such as "*espiritismo, curanderism*, [and] *brujería* [witchcraft]" (Espinosa & Garcia, 2008, p. 20). It is interesting to note that one of the powerful elements of *curanderismo* is the "talking circle," or roughly what we would call a support group. "We use this circle as a way of relating, sorting, integrating and staying connected" (Avila & Parker, 2000, p. 330). In *curanderismo*, as in other belief systems, including Catholicism, praying to the saints is also a common practice: "In the Hispanic tradition we believe that each saint was human once and learned something very profound in his or her walk upon this earth. For this reason, each saint has a special gift for us" (Avila & Parker, 2000, p. 140). According to Avila and Parker saints have a special place in most Hispanics' lives, and it is customary to light a candle to them so that they can pray to the saints and ask for favors.

RELIGION AT THE END OF LIFE

Our religious beliefs permeate many aspects of our lives. Arguably the times when religious beliefs are most salient is at the moments when one is close to death. There are many spiritual practices that could aid a person who is close to death and whose demise may represent a loss that has a great impact on your client. The Dalai Lama, in his book *Advice on Dying and Living a Better Life* (2002), reminded us how necessary it is to be mindful that all of us are going to die and how to apply mindfulness so as not to be so attached to the person who is dying, because attachment is the cause of suffering, not only for the surviving person or persons but also for the dying person. Hispanic families, because of their strong emotional attachment to their loved ones, may display grieving behaviors such as crying when they are next to a dying person or holding the person's hands in such a way as to not want to let go. This behavior may prevent peaceful conditions for the dying, which generate a desirous attitude to live instead of providing, if the patient has been religious, "the right conditions for the generation of virtue by reminding the person of religious instructions and practices," as the Dalai Lama suggests (p. 110). In the case of Latinos, the majority of whom are Catholics, family members often share their thoughts about God, Jesus, and the Virgin Mary to give the dying person peace and comfort in the last moments and so that he or she can be prepared to accept death in a less fearful manner. When a patient is very religious, he or she may see death as the will of God and find comfort in his or her religious practices and faith.

Keep in mind that if we are to understand how a person deals with grief and loss, we need to learn about that person's spirituality and religious beliefs. Many people base their behavior on their religious beliefs; therefore, if counselors expand their knowledge about their clients' spiritual beliefs, they will be able to care better for their well-being in a holistic manner. When counselors and other mental health professionals work with people, the success of their therapy is greatly influenced by their clients' belief systems and expectations.

HELPFUL SUGGESTIONS

- Keep an open mind when working with people whose religions and belief systems may differ from your own. The focus should be on your clients' beliefs and how those beliefs help them cope with their grief. If you find yourself judging a client or feeling uncomfortable because of his or her beliefs, it will be better to refer them to another counselor. When a counselor rejects the religious perspective of another person, even unconsciously or unintentionally, the client may perceive this, and instead of sharing his or her thoughts with you in a relaxed manner, he or she could withdraw feeling that his or her spirituality or religion has not been validated.
- If you are unclear about a religious concept or belief expressed by a client, ask. You do not need to know everything about every religion or belief, but you do need to show real concern about your clients'

beliefs. This will allow you to enter their worldview and be empathic regarding how they use their beliefs when dealing with crises or losses.

- Be in touch with your own spiritual or religious beliefs. If you want to enter the worldview of you clients it is helpful if you are aware of yours. The most valuable thing we as counselors can do is to never impose our religious beliefs on our clients or indoctrinate them based on what we think is best.

PERSONAL REFLECTIONS FOR THE COUNSELOR

- Are you comfortable exploring belief systems different than your own?
- Can you respect the fact that many Hispanics base their beliefs on concepts such as miracles or folk healing practices?
- Are you able to integrate elements of such practices or beliefs into your counseling in an empathic way when working with Hispanic clients?

PART II

Loss and Grief

CHAPTER 5

Hispanics and Their Losses

THE MEANING OF LOSS

Besides the major losses we may experience in life—the death of a loved one; the loss of one's health; the loss of a relationship through divorce or separation; and/or loss of a job, one's savings, a pet, or one's country (i.e., by emigrating)—we may also experience the loss of hope, self-esteem, or our dreams. These losses influence how we live our lives.

As Neimeyer (1998) observed, losses are part of life, and although they can have many different meanings for people, they are a universal experience. In my book *Transform Your Loss: Your Guide to Strength and Hope* (Houben, 2009), I offered the following description:

> We experience a sense of loss when something or someone that belonged to us and was of great value has been taken from our lives, leaving in their place a void that we are sometimes unable to fill. This emptiness leaves us baffled, stunned, and with doubts about the next steps on our path. Loss is an experience of our own human condition. (p. 12)

When a person suffers a loss, he or she experiences a lack of direction as well as a lack of equilibrium and stability. This can be manifested physically, emotionally, socially, and spiritually. As we live our lives, we encounter transitions. Although we may consider some of these transitions, such as the opportunity to move to another country, to be positive events, they may also bring feelings of despair and subsequently turn into losses. Giddens and Giddens (2003) provided the following analogy:

> Loss is an experience that you live and grow with. Some losses can be considered in a positive light like a move to a new home. You may feel the loss of your old house, yet you may be moving to a better neighborhood and bigger home. (p. 4)

In the case of emigrating in general, moving to another country is a transition that may bring mixed emotions—both excitement and despair. One of the most salient emotions emigrants experience is nostalgia for their homeland, and in many cases they do not have the option of returning to their home country. This sense of impotence produces a feeling of loss, and it is with this perspective in mind that I explore some of the most prevalent losses Latinos confront as they find themselves far away from their homeland. Because each person has a unique set of coping skills, and because each person's life circumstances will vary, some of these experiences may be traumatic and harm the individual. Other people may take the opportunity to grow despite their grief when experiencing a trauma.

There is an incredible array of situations that may be pertinent to a loss that Hispanics may face, but space constraints require that I narrow these experiences to those I have considered most salient in my personal and professional experience as a grief counselor.

TRAUMA FROM LOSS

Teresa Descilo, who trains health care professionals in how to help clients deal with trauma, stated, "Trauma occurs when an actual or perceived threat of danger [or loss] overwhelms a person's usual coping ability" (2009, p. 6). This definition was originally given by Beverly James (1994, p. 9) in her discussion of trauma and children, but Descillo added the term *loss* because situations such as the death of a friend or family member, or learning that one has a fatal disease, may become a trauma.

Responses to a disaster vary among people. As Lopez-Ibor, Christodoulou, Maj, Sartorius, and Okasha (2005) observed, "The majority of people exposed to trauma and disasters do well. However, some individuals experience distress, others have behavioral changes and some develop psychiatric illness post disaster" (p. 13).

What are the factors that influence different responses to disasters? According to Lopez-Ibor et al. (2005), being Hispanic is one of the risk factors for developing posttraumatic stress disorder, which is valuable information for mental health professionals who work with this population. In their description of posttraumatic stress disorder, Lopez-Ibor et al. included the following psychological responses, which can be present in some Hispanic clients after they experience a trauma or loss:

- Grief reactions and other normal responses
- Change in interpersonal interactions (withdrawal, aggression, violence, family conflict, and family violence)
- Change in work functioning (e.g., in ability to do work, concentration, effectiveness on the job, absenteeism, quitting)
- Change in health care utilization
- Change in smoking
- Change in alcohol use (p. 23)

POSTTRAUMATIC GROWTH AFTER LOSS

How should one define *posttraumatic growth* (PTG)? Lawrence G. Calhoun and Richard G. Tedeschi, in their groundbreaking book, *Handbook of Posttraumatic Growth: Research and Practice* (1998), presented the perspectives of various scholars and researchers on the subject and postulated that PTG goes beyond just positive changes or benefits experienced by survivors. In my experience I have found that working toward PTG is extremely helpful for the grieving person because it involves a process of transformation, an internal change in an individual, and not just that person's response to his or her external experiences. This growth relates to how the person understands himself or herself and the world at a cognitive and emotional level as a result of a disaster. It also involves disrupting the individual's assumptive world. One may recognize a trauma when the person uses narrative terms such as *before* the event and *after* the event, which can initiate the cognitive engagement that produces PTG (Calhoun & Tedeschi, 1998, p. 9).

This view of PTG does not mean that researchers devalue the pain and suffering that follows a traumatic event, but they recognize

the coexistence of a very different set of responses, a cluster of reactions that seem positive rather than negative, expansive rather than

constrictive, indicative of growth and development rather than re-
gression and decline. Against a backdrop of trauma, growth is not
only unexpected and thus inherently interesting, but speaks to the
multifaceted, inventive course of human coping and adaptation.
(Janoff-Bulman, 2006, p. 81)

Despite the need for further investigation of PTG, the possibility of
personal growth after a trauma is an area of much interest to scholars
such as Caplan (1964), Dohrenwend (1978), Frankl (1963), Maslow
(1954), and Yalom (1980), but it was not until the last 15 to 20 years that
"systematic attention [has been given] to trauma-related positive change"
(Calhoun & Tedeschi, 2006, p. 4).

The research emphasis on PTG is also the result of data provided
by persons who have experienced a major traumatic life event. Based on
this research, both quantitative and qualitative, the major domains of
growth are "changes in the perception of self, changes in the experience
of relationships with others, and changes in one's general philosophy of
life" (Calhoun & Tedeschi, 2006, p. 5). The perception a person has of
self determines how that person responds to life events and how he or she
acts because of such responses. People may know they are vulnerable but
still strong and able to pick up the pieces after their assumptive world has
been shattered. A major component of this capacity is the person's cognitive ability to reframe the situation and even find new possibilities after
a major, painful life event. An example of this is Rosa, a bereaved parent
who told me, "I've been through the most terrible situation I could imagine. Still, despite of all this pain, I know I can handle it. My daughter is my
inspiration to live a better life."

According to Harvey and Miller (2000), several factors influence PTG,
including "an active coping style, optimism, perceptions of control over
life events, a strong sense of self, as well as the nature of the stressful
experience itself" (p. 12). However, variables that can make adjustment
or adaptability difficult after a trauma are "a personality marked by negativity, [and] a severe prior traumatic experience, such as victimization,
disaster, combat experience, and physical or sexual abuse" (Harvey &
Miller, 2000, p. 12). These vulnerabilities may cause individuals to have
maladaptive responses to stressful events or crises.

Although many people respond negatively to traumatic events
long after the event itself has occurred, many studies show that the
majority of survivors perceive a benefit after experiencing a trauma

(Harvey & Miller, 2000). Like many mental health professionals, I have applied elements of positive psychology when working with clients because as a counselor I have witnessed the capacity people have to face painful situations and even to grow at a personal and spiritual level through those experiences. I consider myself aligned with mental health professionals who focus more on growth after a painful experience than on the nega- tive aspects or characteristics individuals exhibit in response to the pain. As Neimeyer (2001), a leading authority on grief and meaning, asserted, if mental health professionals help clients focus on finding meaning from difficult experiences they have had, they can grow and develop purpose.

Many people view their suffering or trauma as a path to a posi- tive change in their lives; otherwise, they might stay on a path to self- destruction. Although the expectation of psychological growth after a trauma is not surprising, what is amazing is how often this growth happens. Many people develop wisdom after confronting circumstances that seem at first to be adverse or negative. I have seen some of my clients who, after losing a loved one, leaving their homeland, or losing their job, develop a change in priorities, a revision of their lifestyle, and an evaluation of what is meaningful in their lives. Many people experience a spiritual trans- formation, and although it is true that many lose faith and hope when confronting a major loss, in my experience in working with clients who have experienced a loss, many have reported the opposite, including a religious change that is positive rather than negative.

Traumatic events can change the way people view their lives. The "over- whelming feelings of grief and bereavement" leave people trying to find ways to understand and searching for meaning in their lives (Becker, 2009, p. 3). In chapter 8 I explore different resources for working with clients who are dealing with grief and elaborate further on reconstructing meaning.

IMMIGRANTS AND SOME OF THE LOSSES THEY MAY EXPERIENCE

For many Hispanics in the United States, as with other groups of people who have immigrated, the uprooting and losses associated with immigra- tion are common denominators in their lives (Schwarzbaum & Thomas, 2008). Among their losses are the loss of their homeland, along with its customs and traditions; the loss of the presence of family and friends left behind; the loss of a unique cultural lifestyle, including traditional foods and rituals; and the loss of a familiar language environment. Hispanic immigrants often do not anticipate their losses, and the impact of those losses, until they have arrived in the United States.

We build our world based on our life experiences, our environment, the messages we receive during childhood, and what we expect to happen in the future as viewed through our unique frame of reference. Therefore, when a person suffers a loss or crisis, the world that person knows—his or her *assumptive world*—gets shattered, and that person needs to find his or her place in the new world:

> We struggle to find meaning in a seemingly senseless event, to find a new understanding of the universe and our role in it, and to construct a new and modified identity which can incorporate the loss and the overwhelming feelings of grief that bereavement brings with it. (Becker, 2009, p. 3)

The losses experienced by immigrants can leave a tremendous void, which can morph into grief. The best way for the immigrants to work through these losses is to find a new way to understand who they are and how the world around them functions (Harvey & Miller, 2000).

Another variable that may intensify an immigrant's sense of a void is the environment. Bereaved persons living in countries with a religious or cultural background different from theirs feel the burden of not being part of the mainstream; therefore, when a crisis occurs they may feel especially isolated (Leick & Davidsen-Nielsen, 1991).

Refugees and other immigrants who lack the company of some of their people need great support when facing their losses after emigrating. Often they miss not only a social system or connection but may also mistrust people and systems in their new world. In addition, at times of loss they may miss the religious rituals used in their homeland (Leick & Davidsen-Nielsen, 1991).

In chapter 10, I discuss in more detail the process of assessing loss among Hispanic immigrants, but for now I want to emphasize on the importance of the values of *connectedness* and *trust*, especially when the person's immigration was forced or necessary. Patricia Hynes (2009) cited four forms of trust that help to conceptualize types of forced migration: (a) social, (b) political, (c) institutional, and (d) restorative. Although Hynes is referring to the government policies of the United Kingdom, she considers trust to be an essential component for promoting "social or community cohesion [and] community engagement" (p. 1) in any country.

After suffering a loss, whether real or perceived, people may experience an array of emotions, such as anger, loneliness, or guilt. They may feel cheated, betrayed, or hopeless. Because going through a loss or trauma is painful and difficult, people often feel compelled to make sense of the circumstances and to find meaning in the event. In chapter 9, I introduce techniques for helping immigrants deal with difficult emotions and provide a perspective for helping them find meaning in traumatic events as a resource for coping with their loss. For immigrants, a loss of hope can have a significant influence on how they see themselves as part of a greater culture. It is important for health care professionals to know how strong their clients' attachment is to their native country because this will determine their attitude toward life in the United States, their homeland, and their perception of themselves as immigrants.

It is especially difficult to deal with losses when one does not have the support of a community or family, especially because of physical (i.e., geographic) distance. Immigrants who have left their families behind to come to the United States may find themselves isolated and dealing with their losses without any kind of support. Relevant questions to consider include the following: How can the immigrant deal with this situation? What kind of physical, emotional, and cultural support can he or she get? How can a health care professional provide the best care for this individual?

The immigration experience provides special insights into how people learn to let go of what used to be, to embrace the new. As Boss (1999) observed:

> Personal narratives illustrate the bittersweet legacy of ambiguity about psychological presence and absence for immigrant families, especially when the psychological family is not in accord with the physically present family. Unless people resolve their ambiguous loss—the incomplete or uncertain loss—that is inherent in uprooting, and bring their psychological and physical families into some congruence, the legacy of unresolved grief may affect their offspring for generations to come, compounding itself as more ordinary losses inevitably occur. This is the legacy of immigration that lies at the root of many personal and family problems. (p. 3)

In my work as a grief counselor and coach of Hispanic clients and in my everyday relationships with other Hispanics, I have come to realize how prevalent losses are in their lives. There are several valuable books about Latinos' values and traditions, but most emphasize the cultural and sociopolitical aspects of their lives, including religion; none goes into the specifics of their losses and grief. Although I would like to expand on all of these valuable perspectives, a thorough discussion of each one is beyond the scope of this book, so instead I will weave these dimensions into the text as I explore Hispanics' losses and show how this background can help counselors understand their grieving process. Consistent with my own perspective, and based on my work with Latinos and their families, I can see a thread that unites us all: We belong to one big family, but we are still unique in our own cultural nuances. These nuances need to be respected and included in a blend of traditions and cultural constructs. For many Hispanics, moving to the United States has been the best thing that has ever happened to them. For others, whether they immigrated by choice or because of circumstance, adapting to U.S. culture has been difficult.

Although Hispanics may experience all or only some losses owing to immigration, it is of great value to explore them all, because many are intangible losses that can cause grief and maladaptive behavior. It is also quite important to evaluate whether the situation in which a Hispanic client is living is real or is being perceived through the lens of his or her own assumptions. For example, if a person believes that because of skin color or accent he or she will be rejected by members of the mainstream culture, that person may behave in a manner that predisposes him or her to failure or rejection, a phenomenon known as the *self-fulfilling prophecy*. In such a case, the mental health professional will need to evaluate the client's history and find out the client's previous experiences to help the client avoid making generalizations. Then therapist and client can find ways to work on cognitive processes and emotional responses, which I discuss in more detail in chapter 8. According to Iris Marion Young (Gracia & De Greiff, 2000), Hispanics as a group experience "disadvantages concerning citizenship and inclusion, language use, and racism and stereotyping" (p. 11). Young continued, "Hispanics/Latinos are frequently positioned as foreigners, and that so many who are illegal or even legal residents do not enjoy the same rights as citizens, has determinate consequences for Latinos' economic, social, and political opportunities" (p. 11). As one can easily see, these consequences influence Hispanics' quality of life and the way they interact in mainstream culture.

People in any society live under a system of meanings through which they identify themselves and the world around them. These systems of meaning, or *worldviews*, are what anthropologists call *culture*: "The symbols, rituals, attitudes and perspectives about life that constitute 'culture' enable human society to cohere and function" (Sheldrake, 2001, p. 3). Stroebe, Stroebe, and Hansson (1993) added the following observations regarding grief:

> The United States is culturally diverse. What is ethnically "normal" for one individual may be deviant for another. . . . Americans may not be prepared to appreciate how people differ in their grieving. This can lead to intolerance for the way somebody from another ethnic group grieves and to blocking emotional support for that person. (p. 105)

What is the role of attachment in the losses Hispanics experience as they move to the United States? According to John Bowlby, a well-known British psychiatrist who developed attachment theory in the late 1960s, human beings engage in affectionate relationships that form bonds. When these bonds are broken or threatened, the person experiences a sense of loss (Worden, 2008). According to Bowlby's theory, the bonds of attachment are formed because of a need for security and survival. If we apply attachment theory to the Hispanic immigration experience, which bonds could we say have been broken as a person leaves their homeland? Family? Friends? Legacy?

Consider the case of Rodrigo, who moved from Guatemala to Los Angeles to start a new career as manager of a popular American restaurant chain. The salary is good, and the opportunity, as he stated, *es una bendición* [is a blessing] for him and his family. Nevertheless, he misses the conversations he had with the employees who knew his father and his grandfather in the club where he worked in his home country. They would sit and tell Rodrigo stories about how his father, Rodrigo Sr., became an entrepreneur, and Rodrigo enjoyed learning about the difficult times his father had while starting a supermarket chain. It gave him a sense of history, of legacy. In Los Angeles, his story was different:

> I do not have a history in the United States. I feel rejected by many who notice my skin color and my strong accent. At times people laugh at how I say something or tell me [that I] "better say it in Spanish." But the worst thing is to feel that many people think that *no tengo los papeles* [I don't have the (legal immigration) papers].

It is difficult for people to feel different or rejected because of their ethnicity, including the color of their skin or their accent. Mental health professionals can evaluate how the perception of others has bearing on their clients' self-perceptions, which should be part of the initial assessment and included in the therapeutic relationship.

Although Rodrigo's situation provokes despair in him, he chooses to remain in the United States to work because of his financial need. He plans to eventually return to Guatemala and join the family business to continue his father's dream.

When people experience a loss, their grief reactions are manifested in many ways, and their emotions are very complex because the loss affects them both individually and as part of the larger culture. When there is a loss at a cultural level, people may experience a deep sense of nostalgia for what has been taken from them or for what they have left behind.

LOSSES SPECIFIC TO HISPANICS WHO IMMIGRATE TO THE UNITED STATES

Hispanics may experience some or all of the following universal losses, depending on their individual circumstances: the death of a loved one, divorce, loss of job, or diminished health. In this section I focus on the intangible losses people experience as they immigrate to another country. I want to emphasize that even in the case of immigration by choice, some of these losses become real as one begins to miss the familiar environment, including the way one relates to others. The immigrant's life changes, and the individual must adjust to the new circumstances. To make this adjustment, however, the immigrant must first *accept* the loss or transition he or she is facing in order to transform it.

In the paragraphs that follow, I discuss losses that many Hispanics experience as they leave their country of origin. Because of its uniqueness, I reserve my discussion of the loss of a loved one for chapter 7.

Loss of Traditions

One of the most cherished celebrations in Latin America is Christmas, and many Hispanics experience nostalgia and grief when remembering these traditions in their country of origin. Carlos, a 51-year-old Venezuelan, provided the following explanation:

> At Christmastime people didn't think about shopping. People loved to party and share with others. It was such a joyful time.

On December 24, *La Misa de Aguinaldo* [a Catholic Mass that is almost entirely sung] was very special, and generally all the family went together to church.

Maria, also from Venezuela, shared her experience of Christmas:

> Here in the USA, during Christmas, I hardly see my family or friends because everything is work or going shopping. People are stressed out all the time because the priority is on the gifts one needs to buy. Because I work in a retail chain store I am supposed to stay until 6:00 p.m. on the 24th, which is the day we have our family dinner. I explained to my manager I needed to leave earlier because I had to pick up my elderly mother who lived on the other side of the city, but he didn't care. He said those were the rules and if I didn't like them I could leave. He didn't understand how important family is for us. It was then when I realized how much I missed my country and how I long to go back, but for political reasons and safety I need to remain in the United States.

In such cases the counselor can engage the client in talking about family and cultural traditions, show real interest, and prompt the client to incorporate some of them, when possible, into his or her new life in the United States. Counselors need to know the resources, such as support groups, that exist in the community where Hispanics can share their experiences with other Hispanics. Some of their issues are most benefitted when shared only with other Hispanics.

Despite the challenges Hispanics may face to maintain their traditions in a new country and culture, many choose to continue celebrating important festivities, rituals, and traditions to preserve their cultural identity. Lourdes, an American whose parents are from Honduras, made the following observation:

> My father was very strict regarding family bonding time. He made sure that we had dinner together every night. No TV was allowed, no video games, and we talked about whatever issues were brought up. We used to tell jokes and shared our everyday experience. Now that we got older that has changed. My parents separated, and my father went back to Honduras. I miss those special times that I shared with my family.

Loss of Homeland

Although immigrants may start a new life and adapt to a new culture, they may still feel melancholic as they think about their country of origin. Therefore, besides being homesick, they may experience uncertainty about who they are and where they are going. Furthermore, Hispanics who leave their country may encounter two types of loss: (a) the loss of home and (b) the loss of their dreams. The former involves a loss of one's country because of war, political unrest, or natural disaster, and the realization that one cannot stay there any longer. The latter comprises moving to the United States yet being unable to live the "American dream" of material prosperity, which is supposed to bring happiness and well-being (Cullen, 2004).

When Hispanics leave their home country and move to the United States, many realize that their dreams and hopes are not being fulfilled and that their expectations have remained unmet, as Cristobal, a 31-year-old Colombian, expressed tearfully:

> When I left my country, Colombia, I thought that I would be happy living in Miami (Florida), but I find myself working two or three jobs in order to send money to my children who stayed in my country. I hardly have time to spend with my elderly mother. I made the mistake of bringing her to live with me. Back in my country, I would visit my mom every day and spend time with her. Now, although she lives with me, we hardly see each other. She complains every day of how lonely she is, and I feel guilty and frustrated.

For Hispanics, the well-being of the family has a pivotal role in how they function as members of society. A counselor's knowledge of the relationship their clients have with their families is a vital aspect of therapy, and I expand on this in more detail in chapter 9. Many Hispanics have emigrated to the United States because of the political situation in their country, as was the case with Amalia, a Venezuelan:

> Venezuela was such a beautiful country, and now everything has changed. I miss living in my country, but I cannot go back because my father was involved in politics. Still, I call home every day. Now with Skype it is so easy. We also e-mail each other, and my cousins send me pictures of my nieces as they grow up. I also ask [them] to send me pictures of *El Cerro Ávila* [the mountain El Ávila] to have

some kind of connection with my country. I live in a Venezuelan community in Florida because at least I feel a little "at home" eating *arepas* [cornbread tortillas] and reading the Venezuelan newspaper. I hope the situation changes one day so I can go back.

As Anita noted, some Latinos try to keep a bond with their country, wherever they go or whatever they do:

> A lot of Latinos come here to the United States but only try to make contact with people from their own country, go to the restaurants that serve their country's food, or listen to their own music. It's like you're searching for your own culture. It is a constant searching to feel you are at home. I think people behave like this because it's a loss, a loss of culture, a loss of the city you're from. You keep searching for things you know because when you do find it, the key phrase is "I feel like I'm home." It's a great feeling to be in such a developed country, achieving all these great things, *y sentirme como en casa* [and to feel I am at home]. I imagine that's why many Latinos would feel strange in North Carolina and Virginia because it's so Anglo. Miami is like another country in America.

A prevalent emotion that the counselor needs to acknowledge is the client's nostalgia for the home country, which translates into the need for feeling connected, a need for a sense of belonging in the new country. Denying these feelings in the client can be detrimental to the outcome of the therapy. Therapists would do well to recognize these feelings in their clients and find ways to work through them with the client in an empowering manner.

The Pew Hispanic Center reported that 63% of Latinos maintain moderate attachments to their homeland: "Those with the highest levels of engagement have deeper attachments to their country of origin than immigrants whose connections are less robust. They also have more favorable views of their native country in comparison with the U.S." (Waldinger, 2007). As a Hispanic and a grief counselor, I have worked with many individuals who experience loss on a regular basis. Many Hispanics whose families have remained in their countries phone them every day. With the advances in telephone and computer technology and free computer software such as Skype, this is easier now; however, not too long ago low-income people spent a large portion of their income on phone calls just to hear the voices of their loved ones.

Some Hispanics leave their home country because of war, political conflict, or natural disaster; these include many Central and South Americans, including Salvadorans, Nicaraguans, and Colombians. In the following section, I briefly explore what a disaster is and its implications regarding trauma for the victims or survivors.

Loss of Self-Esteem

The concept a person has of himself or herself is what gives that person the value of who he or she is. This concept of self may be the result of messages one receives in childhood from authoritative figures as well as those from society. As Hwang (2000) observed, an individual's poor self-concept could have a tremendous influence on that person's self-esteem:

> Self-esteem is often defined as an appreciation of self and self-worth. This acceptance and valuing of self are extremely important in the development of a healthy personality . . . [conversely,] low self-esteem is at the root of many social problems, such as crime, violence, drug and alcohol abuse, academic failure, [and] chronic welfare dependency. In the United States we find from articles in magazines to manuals on how to have higher self-esteem and rely on the self instead of also paying attention to personal and social responsibility . . . but to promote self-esteem without advocating personal and social responsibility will result in psychological emptiness and emotional bankruptcy. (p. 2)

Many studies have focused on the effect of self-esteem and a person's relationship to their social environment. Feelings of security have been linked to a stable attachment system (e.g., Bowlby, 1993). This has a direct impact on how people feel when they experience a lack of security in regard to attachment, which can provoke feelings of aggression, anger, and heightened defensiveness in people (Foster, Kernis, & Goldman, 2007). This may be a good explanation for Hispanics' behaviors when they feel separated from their homeland and have severed all ties of attachment. Foster et al. explained:

> According to attachment theories, two elements lie behind the way people think, feel and behave regarding relationships. These are anxiety and avoidance. Attachment anxiety describes the tendency to

worry about social rejection and the availability of others when needed for support, whereas attachment avoidance describes the tendency to avoid intimacy and closeness in relationships. Attachment anxiety develops out of interpersonal experiences characterized by inconsistent availability and support by attachment figures. Individuals with high attachment anxiety have learned to expect inconsistency in the availability of others when needed, and they are highly sensitive to signals of acceptance and rejection. Based on these considerations, we predicted that attachment anxiety would relate to greater self-esteem instability. (p. 66)

There are two types of self-esteem that directly relate to Hispanics: (a) *global self-esteem* and (b) *earned self-esteem*. Global self-esteem has to do with feeling proud of oneself for no specific reason or achievement, whereas earned self-esteem is based on a person's achievements or accomplishments (Hwang, 2000). If Hispanics feel that they are being treated as an inferior minority group and do not feel valued as human beings, it is difficult for them to gain a sense of global self-esteem. However, if they are not given the opportunity to pursue formal education so that they can achieve goals or advance in their careers, they may also have low earned self-esteem because they don't think they have the capacity to do so. They may feel inadequate and may unconsciously perpetuate this self-perception (e.g., by not pursuing any educational opportunities that are available), owing to lack of motivation to better themselves.

Loss of Hopes and Dreams

As I mentioned in my discussion of the loss of homeland, Hispanic immigrants may face a loss of hope in different ways. They may suffer the loss of hope if they find themselves in a situation in which they do not see a brighter future, or if they continuously suffer from low self-esteem. Joaquin, a Cuban, shared his experience of losing hope for a future dedicated to helping and serving others:

> In Cuba I was a physician. I cannot say I am still a doctor because I haven't seen a patient in the last ten years. I had the dream to contribute and enhance the well-being of my patients. Now I am living [in the United States] because my parents were really missing me. I work at *la bodega de mi papa* [my father's grocery store], but I miss my patients.

Antonia, a Colombian, shared the loss of her profession:

> In Colombia I was a lawyer and worked closely with abused women. I had the vision of having a foundation and making a difference in the lives of these women, but I had to leave my country because it was not secure and my family was in danger. Now that I am in Miami I need to find something else to do. I don't know the law, and I don't have the [financial] means to continue studying. Now I need to concentrate on supporting my family.

A counselor can be of great help in working through these issues with clients to help them regain their confidence, trust, and hope for the future and to find new ways to find new meaning in their lives.

Disaster and Loss

There are many definitions of a *disaster*; according to Lopez-Ibor et al. (2005), "A disaster is a consequence of a danger, the *actualisation* [italics added] of the risk," and the following elements should be taken into consideration to define it: "human losses, number of injured persons, material and economic losses and the harm produced to the environment" (p. 1). In this context, *danger* is defined as "an event or a natural characteristic that implies a risk for human beings, i.e., it is the agent that, at a certain moment, produces individual or collective harm" (p. 1).

One may experience both personal and collective disasters, such as a natural disaster or a war. Rosita, a Nicaraguan woman who moved to Miami after the civil war in her country, remembers how the war brought back memories of the earthquake that destroyed the Nicaraguan capital of Managua in 1972:

> As I heard the gunshots and saw the guards coming to my house looking for my fifteen-year-old boy, I felt in my stomach the same sensation of nausea I felt 20 years before when my house was destroyed by the earthquake in Managua. I lived very close to downtown, and everything went into ruins. It was a widespread destruction. I felt totally numb. . . . I couldn't believe I had lost my house. I was glad I didn't lose any family members, but I know of many, many people who lost loved ones. I don't understand why that feeling came back to me when I feared for the life of my son. . . . Why those memories again? I didn't think about the earthquake for years.

Clinicians need to be able to take a history of their clients' lives, including where they come from, the political and economic situations in their country of origin, and memories of events that may be distressing to them. In taking a client's history, the counselor should consider losses, disasters, wars, or safety issues as part of the assessment.

> **Helpful Questions to Ask Your Clients:**
>
> - Have you experienced any natural disaster, such as hurricane, flood, or earthquake?
> - What is the political situation in your country?
> - Did you lose any civil liberties?
> - Did you have curfews?
> - Was there an ongoing civil war in your country?
>   - Were you exposed to bombing?
>   - Did you lose any loved ones in the war? Friends?

Rosita's case is typical of someone exposed to a natural disaster who internalized her feelings that surfaced years later when she was confronted by a personal disaster because of war. The effects of war may remain latent in the psyches of people because of the danger, the lack of safety and protection; as Rosner and Powell (2006) observed: "In contrast to individual traumatic events, war exposes people to a combination of multiple events in a persistently unsafe environment" (p. 200).

Emigrating from Latin American countries that are at war is not uncommon, and although many Hispanic immigrants may have had this experience, not all of them will react to it in the same way. However, the consequences of war affect people's living situations in three main ways:

> Those who stay at home and are not displaced, those who are forced to leave their homes, but do not cross a national border (internally displaced persons), and those who are forced to leave their homes and then also leave the country (refugees). (Rosner & Powell, 2006, p. 200)

When it is possible to leave a country engaged in war, generally it is the head of the household who makes the decision and takes other family members along. When they move to a safe place for their family and begin a new life, "all refugees have to adapt to different cultures and often to learn new languages" (Rosner & Powell, 2006, p. 200).

When people live through a disaster, their suppressed memories may be triggered by a stressor, and the person may relive the whole situation again. Later in this chapter I explore what trauma is and discuss its relation to the disasters Hispanics may have experienced at personal as well as collective levels.

LANGUAGE-RELATED ISSUES FOR HISPANICS LIVING IN THE UNITED STATES

Loss of Language

As the English poet John Donne said, "No man is an island." People need each other. We all are interconnected. As human beings, communication is necessary to relate to others. Probably the most important way of communicating is through speaking. The concept of linguistic rights has a direct implication for Hispanics and their use of the Spanish language. Do the members of this minority group have rights concerning their language? If one considers the language as part of one's identity, but it is not recognized by the mainstream culture, part of the person is not validated; therefore, this represents a loss.

When Hispanics move to the United States, many look for opportunities to communicate with others in their native language. Margarita told the following story of her struggle with English after she emigrated from Colombia:

> When I arrived [in] the United States I knew English somewhat. I had taken English language classes in Colombia. However, once you arrive [in] this country you realize you really don't know as much as you may have thought you did. For example, when I first arrived here I went to the post office. It was terrifying. The terror you feel to speak the language, because you're in America, such a developed country, is tremendous. You have this perception, at least most of my family members and I did, that you cannot fail. You fear not being able to follow the strict laws of the United States. . . . These are all things that make you feel pressure. As I was saying, when I went to the post office, I was so fearful of speaking English, and I kept asking everyone if they spoke Spanish. Someone responded with "Ma'am, this is America." In other words, he was letting me know that they did not need to speak Spanish, and I understood then. I thought to myself "How could all these foreigners, like me, come to the

United States, and not expect to speak the language?" Another thing that hit me was that although I'm from South America, for Anglos when they use the term *America*, they are only referring to North America—the United States and Canada, and only refer to North America as America.

Anita's comments show the mixed emotions many Hispanic immigrants experience as they try to communicate in their new language, English. They have a sense of fear, but at the same time a resolve to "make it." It is important for therapists to assess similar situations faced by their Hispanic clients when these emotions have emerged and to discuss with clients how they have dealt with them.

As human beings we have the right and the need to communicate with one another. If we are unable to use our native language in important matters such as expressing our feelings, our political views, or even applying for a job, our sense of identity and self-worth suffers, and we feel alienated and isolated. We may even feel guilty for not speaking the mainstream language. It is understood that when a person makes the decision to migrate to another country, that person should learn the language of that country if he or she expects to communicate with others and feel part of society. However, what if a person doesn't have the means to pay for language classes, or doesn't have the time to attend school because they need to take care of their children or an aging parent? Because of issues such as these, some people have suggested that the United States formally support immigrants' learning of the English language: "Free instruction and support needs [sic] to be provided so that every Latino can, without undue burden, learn English (Gracia, 2008, p. 114). What if a person feels he or she lacks the ability to learn the language even if given the opportunity? Keep in mind that a person's sense of capability has a great influence on how that person carries out a task, even if this sense of capability represents a personal advantage. The feeling that one is linguistically incompetent may represent a loss that influences many areas of a person's life, such as social and economic status, and even family relationships.

Language, Communication/Translation Difficulties, and Self-Perception

In addition to the challenge of the language itself, immigrants may feel intimidated if they have a strong accent, especially if people of the dominant culture make fun of it. This could have a great impact on the way they behave, the occupations they look for, and the perceptions they have of themselves, all of which may affect their self-esteem, causing yet another loss.

It is generally expected that the more acculturated a person is to the mainstream U.S. culture, the better English that person will speak, but this is not always the case. Even if a Hispanic person can speak English well, it doesn't necessarily mean that person can express exactly what he or she means because of problems with translation. We know how important it is to use the proper words and in the correct context so that we express our feelings accurately. When we use words to express strong affection, we want to be sure we have been understood. Levine and Padilla (1980) offered the following example:

> In English, we use the verb *to love*. In Spanish, nurturing love can be expressed by either *te amo* [I love you] or *te quiero*. *Te quiero* literally translated into English means "I want you" or "I need you." This expression has a connotation of ownership when it is translated into English that is not present in Spanish when it is used to express affection. (p. 46)

If a Hispanic client is trying to communicate with a counselor and does not find the proper words to express himself or herself, this may hinder the therapeutic relationship. A counselor who perceives hesitation on the part of the client could ask the client to phrase what he or she is trying to say in another way or to use examples to be understood better.

In any relationship, communication is key, and a Hispanic who feels he or she is not being understood will either stop using the language or constantly feel embarrassed to the point of developing a complex because of self-perceived inadequacy. Hispanics who spoke English in their homeland may become shy about speaking it in a native English-speaking country because they fear being ridiculed or not respected; what was considered acceptable English in their country has now been deemed substandard and thus a source of embarrassment and shame. Alfonso, a bereaved parent from Nicaragua living in Miami did not seek help for many months because he felt his English was too limited and did not know of any Hispanic therapist who specialized in the treatment of grief. He was desperate to express how he felt, but he did not have the resources either to find a counselor or to talk about his feelings with others.

Because of globalization and the great influx of Latinos into the United States, Spanish is spoken in many places, although the official language of the United States is English, and many services are offered only in this language. Even if a person could speak English, "Complete native speaking and writing command of two or more languages is difficult and quite rare" (Schwarzbaum & Thomas, 2008, p. 191). Immigrants who have learned a second language often find themselves translating their thoughts so they can talk in a way that others can understand. They may also feel embarrassed by their accent.

Monica, a woman from the Dominican Republic, shared how upset she was when she was interviewed for a job and the human resources manager asked her, in a very patronizing way, "Where does that cute accent come from?" She knew that his question meant that she had a strong accent, and instead of feeling proud of being able to speak English, she felt embarrassed.

Frustrations With Acquiring a New Language, Generational Language Differences, and Resentment

Some Hispanics are more inclined or capable than others of acquiring a new language, and when this is not the case, the individual may feel insecure and lack the necessary resources to succeed in the new environment. Some immigrants lack English proficiency and may even reject acquiring knowledge of the new language to preserve their Spanish language of origin. However, because there are so many immigrants in the United States who speak Spanish, some may find it unnecessary to learn English because they can communicate with others and choose to relate with Hispanics alone. This rejection of the English language may cause a conflict for Hispanic children, who may not want to speak their parents' native tongue.

As I observed in chapter 2, it is common for Latinos to have in their homes members of extended families, such as grandparents, who in most cases come to the United States as older adults and for whom learning English is difficult, if not impossible. Many Hispanics who live in barrios speak only Spanish at home even if they have lived for many years in the United States. They watch television in Spanish, listen to a Spanish radio station, and if possible, read the newspaper from their country.

One of the main factors regarding the preservation of language is the level of acculturation and how favorably the native language is viewed in the larger community or mainstream culture. One can find a contrast in this regard between first- and second-generation immigrants. Often, many Hispanics speak both Spanish and English but master neither. Children of first-generation immigrants may speak English at school or with friends but Spanish at home with the family, especially with their *abuelitos* (grandparents). They may talk to their parents in English and be answered in Spanish. When grandparents want to communicate with their grandchildren they usually have to do so in Spanish. This may create resentment in the children, who may feel a disconnect with these family members who have not fully assimilated. Angela is a second-generation immigrant who was 2 years old when she moved to Miami from Colombia. As she learned to talk, she mainly spoke English because of the influence of television and her friends in school, who were also children of first-generation immigrant Hispanics, so she wanted to speak only in English. Such children might feel ashamed to speak Spanish and might reject other aspects of Latin culture, such as Latin music. I discuss the conflicts between generations of immigrants in more detail in chapter 10.

One of the reasons for resentment and a feeling of being caught between two cultures could be the fact that some children may be reprimanded for speaking their native language at school. Jose, a Colombian, shared his experience as a teenager:

> I remember that when we were speaking in the hallways the teachers would call our attention if they heard us speak in Spanish. They told us to speak that language *tan feo* [so ugly] at home. Also, they told us we were too loud, that we made too much noise.

"Therapists may have a difficult time with clients' accents in English and may become frustrated at not understanding what [they] are saying" (Schwarzbaum & Thomas, 2008, p. 212). This frustration may be projected onto the client, who in turn may feel embarrassed and rejected and may refuse to continue therapy. When one of my clients, Lorena, came to see me, she was really frustrated. She had just moved from Las Vegas, where she had looked for a grief counselor but didn't find any who spoke Spanish. She had just lost her husband and was feeling sad, with no hope for the future. Although Lorena spoke English, she felt her feelings were better expressed in her native language.

Some clients, because of their limited English proficiency, may bring another member of the family to therapy who acts as a translator. This suggests the need for more counseling services in Spanish.

Lacking confidence when speaking English can have a negative influence on a person's performance, including test taking, speaking in public, or having an interview. Lucia, a 30-year-old Guatemalan who studied for 3 months to take the bar exam, said she knew the material but felt very insecure because of her lack of proficiency in English. She didn't pass the exam. A counselor who works with this population could help Lucia work on her fears and lack of confidence by helping Lucia realize that one's self-perception has a direct influence on one's behaviors, actions, and personal achievements.

The story of Esteban, a Cuban immigrant, is an example of the pain of learning a new language by necessity: "English was not spoken at home during my childhood and early adolescence. I had difficulties once I arrived in the United States. The acquisition of English has been a painful process and an instrumental component of my 'identity construction.'"

One can see Esteban's reluctance to let go of his identity when he speaks of his resistance to the acquisition of (or serious attempts to learn) standard English phonemes as a strategy for not being assimilated by the dominant culture, to keep his Cuban identity intact. This is a common reality of many immigrants who share their frustrations with me when they realize I am Hispanic.

When a Hispanic is trying to communicate with a native speaker of English, the Hispanic individual may find that it is not possible at times to do a literal translation because it may confuse the other person. Clinical psychologist Pamela Hays (2001) shared the following example:

> For awhile, I had a tutor for Spanish. She was an Argentinean woman who was fluent in English but wanted help with some of the pickier points of English, so we exchanged services. (I got the better deal.) During one of our lessons, she was quite distressed about a series of events that had occurred. As she was describing her day (in English), she said something about feeling like she was just "going forth and back." I interrupted to tell her that in English, the phrase is "going back and forth." She was annoyed by this, and said, "Well, in Spanish, it's 'para adelante y para atras,' meaning 'going forward and then back,' because you cannot go back until you've gone forth." I could see her point; the English was confusing. Furthermore, the illogic of it only added to her annoyance and distress. (pp. 99–100)

One of the main issues that presents a problem for English-speaking persons working with Hispanics is in not understanding the Spanish language and how this may pose risks when working, for example, with a depressed person, especially one who has been engaging in suicidal ideation. An example of this was reported by Ricardo Muñoz, PhD, a major investigator in depression prevention research for the National Institute of Mental Health. He described a Hispanic woman who went to the emergency room saying something about pills. The doctor did not understand her well because he was not proficient in Spanish, and after asking her to promise she wouldn't try to commit suicide sent her back to the halfway house she was living in. The doctor didn't realize that what she was trying to say was "that she'd already taken a lethal dose of pills and was trying to get help" (Comas-Díaz & Greene, 1994, p. 115).

Language and Identity

Many Hispanics, knowing the value language has for preserving one's identity as a member of a group or as part of a culture one feels proud of, demand that their children speak Spanish at home to retain their original language. They generally would say *"Aqui en la casa se habla español"* ["At home you speak Spanish"].

Lourdes, 28 years old, was born in New York, but her parents are from Honduras. She told me how she remembers how important it was for her parents to teach her and her three brothers Spanish:

> Since I was a child I spoke Spanish. I learned to speak Spanish first. I remember that my parents on purpose spoke to us in Spanish. When I started school I learned to speak English, but still my father would buy me books in Spanish so I could learn. Eventually, as we grew older, my father spoke to us in English, in order to have more of a connection, because we were always talking in English my brothers and me, among us. The only time we spoke Spanish was with our family. My father felt he would bond easily with us if he spoke in English to us. My mom felt embarrassed because her English was broken, so she would rather speak Spanish to us. In her job, if she had to, she spoke English, but if she didn't have to, she would prefer to speak in Spanish. We grew up with *novelas* [soap operas]; that is how we bonded. After dinner, my mom and I would sit down and watch *novelas*. On Saturdays, as a family, we would watch *Sábado Gigante* [Giant Saturday], a famous variety show. It was our weekly opportunity to bond.

Heidi, 27 years old, shared how important it has been for her to keep her Hispanic and Mexican heritage, through her language:

> Although I was born in California, my parents, who are from Mexico, wanted me to learn their language. In my house, until I started middle school, we spoke in Spanish. I am glad I did because I have the Mexican accent. It is part of my heritage.

IDENTITY-RELATED ISSUES FOR HISPANICS LIVING IN THE UNITED STATES

Loss of or Diminished Self-Identity

The way the members of a culture identify it has an impact on how they perceive the world and how they behave. As therapists work with clients, this perspective becomes extremely relevant if the therapist is to understand the client and assist him or her in ways that encompass his or her culture. Because the United States is the home of many cultures, issues concerning cultural identity development have received considerable attention in recent times. According to Pope-Davis et al. (2003),

> [This actually originated] with Cross's (1971) theory of Black racial identity development, [but now] this area of study has expanded to include various models of cultural identity: racial identity development . . . ethnic identity development . . . sexual identity development . . . and womanist identity development . . . Of these, models of racial and ethnic identity development continue to dominate cultural identity research. (p. 38)

As Thomas and Schwarzbaum (2008) observed, "Personal identity is cultural identity. Culture is a powerful organizer of people's lives. How we view ourselves and who we are as individuals, cannot be separated from when, where, and how we grew up" (p. 45).

The concept of self is ingrained from the time we are born. Nobody has to tell us what our identity is. It is basically the concept one has of oneself and how this is manifested. We develop this sense of a persona by who we are individually, but the sense of being part of a group or particular culture also is part of one's identity.

As I discussed at the beginning of this book, a person can be, for example, either a Nicaraguan or a Venezuelan; however, when people move to the United States they are labeled *Latinos* or *Hispanics*. How does a person remain culturally intact with this new, generic identity? What about the individual's particular self? Does being grouped into a collective, catch-all identity alter the perception a person has of himself or herself? Does a label define a person's identity? These are all valid questions therapists can explore with their Hispanic clients.

As Nydia Garcia-Preto observed, labeling diverse groups of people as *Hispanics* or *Latinos* takes away their nationality and "symbolizes a loss of identity" (McGoldrick, Giordano, & Garcia-Preto, 2005, p. 155). This could also happen when the person lives in the United States but experiences a disconnect with his or her new reality. With tears in her eyes, Maria contrasted her experience in the United States with that in her native country:

> Here there are no familiar smells. There is a lack of history. Sometimes when I am walking I would get the smell of certain times of the year and would think of my country, Nicaragua. I remember for Christmastimes apples were imported, and we had a tradition to go shopping on Wednesdays: *La familia gatuna a la luz de la luna va de compras* [The feline family goes shopping under the moonlight]. Each time I smell apples at Christmastime those memories come to my mind immediately. To think that I have lost that is just unbearable. Although I am grateful to live here, there is still a lack of recognition, the feeling of being out of place, being a stranger. It is basically like . . . I am different. I don't know who I am anymore.

It is important to assess which cultural traditions Hispanic clients have been able to keep, the meanings those traditions have for them, and the traditions they would like to incorporate into life in their new country. An assessment of various Hispanic traditions is included in the Appendix.

The largest cultural identity problem facing most Hispanic immigrants is that the person feels split between two countries. Nostalgia for one's homeland, if it is too strong, does not allow the Hispanic individual to form a new and functional identity, which, according to Erez and Earley (1993), "anchors the self in the social system" (p. 27).

Kelly (2009) used the term *solastalgia* to express how nostalgia is intrinsic in such a loss:

> The emotive force of nostalgia lies in loss, in the impossibility of return, not just physically, to a place, but also to a time, and importantly, to an earlier version of ourselves attached to that time and place. But, what happens when the place to which one is attached is lost in a different way, catastrophically changed for those who continue to inhabit it? (p. 103)

Closely related to one's social identity is one's self-concept, which "derives from his or her knowledge of membership in a social group, together with the value and emotional significance attached to that membership" (Schwarzbaum & Thomas, 2008, p. 52). When a person is removed from his or her social group membership and transplanted to another country, that person's self-concept and social identity may be confused or altered, causing a sense of imbalance.

Another aspect to consider when referring to self-identity is the relation a person has to the social system. Hispanics' sense of family, including extended family and the interdependence among family members, contrasts with the value that Americans in the United States generally have for their personal independence. For this reason, many Hispanics who move to the United States believe that, if given the opportunity, they would return to their country of origin. Therefore, counselors who value an individualistic perspective may misinterpret the interdependence among family members of Hispanic culture as a sign of enmeshment or codependency (Hays, 2001).

Family relationships are quite strong for Hispanics, as illustrated by my recent encounter at a restaurant I visited. The waiter who served me was from Chile. When I asked him how he felt about living here, he shared that although he had adapted to living in the United States, he missed his home country but was here in order to support his elderly mother back home:

> Many people think I want to stay here. . . . I don't. Here one feels like an island. I just want to save some money and then go back to my country. I want to be buried next to my parents in *la casita* [the mausoleum] they bought in *el Cementerio General* [the General Cemetery].

This sentiment is not uncommon among Hispanics, and if they are intent on going back to their country of origin if things don't work out in the United States, then the possibility of developing an identity with a group in this country is even more difficult. Counselors can be influential in helping their Hispanic clients assess their feelings, noticing whether they experience anger, sadness, or fear because of their newly acquired immigrant status.

Helpful Questions to Ask Your Clients:

- Are you experiencing anger? If so:
  - What is its origin?
  - Against whom is the anger directed?
  - How do you express your anger?
- Are you experiencing sadness? Explore it:
  - What is its origin?
  - When do you feel sad?
  - What makes you feel better?
- Do you feel that fear of the future is dominating your life? Ask yourself the following questions:
  - What am I afraid of?
  - When do I feel most afraid?
  - Why do I feel like this?
  - How long have I felt like this?

Economic Losses and Identity

Because of the recession in the United States that began in the first decade of the 21st century, many people lost their jobs. At the time, native-born Hispanics had the second highest rate of unemployment, after African Americans. In the case of foreign-born Hispanics, although the rate was higher, it was still less than the rate for African Americans (Kochlar, 2009). One of the major determinants of the economic status of the Hispanic is, as noted before, their lack of proficiency in the English language: "English language skills are one of the main determinants of employment levels and success. Individuals with limited English language skills are frequently unemployed or working low-skilled jobs with little upward mobility, such as catering, cleaning, and factory work" (*Fortaleciendo la Familia Hispana* [Approaches to Strengthening the Hispanic Family], 2009, p. 9).

Many Hispanic immigrants come to the United States looking for a brighter future, only to find themselves unemployed and/or living below the poverty line. This may make it difficult for them to obtain services such as counseling/therapy. However, if they do have the opportunity to access any of these services, they may feel too embarrassed or ashamed to share their situation with others, as in the case of Linda, a Venezuelan professional, who works as a maid:

> In my country I was a lawyer, but when I came here I found myself with little money because I wasn't able to take it out from Venezuela. I tried to work as a paralegal, because to be a lawyer I needed to study the laws of the USA, and without the language, it was very difficult. Because I need to pay my bills, I am working as a maid six days a week, and on Sundays I study English. My mother, who stayed in Venezuela, thinks I am working in a firm of lawyers. I feel bad because I lied to her, but *ella se moriría* [she would die—a colloquial expression] if she knew the truth.

What is the counselor to do in this case? Besides her economic losses, Linda is confronted with issues of self-esteem, self-identity, and status. In this case the counselor could focus on Linda's strengths and how she could apply them in her new situation. In chapter 6, I expand on the approach of *strength-focused therapy*, which would be an appropriate perspective to apply with clients facing situations similar to Linda's.

One thing that may influence Latinos of a lower economic status is their fatalistic worldview, including their belief in fate, that things happen to a person independently of their free will. In this matter religion also plays a role. The saying *"Lo que Dios quiera"* ["It is God's will"] is common among Latinos. Suffering is accepted as part of life, and although this attitude may work as a coping skill, it also can cause a sense of hopelessness and encourage feelings of powerlessness (Schwarzbaum & Thomas, 2008).

Despite many Hispanics' low economic status, many do own a business, their own houses, and have great buying power. According to the U.S. Census Bureau, "The median income of Latino households in 2000 was $33,447 . . . and about 79% or 28 million Latinos were above the poverty line in 2000" (Hablamos Juntos, http://www.hablamosjuntos.org/resourcecenter/pdf/00306272003.pdf). Counselors who use cognitive behavior therapy, which I cover in chapter 9, can help their Hispanic clients change their perspective from believing they are an oppressed people to seeing possibilities and growth.

Loss of Social Status and Identity

The loss of a person's social status is closely related to economic loss and low self-esteem. The *New World Encyclopedia* (online version, 2008) defines *social status* as "the standing one holds in society based on prestige. It is also affected by a number of factors such as occupation, wealth, education, and family background." Diminishment of any of these factors can contribute to a loss of social status and can have a great influence on the lives of Hispanic immigrants.

To illustrate the loss of status and identity, consider the story of Emilio, a Nicaraguan man who was a physician in his country until the civil war in 1979, when he had to flee his country and take asylum in the United States. After so many years in the United States he still feels frustrated and angry because he was never able to practice again due to his inability to learn the language and qualify to work as a doctor here. With much nostalgia, he remembers his patients and the respect and the role he had in his Nicaraguan community. As he explained, now he feels he is *un don nadie* [a nobody]. He said he drinks every night after his shift as a courier is over and does not have any hope for a brighter future.

The Law of Identity

According to Ridley (2005), when talking about identities the model used most often in the Western world is the "either–or thinking" that originated with Aristotle's philosophy that states that it is not possible for something, at the same time, to belong and not to belong. One of the laws on which this philosophy is based is the *law of identity*, which has very powerful connotations when applied to race or ethnicity because it may imply that racial groups are totally separated one from one another. Ridley further stated that this either–or thinking may bring "the notion of group superiority and involves a dehumanizing process. Members of the dominant cultural group devalue members, cultures, and customs or minority groups" (p. 15). For Hispanics, to feel devalued and inferior may bring a profound sense of inadequacy and grief. Counselors may want to explore whether their clients have faced any situations in which their identity has been challenged or mocked.

Helpful Questions to Ask Your Clients

- Have you ever felt ridiculed or looked down upon?
- Has someone made fun of your culture?
- Have you ever been called derogatory names regarding your Hispanic heritage?

Counselors need to be aware of their own possible misperceptions and biases to avoid making their clients feel inferior or invalidated, which could make the situation even more problematic because, as Ridley (2005) observed, "Many counselors are ineffective with minority clients because they fail to see 'the big picture.' That is, they overlook societal factors that influence the behavior and adjustment of these clients" (p. 15). The method of evaluation I present in chapter 9 can help counselors gain awareness of their own potential bias regarding Hispanics.

Immigrants—specifically, refugees—undergo a process of adaptation and transition to their new cultural status. In this journey they may lose the personhood with which they identify to acquire the new identity. Flores-Borquez (1995), in her own transition as a political refugee from Chile, observed that despite the fact that she maintained her own integrity, she had to acquire an identity that felt strange to her.

Latin Women and Identity

I include here a separate section for Latin women (Latinas) because their identity has undergone a tremendous development, from the traditional role of the stereotypical Hispanic family to an independent and contemporary one.

Women in Latin cultures have historically experienced oppression because of the patriarchal society structure. "Women in World History: Health in Latin America," a project of the Center for History and New Media at George Mason University, indicated that "historical documents on Latin American life in the 20th century are marked by an absence of women's voices, and a presence of the more powerful to speak for—or, on behalf of—women" (Mooney, n.d., http://chnm.gmu.edu/wwh/modules/lesson15/lesson15.php?s=0).

Although advances for women in Latin American countries have been made, their inferior/submissive status is still upheld in some families. This may represent struggle and a conflict of identity for Latin women living in the United States. In traditional Latin families, women may be expected to act submissively, although this has dramatically changed in Latin American countries with globalization and the exposure to the modern lifestyle that emphasizes equality between men and women. This stereotype of Latin women as being submissive may influence the way they are perceived and treated in U.S. society, including in counseling situations. "The reality of a Latina is *un choque* [a clash], a cultural collision constructed from numerous experiences and identities that form her new and unique existence"

(Gloria, 2001, p. 3). For example, according to Comas-Diaz, a Puerto Rican–descended woman "must simultaneously stand against a society outside her community that discriminates against her as a Puerto Rican and a society within her community that demands her submissiveness as a woman" (cited in Gloria, 2001, p. 4).

The National Council of La Raza, which is the largest national organization involved with civil rights and advocacy for Hispanics, offers the program *Alternativas para Latinas en Autosuficiencia* (ALAS; Alternatives for Latin Women in Self-Sufficiency) to provide Latin women living in the United States more opportunities to be self-sufficient and live a better life. ALAS, which is offered in Spanish, consists of training women to be self-employed so that they can improve their economic situation. This initiative is very meaningful because, according to ALAS, many of these women do not have roles as business owners, and in general they are not supported or encouraged by their families or communities. The training involves business planning as well as computer and English classes and actually encompasses a holistic perspective: "Through culturally and linguistically competent training, micro-financing, and ongoing support services, ALAS helps low-income Latinas overcome barriers, build self-confidence, and achieve financial independence for themselves and their families" (*Fortaleciendo la familia Hispana* [Approaches to Strengthening the Hispanic Family], 2009, p. xx).

Because there are certain identifiable values within Hispanic traditions, some therapists or counselors may assume that when a woman makes a choice, it is based only on these traditions, not taking into account her individuality, even if she displays a restrictive behavior that could be considered part of her culture.

We all have our own histories and base our choices on our perceptions of the world. A Hispanic woman may find herself making choices that could resemble a "cultural norm" expected from being Latina. However, if the counselor bases her or his assessment of the client on a superficial understanding of her culture, a misunderstanding of the motives of her choices could result, eliminating the client's individuality (Espin, 1999).

Identity and Race

A person's sense of self self-esteem may be greatly influenced by that person's race (Schwarzbaum & Thomas, 2008). For example, physical features, such as skin color, hair texture, and facial features, have been historically identified with the race/ethnicity to which an individual belongs and, in some milieux, that person's social status. For example, among Hispanics are people with both dark and light skin. People with lighter skin, according to Gomez (2000), experience less discrimination in the labor market and reach higher socioeconomic levels. Hence, there seems to be an association between physical racial characteristics and racism.

Racism, according to Ridley (2005), is "any behavior or pattern of behavior that tends to systematically deny access to opportunities or privileges to members of one racial group while allowing members of another racial group to enjoy those opportunities or privileges" (p. 29). One of the key features of Ridley's approach is *preferential treatment*, which has to do with the lack of equal opportunity for members of racial/ethnic minority groups compared with the preferred group.

Because of the aforementioned limitations of race, some Hispanics deny their ethnicity and choose to overidentify with mainstream culture and engage in civic activities that relate them to North American culture. The problem with this denial of one's ethnicity is that it can bring emotional distress because the individual's cultural values may become mixed and confused (Levine & Padilla, 1980). These conflicts may be reflected in their personal and professional lives.

People who feel embarrassed by or devalued for being of a certain race often project these negative sentiments onto others, and it is likely that most people won't accept them because of this. One strong emotion experienced by Hispanics who have encountered racism is anger, and counselors need to pay special attention to this response because "it is adaptive for the client to express the anger associated with this subjective discomfort" (Levine & Padilla, 1980, p. 88). In chapter 9, I introduce different ways to help clients use techniques to cope productively with discrimination, racism, and stereotypes.

RACISM IN THE HEALTH CARE SYSTEM

One of the areas where racism is perceived by Hispanics is in the health care system, where they have difficulty obtaining services owing to a lack of health insurance because they cannot afford it, their employer does not provide it, or they are not in the United States legally. If they are illegal immigrants, they are not entitled to most elective services other than emergency treatment at a hospital. Abigail, a Salvadoran who has lived in the

United States for 10 years, shared the scare she had when she got sick and was unable to get help because she did not have health insurance:

> I was suffering from terrible pain on the right side of my torso but didn't know what it was. I thought it was a stomach congestion [sic] and took a couple of *Sal de Andrews*, you know, they are like Alka Seltzer, but I buy them in the Latin grocery store.
>
> I work as a maid and had to do my job with the constant discomfort. One day I could hardly move. I got scared. I went to the hospital and they refused to see me due to my illegal status and [because] I didn't have health insurance. That is when I decided to go to El Salvador, where I have a sister who is a doctor.
>
> The moment I arrived they took me in [the emergency room] at the hospital and saw that my gallbladder was totally swollen and that I needed surgery. I got even more scared, but they told me I would be fine. But they didn't contemplate the possibility of my gallbladder erupting, and I almost died in surgery. When I was in recovery my sister told me I was very irresponsible. She was angry with me because I didn't take care of myself and waited too long to go to the doctor. I told her I had been denied assistance, but I felt guilty for not going back to my country sooner. She recommended I stay in El Salvador, but I couldn't. My husband was waiting for me in Miami, and besides, I had to earn money in order to pay for my son's law school. I don't care if I have to sacrifice for him. I want for my son a better future.

According to the United Nations, in most countries 10% of the population has some kind of mental, physical, or sensorial disability, and the number of people with disabilities had reached 500 million people by 2006 (Martz & Livneh, 2007). There are many reasons why these disabilities occur, but treatment and prevention may be of great help if people understand and are educated about the relevant issues (e.g., not delaying seeking health care treatment).

Martz and Livneh listed some variables that contribute to disabilities, which may be found among many Hispanics living in the United States:

> Wars, poverty, and epidemics; overcrowded and unhealthy living conditions and pollution in the environment; low literacy levels and the related lack of knowledge about health measures or services, as well as inaccurate understanding about the cause and treatment of disability and the range of possibilities in life when having a disability;

lack of health-care infrastructures; lack of access to available health-care resources. (p. 3)

THE NEWS AND ENTERTAINMENT MEDIA'S INFLUENCE ON HISPANIC SOCIAL IDENTITY

"Anyone in the United States who believes that he or she is immune to cultural attitudes about race underestimates the power of modern advertising" (Ridley, 2005, p. ix). The news and entertainment media influence the way people perceive other cultures, and the messages the media outlets send, whether obvious or implied, may provoke stereotyping and develop biases. "Negative stereotypes, a form of psychological and sometimes physical violence that impacts all aspects of Latino and Latina lives, are perpetuated (implicitly and explicitly) in the media and in economic and social systems" (Utsey, Bolden, & Brown, 2001, cited in Atkinson, 2004, p. 90).

The news media (television, newspapers, and radio) and the advertising used therein have an impact on how people form stereotypes concerning cultures different than theirs. Sometimes people get the wrong impression of their own culture! The media have a huge influence on prejudices, biases, and negative attitudes toward members of racial/ethnic minority groups. Psychologist Linda A. Jackson (1995) stated that Anglos tend to perceive Hispanics in ways that may not be positive and noted some common stereotypes of Hispanics:

> A review of the handful of studies that have examined stereotypes of Hispanics suggests that perceptions are generally unfavorable (Bernat & Balch, 1979; Fairchild & Cozens, 1981; Guichard & Connolly, 1977; Simmons, 1961). For example, Hispanics are viewed as lazy, cruel, ignorant and pugnacious, but also as family-oriented and tradition-loving (Fairchild & Cozens, 1981). Other evidence suggests that Hispanics use the same stereotypes in describing themselves. (p. 3)

Jackson also mentioned that some Anglos perceive the following traits or behaviors of Hispanics:

> Stereotypic characteristics and values indicated generally negative perceptions of Hispanics (e.g., [that they are] less productive and intelligent, more physically violent and rebellious). (p. 2)

It is safe to assume that some of these negative portrayals have a detrimental impact on how Hispanics see themselves and therefore may play a role in lowering their self-esteem.

HISPANICS DEALING WITH MULTIPLE LOSSES

As a Hispanic as well as a grief counselor, I have worked with many Hispanics who experience loss on a regular basis. For example, for Hispanic clients who feel homesick, and wonder why they have to be so far away from home, counselors can help them realize their purpose for coming to the United States in the first place and help them clarify what they are doing or achieving now. If one wants something, one has to make sacrifices. Are these sacrifices worthwhile? Is there any benefit the client is not seeing because he or she is too focused on the problems? The first step that I find necessary as a person faces a loss is to accept it. According to the Rev. Mel Lawrenz, PhD, people in the United States live in a society of denial regarding losses and think they shouldn't happen to us. Thus, "When we suffer loss or [believe] that losses ought not happen in life" (Caine & Kaufman, 1999, p. 365), we feel like victims. Some clients may be facing multiple losses, feel overwhelmed, have a fatalistic view of the future, and feel like victims. For example, Joaquin mourned the loss of his job and the impossibility of making payments for his house and faced the possible loss of his home owing to foreclosure. For these reasons, he assumed that his wife would leave him and go back to the Dominican Republic. Therefore, he anticipated his grief if his wife were to leave. He imagined that he would be left alone, without the possibility of going back to his country because he didn't want to show others he had failed. He was told that there was a support group run by men who were in a similar situation, but it was conducted in English, and he didn't feel he could express his feelings in another language. Furthermore, he thought support groups were better suited to women. He indicated that he is un hombre [a man] and has to be strong. Central to Joaquin's despair were his feelings of inadequacy and loss of self-esteem.

Joaquin is typical of someone who has experienced a major loss and has secondary losses subsequent to the first. Some of his losses were real, but some were fabricated by Joaquin's pessimistic outlook. Nonetheless, it is important for counselors to assist clients in evaluating their losses in a realistic manner and to help them realize what strengths they have to deal with them. A special section on how to use strengths and values, which can be a valuable tool for clients and therapists, is included in chapter 9.

Neimeyer (1998) offered a straightforward perspective, stating that people don't "get over" many losses, as suggested by other theories; on the contrary, one learns to live with the loss, which is a philosophy I share. The losses "become part of who we are" (Houben, 2009, p. 235).

Coping Mechanisms

It is common among people who have experienced a traumatic event, such as losing a loved one owing to death, losing a job, or having a health scare, to develop "clinical depression and anxiety within a one-year period" (Bifulco & Brown, 1996; Finlay-Jones & Brown, 1981, cited in Harvey & Miller, 2000, p. 12). However, people are unique, and they respond in unique ways to stressful events or losses, both negatively and positively. Therefore, it is not easy to predict a positive or negative outcome in clients who experience a loss. Vulnerability factors for anxiety and/or depression after a loss include "a personality marked by negativity [and] a severe prior traumatic experience, such as victimization, disaster, combat experience, and physical or sexual abuse" (Updegraff & Taylor, 2000, p. 12). Adaptive personality traits, including an active coping style, optimism, perceptions of control over life events, and a strong sense of self as well as the nature of the stressful experience itself seem to help a person react to an event in a more positive manner. Harvey and Miller (2000) found these elements to be "potential determinants of stress-related growth and vulnerability" (p. 12). In the case of Hispanics, this information is valuable because the counselor can conduct an assessment to evaluate how many of these characteristics the client possesses.

Rebuilding Self-Esteem After a Loss

Jose thought his world had ended after the death of Lucia, his spouse of 23 years. They had moved to the United States at the beginning of the 1990s, and after many sacrifices established a courier business. Jose was devastated after Lucia's death, but despite his pain he was able to continue working and, inspired by his wife's resilience during her illness, started a support group for men. The idea was to offer help to husbands who didn't know how to cope with the loss of their spouse.

Therapists need to be cognizant of the role men have in Hispanic culture and at the same time keep in mind that all Hispanic men are not the same. Some men do not believe in support groups; others do. Ideally, the counselor should explore the client's concept of how men should behave, their role when facing a loss, and how they can evolve as human beings.

Even if the possibility of growth after a trauma exists, therapists need to be cognizant of the pain involved after a trauma, because this experience "usually produces distress, disrupts one's understanding of the world, makes salient one's vulnerabilities and lack of power and control . . . and extreme doses of trauma may simply overwhelm the psychological resources of most persons" (Calhoun & Tedeschi, 2006, pp. 9–10).

The Individual's Emotional Response to Loss

As people go through the transitions that follow a loss or major life event, they may experience an array of emotions that could prevent them from moving forward. Shaver et al. (1987, cited in Shaver & Tancredy, 2001, p. 70) stated that human beings experience five basic emotions: (a) love, (b) joy, (c) anger, (d) sadness, and (e) fear.

In the following example, one can see the array of feelings that Amalita, a woman from Colombia, experienced during her different transitions:

> I remember that when I moved to Miami I cried every day. I had never left my country before. I hardly spoke English and felt totally disconnected from this lifestyle. I had a young child of two years of age and found myself with no help and was trying to find a new life for both of us. I had just divorced my husband and wondered if I had done the right thing. I felt devastated because my family were traditional Catholics, [and] divorce was considered something wrong. I felt ashamed and embarrassed to say I was a divorced woman. I sometimes would lie, saying that my son's father was in my country working but would be moving very soon with us. In the meantime I had to find a way to function despite my lack of desire to leave my bed or even prepare food for my child. My mother, who stayed with me for some time to take care of my child, would also cry every day because she suffered for my own situation. She would say, "Amalita, mothers feel pain when their child suffers. You will see when your child grows up." It didn't help me much because I felt guilty for having my mother be in that situation. On top of that, she didn't speak a word of English, so I needed to be translating for her all the time, and that also made me feel irritated. Why couldn't she understand a word? For some time I considered going back, but in my country the civil war was increasing, and it was not safe.

Here in the USA, if one proved we were fleeing due to political problems, we were granted asylum, so I decided to put all my papers in order and, against my real desire, applied for it. The day that I had the interview in Immigration I was really scared. I remember asking myself the following questions: What would they say? Would they ask me about my family? Would they know that Pedro, my brother, was a drunk and hit his wife? And what about if they asked me to bring my mother inside the room? She wouldn't be able to speak because she wouldn't understand English. That would be embarrassing and maybe they would consider her to be *una carga* [a burden].

To understand the emotions a person experiences, we can use the following model of the emotional process, adapted from Shaver and Tancredy (2001, p. 67). This model identifies different aspects of the emotional process and notes how the emotions are the result of a stimulus, the person's response, and his or her coping skills. This model encompasses the following stages:

- A notable change or event in the internal or external environment
- Appraisal of the event in relation to goals, wishes, concerns
- Self-regulation efforts
- Appraisal- and emotion-specific thought and action tendencies (and their underlying physiology)
- Expressions, thoughts, behaviors, and subjective feelings.

As Schaefer and Moos (2001) observed, there is no consensus in the existing literature about the definition of personal growth, but they stated that a wide variety of crises—including natural disasters, war and combat, physical illness, divorce, and bereavement—can be catalysts for personal transformation, and thus they believe that persons who effectively adjust to bereavement may experience personal growth more than people who do not adapt in a similar manner. Schaefer and Moos (2001) developed a conceptual model for understanding positive outcomes that may result from a life crisis or a transition from bereavement, using the following two questions:

1. Are some individuals especially likely to emerge from bereavement with a new sense of self, increased maturity, and a greater appreciation for life?
2. If so, are these individuals' preexisting personal and social resources and coping skills associated with positive outcomes?

What people expect from us has an impact on how we express our emotions (Hochschild, 1979). Hispanic men are generally expected to be strong, *muy macho* [very manly], which may prevent them from fully experiencing grief or showing nonfunctional ways of coping. Marcos, a Nicaraguan who recently lost his mother, shared how he needed to hide his emotions:

> When my mother died I felt my world had ended. She raised me by herself and was very supportive of all my decisions. I had to start working very young because my father left us, and I remember going back home very late at night and my mother would be waiting for me with a plate of *arroz con frijoles* [rice and beans], *tortilla y queso* [tortilla and cheese]. It was not much, but it was cooked with great love. When I moved to the United States due to the political situation, I left her back in Nicaragua, because she was afraid of planes, but every year I went back to my country with gifts. Now that she has died I feel guilty for not bringing her with me. I feel like crying every day but I don't want to show any weakness in front of my children. Men are not supposed to cry. We need to be strong and show we can handle anything.

A meaningful way to maintain or gain control over one's life is to modify or adjust one's goals. Many Hispanics may stress themselves with goals that are very difficult to attain and may become frustrated and therefore experience further loss. However, those who manage to adjust their goals to be more attainable and realistic can acquire a sense of mastery and achievement that could inspire them to try different options and find new opportunities (Harvey & Miller, 2000).

Using Hispanics' Resources

Not everyone who experiences loss will react with obvious distress. There are many reasons why this occurs, including the mourner's customs, whether personal or cultural (e.g., if the person rejects an open expression of grief). The mourner's use of spiritual or global strategies to cope with loss can also reduce the need for an overt expression of distress. The value of support from family, professionals, religious organizations, and the community for the grieving and coping processes are being given increased recognition by thanatology researchers (Becker, 2009).

During my counseling of Hispanics I find it pertinent to take into consideration the most salient issues in the clinical setting, as identified by Schwarzbaum and Thomas (2003): "Their migration experience, their acculturation and acculturative stress, their experiences with racism and discrimination, language issues, and gender roles and expectations" (pp. 68–69).

When Hispanic clients experience a loss, it is of great value to know what, specifically, the loss is, what strengths the clients can use to handle their loss, and their perception of themselves as they have become part of a racial/ethnic minority group in the United States. The conceptual model developed by Schaefer and Moos (2001) notes that despite losses, there can be positive outcomes after a person experiences a transition or crisis. Their model focuses on the resources a person has, both environmental and personal; the individual's life crisis or transition; that person's cognitive and coping responses; and potential positive outcomes, which include social resources, coping skills, and personal resources (p. 151).

Moving to another country is a major life transition. People going through such transitions may encounter three similar stages, as presented in a seminar by Bridges (2004): "an (1) ending, followed by (2) a period of confusion and distress, leading to (3) a new beginning" (p. 8). I have found the third stage to be extremely empowering for clients. If Hispanics can see their challenges as opportunities to grow, they can also see their transition from their home country to the present one as a new beginning.

CONCLUSION

How can Hispanics face their situations, which may seem to remain the same over long periods, and still find strength to continue living with purpose and joy? In my book *Transform Your Loss: Your Guide to Strength and Hope* (2009), I discuss the attitude, expected in U.S. society, of "I'm OK, You're OK." But at times we are not OK, especially as we face a loss and find ourselves grieving and in despair. In chapter 8, I expand further on how to help Hispanics in their grieving process.

When a person faces a loss, it is necessary for that person to reach out to others, to communicate with them. Hispanic people who do not have a support network, friends, family, or a support group are missing an essential aid when facing their loss. Reaching out to help others may also help them get outside of their own situations. Mental health professionals can play an important role in this process.

HELPFUL SUGGESTIONS

- Acquire knowledge of your clients' personal histories, and expand on your knowledge of their country of origin. Be sure to learn about the different situations in each country, such as natural disasters, civil wars, or issues of personal safety. You may not identify personally with these different situations, but learning about your clients' unique and often difficult experiences may increase your understanding and empathy. For example, you can learn about the political situation in Venezuela, the exiles from Cuba, or the war experience in Nicaragua. If you don't know specifics about a client's background, ask. It is always better to ask and establish a bond with your client than to pretend you know and remain absent.
- Engage your clients by asking them to share information about their family traditions and celebrations from their home country. Show interest, and inspire them to tell you stories from their childhood, neighborhood, and life in general. Let them communicate their sorrow as well as their joy for being able to speak about their country.
- If you have a problem understanding a client's English, because of the accent or limited proficiency in the language, do not make the client feel uncomfortable through your body language or words. If language is an obstacle, ask for a translator, or refer the client to a counselor who is fluent in Spanish. It will be a negative experience for you and your client if, owing to lack of language compatibility, the important issues of loss and grief are not addressed in a constructive and meaningful manner.

PERSONAL REFLECTIONS FOR THE COUNSELOR

- Do you find yourself comfortable working with clients who speak English in a foreign accent?
- Do you find learning about your clients' homelands, traditions, and celebrations a valuable aspect of the therapeutic relationship?
- Do you demonstrate an excessive interest in other cultures because of curiosity instead of concern?
- Are you able to understand the sense of loss your clients may be experiencing by not living in a familiar surrounding, including the language they speak and the different kinds of foods they eat?

CHAPTER 6

Hispanics' Health Care, Illness, and End of Life

Geri-Ann Galanti started her book, *Caring for Patients From Different Cultures* (2008), with a question: "What happens when an Iranian doctor and a Filipino nurse treat a Mexican patient?" (p. 1). I found this question so enlightening because it reflects the current situation in the United States. We all come from different places and live under a huge umbrella as immigrants, but we all have our uniqueness, which may cause conflict when making decisions concerning health and end-of-life issues. Although I do not disagree with Galanti's observation that Hispanics may take the attitude of *Qué será, será* [What will be, will be], I do believe that Hispanics know they have some control over nature in the sense that we take remedies or actions to prevent something bad from happening. What I find problematic is, as Galanti observed, that the use of preventive health care measures is not common among Hispanics, which may have negative implications for the actions or decisions they take.

As one faces a health issue or a terminal illness, or confronts end-of-life issues, the support of others takes on greater importance. For Hispanic people, this support may come primarily from the family as the family members get actively involved in the care of the ill person, including his or her physical and spiritual well-being—to the extent of collaboration in making important health care decisions. Cardenas, Garces, and Deborah (2004) observed that:

> In the Latino culture, there is a complex relationship between health and illness, as well as the physical, mental, and spiritual parts of a

person's life . . . [and] . . . the family-centered model of decision making is highly valued and may be more important than patient autonomy. (p. 1)

This may be in conflict with health care practitioners who are not prepared to deal with patients who prefer not to make decisions until they have first discussed the matter with their families (Galanti, 2008).

HISPANIC FAMILY DYNAMICS AND HEALTH CARE

Throughout this book I have presented the role of *familismo* [familism] in the lives of Hispanics. *Familismo* is a value that influences the way health care decisions are handled by many families as well as the interaction of family members when a relative has a terminal disease. Carmen Lucía, a middle-aged woman from El Salvador who was diagnosed with breast cancer, felt that she was not understood by the doctor or nurses involved in her care:

> I was diagnosed three years ago with breast cancer and it was very scary because my mother died in my country, El Salvador, of breast cancer. I remembered how much I suffered seeing her going through chemotherapy and radiation for nothing. I didn't want to take any action but wanted to consult with my family. My doctor suggested I go through a round of chemotherapy and have a breast removed. Maybe that would prevent the cancer from spreading. I told him I needed to ask my husband and three children. My family and I decided not to take that route. We decided to visit a *curandero* [folk healer] for some herbs, and I decided to change my diet to eat more organic food without pesticides. In my country the fruits and vegetable grow naturally, not like here. Maybe I got [the cancer] from eating so many chemicals and hormones. I wanted to go back to basics. I have also been away from the Church. Maybe this was a signal I needed to be more [of] a believer. My family supported me on this, and everyday we prayed a novena to St. Jude and every Sunday we all went to Mass. I am happy to say now that it was the best decision. . . . For three years I was cancer free, now it has come back, but I am at peace. We got even closer as a family and I feel this is my path. My doctor doesn't understand why I had to consult

with my family about my own health and why I have taken such a passive stand.

Carmen Lucía's case exemplifies the necessity of health care practitioners respecting the values of Hispanic families. The doctor's purpose in recommending chemotherapy and surgery was to cure Carmen Lucía's breast cancer, but she chose an alternative modality that was more congruent with her values and traditions.

In addition to the involvement of the family in health care is the issue of health care access. Many Hispanics lack health insurance. Much research shows that members of racial/ethnic minority groups, including Hispanics/Latinos, generally have worse health outcomes than Whites and that a higher percentage "are uninsured compared to non-Hispanic whites" (Jonas, Goldsteen, & Goldsteen, 2007, p. 190). These facts make it very difficult for the Hispanic population to take advantage of preventive medicine or even to see a physician when ill. Therefore, many Hispanics who face a serious health condition or require surgery choose to go back to their country of origin, where the cost is much lower than in the United States. For instance, Luisa, a Nicaraguan, needs to have hip replacement surgery. Because she is not employed full-time, she does not have health insurance. She cannot afford to pay for the surgery, which costs more than $50,000. Therefore, she is contemplating going to Colombia, Costa Rica, or Nicaragua, where she would pay less than $10,000 for the operation. Cases such as this are very common among Hispanics regarding surgeries and health-related issues in general. In regard to a terminal illness, many people choose, if they can afford it, to go back to their country of origin to die. Sometimes, however, this is not possible and, according to the Rev. Hector Figueroa, a chaplain for the Jackson Health System in Miami, Florida, this is a great cause of grief for a Hispanic person:

> The other issue with losses [in Hispanic dying patients' experience] is [that with] people coming from different parts of Latin America and other places, there's the issue of "Oh, I wish I could have gone to my country to see my family" or perhaps there's an issue of where that person is going to be buried and they think, "Oh, I wish I could have said. . . . I wish I could have resolved. . . . I wish I could have the finances to have my family bury me in my country."

HISPANICS AND TERMINAL ILLNESS

Many of us live without any thought of our mortality, often until we are touched by the devastating news of a death of a loved one, or faced with our own impending death. When a person is diagnosed with a terminal illness, many questions and fears related to death and dying arise. The ill person, who must deal with what his or her illness and what eventual death will mean for himself or herself and his or her loved ones, is often riddled with strong emotions. Terminal illness also exposes one to a fear of pain, anxiety about death, and the anticipation of being separated from loved ones and the things we love (DeSpelder & Strickland, 2005). Patients facing a terminal illness need to make several decisions, especially in regard to issues that involve medical care. The family, too, may need education about the illness as well as information about their loved one's options, such as home care, hospice, and legal documents (e.g., durable power of attorney). I have observed an unfortunate lack of education about these issues among my Hispanic clients. María Gómez, a licensed social worker who has worked for one of the largest hospice providers in south Florida for the last 14 years, considers there is a need for advance directives so that the patient's wishes are known. María observed,

> There [often] is nothing in writing. It is just shared with the family. Then we ask, "Did he or she talk about what he or she wanted?" The family responded, "He was so afraid of death, he never talked about it."

Another element of health care that affects patients' emotional well-being is in communicating the diagnosis of a terminal illness to them and their families. Hispanic families have tight bonds, and they are likely to be involved in what is happening to their loved one. Some patients, to protect their family, do not tell them how sick they are. Many health care professionals lack the necessary cultural awareness when dealing with Hispanic families. Dr. Alex Fiuza, a Cuban psychologist, observed the following:

> I feel that education is powerful and only by educating the masses will you be able to help them understand. Again, going back to the traditions and ways things are done, most Latinos are very private

with their discussions of family illnesses and the way they deal with them. The only differences are that some keep it in their own family groups and others don't even mention it.

Talking about terminal illness and life-threatening diseases is rather taboo among many Hispanics, although this differs according to their country of origin. Fiuza continued, "An illness is treated or defined differently in Cuba than it is in Santo Domingo. In Cuba when a person gets sick you cannot talk about it". Such was the case of Pedro, a Nicaraguan man who had to admit his mother to the hospital because she was complaining of stomach ache. After running some tests, her doctor suggested surgery to remove a possible tumor. When he performed the surgery, he realized it was too late; the cancer had spread throughout her abdominal cavity. Pedro was devastated, but because he wanted to spare his mother emotional pain, he told her the following:

> Mamita, the doctor found a small tumor, but it was benign. They removed it and little by little you will start to feel better. You need to pay attention to what you eat. I will start giving you sopa de pollo [chicken soup] and you will see how well you will be. We just need to be patient and pray.

Certain Hispanics believe that if you drink or eat certain foods they will prevent or cure cancer. For example, in my country of Nicaragua, people believe that if one drinks sopa de garrobo [soup of a large lizard] he or she will be cured of cancer. Pedro was giving his mother sopa de pollo and hoping that it would help her recover from her cancer.

Another custom that may be misunderstood by a health care professional of a non-Hispanic culture (e.g., Anglo) is that when a Hispanic person is in the hospital, the family and close relatives will visit the patient and even stay with them after visiting hours. At times, this has been a problem, according to Sonia Martinez, director of consumer relations/volunteer services of the University of Miami Hospital. Some Hispanics do not respect the hospital schedule and regulations. They worry that their loved one won't be taken care of well enough. For example, Susana, who is from the Dominican Republic, shared the following anecdote:

> The moment my mother was admitted in the hospital for heart surgery, I was also admitted. I was with her the whole five days. I didn't

go to work or take care of my house. My cousin came to my house to take care of my children. I needed to be next to my mom all the time. She doesn't speak English, and I was afraid they wouldn't understand her. Also, the hospitals here are so different than in my country. Here people are so cold. They are more detached, and the nurses and doctors seem to be always in a hurry. My mother also had a problem with the food in the hospital. Nothing resembled our food. It is so difficult to be in a foreign place. I remember the first day as I was cleaning her and taking care of her, the nurse told me, "Leave her alone, she is fine." How would she know? She didn't pay attention to the way my mother looked at me or how she wanted to pray with me the rosary.

Hispanic families often want to be with their loved one at the time of death. They may not understand that there are rules and regulations involved in the hospital, and this can be a source of grief as it can bring feelings of guilt and anger, as the following comment reflects:

When Ramon was dying, the doctors wouldn't allow me to be in the room. They said [his illness] may be contagious, so I needed to stay outside for most of the time and just enter the room wearing some clothing that would protect me against any infection. I got so angry! I screamed. I wanted to take him home, but they wouldn't listen. I needed him to be at home surrounded by his family. The day that he died, he was alone. Nobody was with him. That is not a caring way to die.

AIDS and Latinos

Cultures around the world deal with death in different ways. Throughout this book I have discussed ways Latinos deal with death, grief, and mourning. In this section I discuss the ways Latinos deal with deaths caused by diseases such as AIDS, which can be a taboo topic in this culture. This may also be true of other cultures, but Latino cultural values, which are characterized by spirituality, collectivism, and *machismo*, have made these types of death more difficult to deal with (Leong & Leach, 2008). Data from the Centers for Disease Control and Prevention (2010) on HIV/AIDS among Hispanics in the United States show that, in 2006, 18% were infected with HIV. Of those infected with the virus, 73% of Hispanic females were infected through heterosexual contact, 23% by injection and drug use, and 3% by other means. Among the Hispanic men, 59% were infected through male-to-male sexual contact, 19% by injection and drug use, 17% through heterosexual contact, 4% through male-to-male sexual contact as well as injection drug use, and 1% by other means. Furthermore, "In 2006, HIV/ AIDS was the fourth leading cause of death among Hispanic/Latino men and women aged 35–44" (Centers for Disease Control and Prevention, 2007). To create more awareness about HIV prevention among Latino men, Diaz wrote *Latino Gay Men and HIV: Culture, Sexuality, and Risk Behavior* (1998), asserting that the sociocultural factors of "machismo, homophobia, family loyalty, sexual silence, poverty, and racism—internalized through socialization experiences[—]undermine self-regulation and have become important barriers to the practice of safer sex" (p. 19).

Dealing with death often causes painful emotions, but dealing with the impending death of a loved one who has a terminal illness as a result of AIDS is a more daunting task. Although this is owing to the social stigma that the disease carries, culturally sensitive counselors can consider the sociocultural factors that Diaz (1998) discussed and provide holistic care to clients who are dealing with AIDS. Latinos have a tough time coping with the subject of AIDS overall because of its taboo nature in their culture. This taboo has to do, in part, with cultural ideals set for Latino men and masculinity as rooted in the notion of *machismo*. Latinos define masculinity or "male identity in terms of highly prized virtues such as courage, fearlessness, protection, and strength" (Diaz, 1998, p. 63). Men must therefore prove their masculinity by performing acts that display these virtues. When HIV/AIDS was first recognized in the United States, it was predominantly striking the gay community and in turn causing people to view it as a disease that transmitted primarily among gay individuals. However, as HIV has spread to the heterosexual population, it is no longer considered solely a "gay disease."

With a terminal illness comes an array of emotions and fears, which seem more acute among persons with AIDS because of the social, emotional, and physical implications. In the newsletter *The Forum*, Robert Sproul (2009) described the social stigma a 72-year-old retired widow faced when her heroin-addicted daughter died of AIDS. The one place this mother looked to for support was her church, but she was shocked to be shunned instead of comforted. This type of social stigmatization often leads loved ones to experience complicated grief. Confronting the death of a child is a painful transition, which can be exacerbated by the reasons for death and the cultural implications:

> The parent of an adult child with AIDS may not be able to process and accept that the child is gay, has used drugs, or has been sexually active. Given the widespread stigmatization of those with AIDS, parents are often confused, ashamed, or angry as they confront the life and death of their child. I believe that it is not until that parent "owns" and can speak fully of the reality of the child's life that the ultimate grief process can proceed. However, that process may be particularly painful when the child doesn't conform to the judgmental prescriptions of this culture. (Sproul, 2009, p. 8)

Because religion and spirituality have proved to have a positive impact on health, I consider it necessary to explore how these relate to AIDS, and the results I found were not surprising. Koenig (2008) cited studies that show a strong correlation between spirituality/religiosity and long-term survival among patients with AIDS. The results were based on how many times the patients prayed, meditated, or attended a religious service and how these activities effected their psychological well-being, social support, embrace of hope and health, and altruistic behaviors.

Coping Skills of the Terminally Ill

Everyone responds to a terminal illness in his or her own way, and these responses vary according to factors such as personality, psychological makeup, family and social patterns, and environment (DeSpelder & Strickland, 2007). Even the people in the patient's life will cope with the news in different ways. Terminal illness and death are still often taboo subjects. They do not fit the "idealized view of how things should be," and thus people often cope with the news only by avoiding "people, places and objects associated with the forbidden condition," including the patient, creating a "social death" (p. 185). One seldom finds this situation among Hispanics, however, because in general the family members will be constantly with the patient, who may even worry about the well-being of the family. Hispanic patients may feel guilty about their condition, become depressed, and question why this is happening to them. They may feel a burden that is oftentimes extended to their family as everything that comes with the terminal illness starts to affect their family life.

The Rev. Figueroa shared how often he sees the following situation among Hispanic patients:

> What I have observed with people . . . is that the person for some reason cannot let [the issue of the family] go. They are on the brink of death and it takes days and days and what I've observed in them is the issues of relationships going on or issues of "Who's going to take care of my family?" or "Who's going to take care of my mom or my children?" I've seen this a lot, how the children have to go over there to that bedside, and I encourage them. I tell them, "Go tell your parents that it's okay for them to go, that you'll be okay, you will take care of yourselves and God will take [care] of you."

DeSpelder and Strickland (2005) explored three ways patients and their loved ones cope with their awareness of dying: (a) *closed awareness*, in which the dying patient is not aware of the diagnosis and there is no communication from others who know; (b) *suspected awareness*, in which the individual suspects his death is near but that fact is not communicated to him by his loved ones; and (c) *open awareness*, in which the patient and her loved ones communicate openly, acknowledge death, and discuss it. This is to say that not only does open awareness makes an impending death easier to deal with but also the sense of support and coping becomes easier with open communication. Kenneth Doka, a leading thanatologist, provided a model to understand better how people cope with stages of a terminal illness. His model includes the *acute phase*, which is initiated by the diagnosis, in which the individual tries to understand his disease, expresses his feelings and fears, and optimizes his coping strengths; the *chronic phase*, when the individual is already living with the disease and tries to find meaning in uncertainty and suffering; and the *terminal phase*, in which the individual tries to find ways to cope with his or her impending death (DeSpelder & Strickland, 2005).

Many Hispanics take refuge in their religion when coping with a terminal illness. In some cases this may prevent them from taking a proactive stand because they may leave everything to God:

> [The] patient and family may believe that God determines the outcome of illness and that death is a natural part of the life process. Because of this acceptance of the sick role, the patient and family

may not seek health care until the condition worsens significantly. (Cardenas et al., 2004, p. 1)

A study of Catholic Hispanic women diagnosed with cancer revealed that some had an attitude that "their illness was God's will" (Koenig & Cohen, 2002, p. 95). Others resorted to prayer and asked for a miracle. They engaged in bargaining with God; for example, "If my mother is healed I will go to church every Sunday" or "If my spouse gets better I will be a better Catholic." Others used natural remedies to get better and sought out folk healers, looking for a *trabajo* [spiritual work] that would cure them. However, many Hispanics have difficulty talking about a terminal illness. They tend to pretend that nothing is going on. The Rev. Figueroa observed:

> It's the aspect of denial whenever we're dealing with the subject of death, that's one of the first stages, shock, then denial. They cannot believe that it's happening to them. Then it's the secrecy among Hispanics, not to tell the person that they're dying; then the patient sometimes tells the doctor not to tell the family members that they're dying.

Koenig (2008) reminded us that "the influence that emotions have on the natural healing systems in the body is an important area of research if we want to understand the ways that religious or spiritual factors affect health" (p. 37). Counselors who want to understand the worldview of their clients as they deal with a loss of health must be cognizant of this meaningful factor. Koenig (2007) suggested that, when assisting persons from other cultures or who have specific cultural beliefs, one needs to take into consideration those beliefs, including traditions such as *Santería* or *curanderismo* because "practitioners from these traditions may be invited to assist with sick patients" (p. 225; see chapter 4, this volume, for an in-depth discussion of *Santería* and *curanderismo*). This philosophy once again highlights how vital it is to enter our clients' worldview, especially as they face health issues and when faith plays an essential part in their perception of the illness and the expected outcome.

Furthermore, most Hispanic families don't understand when euphemisms are used to communicate the news of illness or death. It is better to communicate with them in a straightforward manner and be open to their demonstration of grief as they receive the bad news. Some people take a stoic stand, saying "*Ésta es mi cruz*" [This is my cross]. They mean that if Jesus suffered for all humanity, one should be able to carry one's own cross without complaints. Above all, a counselor or a health care provider needs to keep in mind the emotional dimension of their clients and the way Hispanics express their feelings when faced with illness or death. Bonding is extremely important, especially within the family, but not all cultures express it the same way. Psychologist Dr. Alex Fiuza made the following observation:

> I would feel the most important thing is that Latinos bond; the bonding trait that unites us all together is family. The Anglo should understand the nucleus of the family as a whole. Latinos honor their parents, their grandparents, and their children. They should understand what this is about, that the cultural bonding within the family is similar among all Hispanics. For instance, the Argentines bond, but they're not as affectionate in expressing their emotions to their loved ones. They're more guarded. They're not as emotionally dramatic as someone from the Islands would be. A person from the West Indies, and I am talking about Latin cultures, would express their emotions dramatically with their loved ones.

Understanding the ways people cope with terminal illnesses and end-of-life issues can give counselors a greater understanding of how to be present for their clients and how they can provide a compassionate and caring hand. As a counselor, I have learned to be engaged in the other person's experience, to see my clients as unique persons. In the end, Hispanics are simply human beings with their unique needs and coping skills. As the Rev. Figueroa observed,

> We all can be put in categories, but we are human beings and [patients] cannot be categorized, depending on the history or where the patient is from. We have to assess that individual person, and let's not take anything for granted, and let us not assume anything just because we have known people from this background or from this country. The other important thing is that all of us have our own story.

Caregivers and Loss

In Hispanic families it is common for family members to take care of elderly parents, sick relatives, and the terminally ill. There are many situations when the family needs to make an important decision regarding an extended and progressive illness. Some Hispanics may be unfamiliar with their options in such situations because of a lack of education or other reasons; therefore health care professionals should take into account the following principles, which, according to Lamers (2001), should be used as a guide for doctors when dealing with all caregivers. Above all, communication is crucial: The doctor should ascertain that the person being spoken to understands what he or she is saying and should ask the caregiver to repeat what he or she has said to them. This is especially important with Hispanics who may not have proficiency in English. The doctor should also give caregivers different ways to contact him or her, encourage them to ask questions, and educate them on what constitutes an emergency. Many times family members fear knowing what is happening to their loved one, but doctors should inform them about the patient's condition and explain what changes could occur in the patient's situation. In addition, caregivers should be informed about any medication the patient is taking and any side effects the patient could experience. Again, if language is a problem, a caregiver may not be able to read the medication literature (e.g., the inserts that accompany prescription medication) and thus may be unaware of any potential contraindications. Furthermore, when taking care of the patient, caregivers should know where the relevant records and documents are and be cognizant of resources available to them, including home health care agencies and social resources. Because Hispanics are used to taking care of their loved ones at home, they may not be aware of these services; however, once they know about them, they may utilize them. Finally, in the case of a terminal illness, doctors need to educate caregivers about nursing and hospice care and indicate whether either would be an option at the end of life. I discuss these issues in the following sections.

The Nursing Home: An Alternative?

In Latin American countries, our grandparents either live with us or live very close to us. It is not uncommon to have several different generations sharing the same home. When Hispanics move to the United States, many of them try to continue this tradition. Some may do it out of convenience—for example, so the grandparents can help take care of their grandchildren—but it goes beyond that. Families are used to being together, to sharing times together, both happy and sad. Therefore, when a person gets too old or frail it is generally very difficult for the family to decide whether to place that person in a nursing home. Consider the following case. When Carla, a woman from Venezuela, came to see me she was very sad. She had just visited her mother at the nursing home where she had placed her, and she felt she had betrayed her:

> My mother always made me promise to her she would never be placed in one of "those places," as she called them. She thought nobody would take care of her and was afraid to die alone. I always told her I would take care of her, until she was diagnosed with Alzheimer's and I couldn't take care of her any more. I lived only with her. I don't have any other relatives and need to work the whole day. Sometimes I need to work on weekends in order to pay the mortgage of the apartment I bought for both of us. Now, I find myself lonely in the apartment and she is lonely at the nursing home. I cannot deal with these guilty feelings. Each time I go home I feel her presence everywhere in the apartment. When I go to sleep, I imagine her in the nursing home, lonely and missing me. How can I live like this?

Families and patients may need to find meaning when facing a terminal illness or life-threatening disease, especially older adults, who because of modern trends and technological advances are now more likely to be placed in a nursing home. William Chovan (2005) reminded us of the impact of these changes on the lives of our elders: "The breakdown of family cohesion and the placement of elderly in nursing homes, together with weakening of family values and religious commitment, have deprived the elderly of major sources of meaning" (p. 9). This reminds me of the story of Lucia, an elderly woman living in a nursing home where I conducted a focus group for a new program. When she heard that I spoke Spanish, she grabbed my arm and said to me in an anxious voice: "*Necesito un sacerdote, necesito un sacerdote*" [I need a priest, I need a priest]. Not knowing what she meant, I sat down with her and asked her what she wanted. With tears in her eyes, she said,

> I have been here for a long time and I know I will die soon and I haven't confessed to a priest my sins. If I die tomorrow I may go to hell. Please tell them I need a priest who speaks in Spanish. They brought one the other day but he just spoke English. I didn't understand a word he said and [felt] even worse trying to talk to him. He would have had . . . difficulty in understanding my English.

After giving her a hug I told her not to worry, that I would talk to the staff so that she could make her confession to a priest who spoke Spanish. That is what I did. The staff nurse was very supportive and understood the needs of this Hispanic elderly woman. In doing this, I realized how little it takes to help others. If you simply pay attention to their needs, you can make a difference in their lives.

Many empirical studies have concluded that because some older adults have gone through multiple losses, including death, they are better prepared to deal with them. On the other hand, to a person who hasn't experienced many losses, or lacks a strong social support network, dying may be more overwhelming (Walter & McCoyd, 2009). Many older adults live by themselves, and this lack of support may be detrimental to their mental and physical health. For Hispanic older adults who were used to life surrounded by family in their homeland and have now been transplanted to the United States, sometimes unwillingly, just to be close to their children and grandchildren, living by themselves or being alone for long hours can make them feel great sadness and despair. Such was the case with Paquita, age 88, who came to the United States from Guatemala and now lives by herself and attends an adult day care center:

> Look at me . . . where I spend my last days surrounded by strangers, and although these people are *muy cariñosos* [very caring and affectionate] with me, they are not my family. I remember that in my country my mother lived with us until she died. Here my two sons are very busy with their businesses and I hardly see them. It is incredible how they have changed. Maybe they changed with me because they married women who are not Latinas. One is from New York and the other from Canada. They don't understand they were very close to me. Now I live by myself, and although they bought me a beautiful TV and I have a lady who comes and helps me three times a week, it is not the same. I miss my sons. Why don't they send me back to Guatemala? At least when I die I [will] be buried there.

Paquita's story reminds me of a presentation I gave on "Life Review and Older Adults" at the Latin American Association of Palliative Care on the island of Margarita, Venezuela, in 2006. During this presentation I spoke of my experience with a group of elderly individuals I facilitate at an adult day care center. As I explained the purpose and nature of this center, a Costa Rican raised his hand to voice his total amazement. He said that if being part of a developed society meant placing our elders in an adult day care center, he preferred to live in an underdeveloped country where elders were taken care of by their families. As we can see from this example, there is a clear difference between what is accepted in Hispanic countries and how their values and customs are gradually changing with globalization and modernization.

However, even though placing their elders in a nursing home is not a custom with which many Hispanics are comfortable, attitudes have begun to change. María Gómez shared the following from her experience as a social worker with the Latino community in hospice care:

> In Latinos something that has not changed in the past 14 years is the not wanting to separate. I try to explain to many that we all need some privacy every so often when we're living and when we are dying. It allows for trust to grow, a genuine trust. When the family knows that the patients are being cared for, they begin to let go a little and trust. I am beginning to see . . . in Latinos the coming to the realization of "I can no longer take care of my father at home. I just cannot do it." The conversation of needing to put a loved one in a nursing home is usually met with resistance. I see it in stages. The first conversation ends with a "No." The second conversation is, "Well, Dad can no longer stay here in my home because it is no longer stable for him," or just knowing you cannot quite give the loved one the proper care and looking at options. Then you move on to the acceptance that you cannot provide private at-home care, so you look at nursing homes. Then you have the guilt. You get a lot of "I promised that I would never do that, but I have to. I just need to find a place that feels like home." The reality is that there is nothing like home.

Hospice Care

Dame Cicely Saunders is the founder of the modern hospice movement and a pioneer in the field of palliative care. When a person is faced with the end of his or her life, most family members are so overwhelmed and distressed by the situation that it becomes extremely hard to focus on what is necessary to help the patient. Hospice is there to provide palliative care for the patient, whether this be at home, in a nursing home, or in an in-patient unit, as well as to provide support for the family. Dame Saunders, a nurse, physician, and writer who worked in St. Christopher's Hospice in England for nearly 30 years, listed in detail the five core values of hospice. She cited them as the mission statement of hospice providers and explained how this philosophy challenges the members of the multidisciplinary team to demonstrate at all times these core values. These values also describe the purpose of palliative care, which is

> [a] to affirm life; [b] not to hasten death but to regard death as a normal process; [c] to respect the worth and individuality of each person for whom we may care; [d] to offer relief from pain and other distressing symptoms; [e] to help patients with strong and unfamiliar emotions. To offer the opportunity to reconcile and heal relationships and complete important personal tasks; to offer a support system for family and friends during the patient's illness and bereavement. (Saunders, 2002, p. 24)

There is much misunderstanding regarding hospice care, possibly because there is a lack of education and understanding regarding end-of-life issues among people in general, and Hispanics in particular. I teach a class on death and dying at Florida International University, and in my experience I realize that end-of-life issues are rarely discussed among family members. Most students ignore what hospice is, unless they have had a family member who has used this service. Every time I teach this class I invite a representative of hospice to talk to the students so that they can become more aware of what to expect from it. Furthermore, most people think hospice is a place, like a hospital or nursing home, rather than a caregiving service. Josefina, a Colombian woman who came to see me because her father had been diagnosed with cancer, was really distraught with the idea of placing her father in an institution to die. I explained to her that she could have hospice care at home for him and that it was actually an opportunity to be present for him, because hospice is family centered.

María Gómez believes that generally we need to have a better understanding of what hospice is:

> I think there still needs to be an incredible amount of education in the field. I think there is a big misconception as to what hospice is. But despite that, with the more education the community receives, the more positive the experiences the families will have. Those families in turn talk to others and discuss their experiences [with] hospice and recommend the service. I think that in these past fourteen years there has been progress, maturity. On the other hand, people still think hospice is a place and not a philosophy, or a concept of care

that can be given in the patient's home, assisted living facility, or nursing home . . . Hospice is the care that you give. The patient can no longer receive aggressive treatment because he or she can no longer tolerate it, and there are symptoms that cannot really be controlled, so an option would be hospice where they could be comfortable and in a community.

Because there is so much misinformation about hospice, people working in this field should approach patients with honesty and sensitivity. Saunders (2002) recounted a time when it was thought that patients should not be aware of their diagnosis because of fears that they may not be able "to face the unwanted truths," but she also discussed how there is now more communication and honesty among patients, family members, and workers in the hospice field (p. 26). According to Saunders, the hospice philosophy as a whole is the basis for how best to help, in a respectful and responsible manner, those faced with death.

The last, and perhaps most important, value of the hospice philosophy is to offer a support system to individuals who will be grieving and struggling with their own thoughts of what their loved one's death will mean to them. Hospice offers support from an array of professionals, including psychiatrists, social workers, and chaplains, who can help family members and friends through the end-of-life journey. Family members who care for their terminally ill loved ones at home are met with many demands and challenges. Because family is central to Hispanics' well-being, I find hospice to be a valuable option that, once appropriately explained, may be beneficial and even welcomed by the patient and his or her family. Hadlock (2004) emphasized how central the family is in hospice care:

The patient's family is key. They are critical to successful hospice care up to the time of death because, as the patient physically and mentally declines, they become competent care givers with a personal interest in the patient's welfare, which permits palliative care to be continuous. Families are not only care givers; they are care receivers as well. As they care for their own, they suffer with the loved one and need support themselves. (p. 3)

Still, cultural attitudes and family traditions may be a deterrent to Hispanics. Carolina, a 26-year-old Mexican woman, was strongly opposed to hospice. She told me that if her mother were terminally ill she would never allow a stranger to take care of her, especially if they did not understand her Catholic beliefs, her culture, or her personal story. As a Hispanic with an elderly mother who is a devout Catholic and hardly speaks English, I understand Carolina's attitude. It is difficult for us to let go of our parents if we fear they may not feel cared for, especially if the services provided are not culturally sensitive. Still, if people are educated about the value of these services and how their lives and the lives of their loved ones can be bettered, perceptions can change. Hospice is not about dying but about living until the last minute surrounded by love, care, and comfort.

HELPFUL SUGGESTIONS

- Learn about the situations members of racial/ethnic minority groups face regarding health care and how accessible health care is to your clients. Evaluate why they don't take care of themselves, whether it is because they don't want help or because they cannot afford it. Provide them with helpful information.
- Take into consideration sociocultural factors when assessing a client who is facing a terminal illness and how these affect the dynamic of his or her family. Explore the communication among the family members and evaluate the coping skills that work best for them. Always show respect, and assist them in a nonjudgmental manner.
- Be open with your clients and let them know about the different options available to them. If they don't ask, offer the information. They may not know what to ask or may be embarrassed to take an active role.

PERSONAL REFLECTIONS FOR THE COUNSELOR

- Do you feel comfortable with alternative approaches to health care?
- Are you sensitive to the excessive inclusion of Hispanic family members in health care decisions?
- Are you able to assist the person who is dying without reservations or biases?

CHAPTER 7

Death, Dying, and Bereavement

When someone we love dies, the grief we experience is universal; it is not contingent on our culture, ethnicity, or race. What may differ are our attitudes toward death and bereavement as well as the rituals surrounding death and the way they are expressed in one's culture.

Of the many losses Hispanics may experience after leaving their homeland, the loss of a loved one to death is probably the greatest and most difficult. As DeSpelder and Strickland (2005) observed, "Of all human experience, none is more overwhelming in its implications than death" (p. 5). This loss can be exacerbated if the bereaved could not be with their loved one at the time of the death, or if the funeral practices or the wishes of the deceased are not honored.

A death influences a family's dynamics, and most of the time some reorganization needs to take place. The way a particular family copes with the death is greatly influenced by its traditions, religious beliefs, and coping styles. In this chapter, as I explore how the loss of a loved is experienced in the Hispanic population, I present cases in which such values and traditions will be obvious, and I explain how counselors can assist their bereaved clients. Because the Hispanic groups living in the United States are so diverse, I have included examples of funeral rites associated with different countries of origin. As you read these cases, please keep in mind that they are merely illustrations; the variety of rituals may be influenced by many factors, including family traditions, region of the country, and financial resources. However, there are some common elements that can provide helpful insight into the richness of the traditions and the way Hispanics express their grief.

Because there is such a close connection among Hispanic family members, when there is a death in the family they all want to make sure the bereaved person is getting the help he or she needs. Once a woman named Ana María, who was from the Dominican Republic, called me to express her concern for her *abuela* [grandmother], who had lost her daughter (Ana María's aunt) and was completely depressed. She was fearing for her grandmother's health and wanted to know whether I worked with older adults in bereavement.

I have also received calls from family members and even friends seeking ways to help a bereaved relative or friend and to ask for suggestions or guidance. I have observed this phenomenon more often among Hispanic clients than among Anglo Americans. For example, Rosaura, a Peruvian, called to ask about her father-in-law:

> I worry my father-in-law is not doing well these days. He lost his wife of 53 years a month ago and he doesn't leave his room. He refuses to talk and is eating very little. The only thing he does is listen to Radio Paz. He used to listen to Mass every day with his wife and now he does it by himself. I know he is very religious and finds comfort listening to this radio station. Are you Catholic? I saw on your page you integrate spirituality when working with clients and I just wondered if you could help him.

When I shared with Rosaura that my religion is Catholic (although I embrace all religions and find meaning in the religious beliefs of every individual), she was very happy, and a bond was immediately established. She said she would make the appointment to bring her father-in-law in the following week. I suggested she ask him first, but she went ahead and made the appointment. Rosaura's case shows the value people find in identifying with the counselor, or at least feeling that their values or religious beliefs are being recognized. She was also happy that I spoke Spanish, because her elderly father-in-law spoke very little English. This is common among older Hispanics.

I have found that Hispanics' attitudes toward death, dying, and rituals are similar to those of African Americans (Barrett, 1998), in that they

- oppose active euthanasia;
- regard death, dying, and the dead with great reverence and respect;
- believe that one's attendance at and participation in funerals represents an important social obligation; and
- prefer in-ground burial for final disposition.

To these customs I would add among Catholics the praying of the rosary and *la novena* [praying nine consecutive prayers]. Because almost 70% of the Hispanics living in the United States are Catholic, the praying of the rosary is quite common in many families. It is customary to see people praying it at hospitals, funeral homes, or in church. Moreover, if the person is Catholic, it is very important for the family to bring *el padre* [the priest] to the house so that the dying person can make his or her confession and receive the last rites.

However, many Hispanic Catholics are converting to Protestantism, as in the case of Sandra, a Colombian, who shared the story of her son's death and how much her religious beliefs helped her find meaning in it:

When he was 9 years old he developed a brain tumor. Between [when he was] 9 and 18 years old I dedicated myself completely to him. We would go to the hospital constantly. At 18 they began to tell me that he had problems with his liver and that he needed a transplant. Everywhere I'd go I'd talk of the Lord's word. The transplant was a Tuesday or a Wednesday. I went to church, to a prayer group. When I returned he said to me, "Mommy, I spoke to God and told him I didn't want to keep living this way." I told him "Are you crazy! You have me still." And he responded with "Mom, if it's God will you will have to understand." I thought about this all day. They told me the next day that they had the organ ready. It usually takes years. So what did I think? I thought God was returning my son to me. The surgery was performed on a Wednesday. The next few days everything turned out fine. By Monday morning I thought it had all been successful. I thought, that's it! God is returning my son to me and he will live many years. My husband told me that he wanted to spend time with our son. I didn't want to leave, and my son asked me not to, but I had to work. My husband stayed with my son and they asked for forgiveness, talked about beautiful things, talked about what they would cook, what movies they'd watch. When he left the room to grab a cup of coffee, he felt his heart heavy and returned. He noticed they had everyone out of the room. When he entered it, he saw that they were trying to revive my son. He grabbed our son and told him "Come back! Don't leave." He said that at that moment he saw a bright light that gave him lots of peace. [My son died of] cardiac arrest due to an excess of morphine. Friends called and said that we could sue the doctors, but for what? Suing them won't bring my son back. The lady that called me told me that God had taken my son from me at the right time, at the adequate moment. Now I'd be doing His work.

Maria, a 46-year-old Christian Salvadoran, also shared the story of her son's death and how her religion helped her cope with her loss:

The loss of my son was very painful. He was 14 years old and his name was Jaime. It was something I didn't expect; as they say, one is prepared to bury their parents but not to bury their children. Despite the fact that I'd gone through tragedies in the past, having buried my mother, my brothers, cousins, friends, this had to be the worst thing I'd ever lived through in my life. I couldn't believe that my son, just starting to live his life, and not even sick, which at least can be understood, a death by illness, but not in the way my son passed away. He was killed, stabbed 14 times while at school by a 14-year-old boy, and that's so painful because one cannot imagine what kind of 14-year-old boy has that much evil in him to be able to do such a thing. It was a shock no one was expecting. I went through a period of denial; instead I preferred to think that he was somewhere else, that he went on vacation, not that he was buried in the cemetery, and I know I was angry with God, until I gave in. I think I gave in because I got to a point where I was tired of crying and, as my pastor said, I think the way I got angry with God was not because I didn't believe in God's existence but that I was sure He existed and He could have taken [my son] away from me, but I grew tired, and one day I said to Him, "Wow, it's been months since I've slept. I'm worn out, cried out." My hands hurt from pounding on the floor, and so then I gave in and said to God, "Well, here I am and everyone says You can help me, but I don't know how, and I know You can give me some sort of sign, to give me hope." I remember that night, I fell to the ground and I passed out. I don't know if I fell asleep or if I was awake, but I saw I was standing in front of Jesus, speaking with Him, demanding from Him, fighting with Him, and that's how I said to Him, "Lord, I give in. I'm fighting against a force so much stronger than me." And of course, only I would think of doing such a thing, and that night, lying on the floor, I said to Him, "I know you can give me a sign, I'm sure of it." And I saw Him but didn't see his face . . . and I can't even describe that image because it leaves my memory when I try to convey it. All I know is that I was demanding of Him that He left my son alone and He responded, "Jaime was not alone. I was with him during that moment." So then I said to [Jesus] that I knew He could bring Him back and He said, "I can, but it's not the time." I told Him it was His fault, but He didn't respond. That's when He told me that . . . He could revive Jaime but that [Jaime] wouldn't be happy, and I said, "Of course he'll be happy to be with his mother." So then He said, "Let's make a deal. If you're sure that he's going to be happy when he returns to you, then it means you will accept this challenge. I will revive him, but you can't give him back to me." I told him "Yes" and I [tried to hug] Him, but I couldn't touch Him. I couldn't get near Him. Then I remember He called Jaime over, and there he was, standing in front of me, and then [Jesus] disappeared. I thanked [Jesus] profusely and was so happy and was hugging my son and then I was telling the people that were at the funeral that Jaime was revived but not to tell him anything because he doesn't know he had been dead. I remember hugging him, but I could feel his sadness and I asked him, "Papi, are you happy?" And he said "Of course, Mami, but . . ." There was a but. And while there were people at my house, there was a party at my house that day, I lost him, and I started look-ing for him and found him crying by himself, crying and crying. I asked him, "Papi, are you sad?" He says to me, "No, Mami, I'm fine," and he wiped his tears away and that's when I said to him, "Papi, no, I feel that you are unhappy." . . . [He] asks how I knew, and I told him I felt it inside of me that he wasn't happy. Then I told him to please forgive me, that I had been selfish for only thinking of myself! Now I didn't know how I was going to get him back after the deal I'd made! I couldn't give him back, and I asked for his forgiveness. That's when I woke up, still lying on the floor of my home, and that's when I said to Jesus, "I give in. You have now given me the signal I needed. Just please help me to withstand this pain because I can't do it alone."

EXPRESSIONS OF GRIEF AND MOURNING

Grief and condolences among Hispanics are in most cases very openly expressed, and people offer their support through hugs, kisses, and crying with the bereaved. If they are religious, they also pray with them for the *alma del difunto* [soul of the dead]. In many traditional families, they hardly talk about the deceased and choose to hide their pictures. They don't dance, laugh, or go out (to celebrations) for many months. They wear black or black-and-white clothing to show they are mourning. When my father died in 1971, my mother wore black for 3 years without putting any makeup on. I was 12 years old and had to wear black and white for a whole year. I was taken away from my piano lessons and could not listen to the radio or watch television for a whole year, out of respect for my father's memory. This was the traditional way of mourning and, little by little, it has changed because of modernization. This could be why mourning is so different between the rural and urban regions in Latin America. The more modernized the region, the more changes one sees in the people's traditions. Furthermore, as people move to the United States and acculturate, they adopt the mourning rites of the country. This is a source of disappointment for older Hispanic adults who don't understand how their children or grandchildren can have such a different view of mourning.

During grief counseling, it is important that clients remember the good memories and realize that they can honor their loved ones by enacting certain traditions. Hispanics, for example, can honor their loved ones by celebrating with a special traditional food from their country. For example, Hortensia, a Venezuelan, cooks a special family dish every Christmas since her mother died:

> My mother Joaquina was known for her *pernil de cerdo al horno* [oven-roasted pork] she cooked for Christmas. She would spend days preparing it. My family wouldn't accept any other dish to eat for this celebration. It made us feel closer to our beloved country. My mom would marinate the pork with *vino y ron* [wine and rum] and cook it in the oven for at least six hours. I remember, as a little girl, helping her in the kitchen. Who would [have thought] that it would be me who would keep the tradition . . . and her memory [alive]?

It is so important that counselors understand the cultural experiences of their clients and have a sense of how painful it is to feel the bond with one's country severed with the death of a loved one. Rosaura has felt that void with her mother's death:

> Since our mother Carmela died, there is a void that only she can fill. She was the core of our family and who kept us united. She is the one who told us stories about our country, Colombia, and cooked our food every Sunday, when we had our weekly reunion. Now, who will

cook for us? Who will make *hallaca* [a traditional Venezuelan dish made of flour and beef, or chicken] for Christmas? Who will tell us the story of our grandparents when they met in Valencia?

HISPANIC FUNERAL TRADITIONS

Wingett, in her article "Funeral Homes Tailoring Services to Hispanics" (2006), elaborated on how funeral homes in a number of states are embracing Hispanic traditions. She described a Mexican funeral in Phoenix, Arizona:

> In hushed voices, the mourners crowded into the central Phoenix home to pray for the soul of Sergio Chávez, dead of a gunshot wound at 28.
>
> A 3-foot crucifix of Jesus hung next to his open casket. Above the coffin were three photos, a cross and Chavez's favorite shirt with the slogan "Viva Mexico." Led by a Catholic deacon, friends and relatives prayed and wept in the small living room, emptied to make room for the visitation. The service, overseen by La Paz Funeral Home, allowed for more intimacy than a traditional service. By catering to Latinos, La Paz has built a thriving business on death. In this area of Arizona, home to more than 1 million Hispanics and about 85 funeral homes, funeral directors are racing to adapt to the needs of the burgeoning immigrant and U.S.-born Hispanic clientele.
>
> They are doing it by offering in-home funeral services like Chavez's, typical in Mexico and other Latin American countries. They are offering culturally themed programs that can include mariachis, overnight visitations and family feasts in mortuaries. They are putting up welcoming signs announcing "*Se habla español*" [We speak Spanish] and buying newspaper ads branded with images of the Virgin of Guadalupe. (p. xxx)

Instead of burying their loved ones back home in Mexico, many Hispanic families are burying them in the United States, and some funeral homes are accommodating them with a service that is meaningful. Wingett continued,

> At funeral homes that specialize in Latino funerals, many families bring in clothes and dress their loved ones themselves. Some fix the

dead's hair and stitch or pin into the fabric-lined coffins, images of the Virgin Mary, photos, rosaries, books, jewelry and poems. Some families request in-home visits or daylong services with rosary services and other traditional Catholic prayers. Viewings can last overnight, and mourners tend to grieve loudly and grip the lip of caskets and kiss the cheeks of their dead loved ones. (p. xxx)

As I read this last sentence, I remember that as I stood next to the casket after my father had died, I did kiss his cheeks. To this day, that loving memory remains in my heart.

Diana de Armas, the manager of the funeral home Memorial Plan in Coral Gables, Florida, shared with me stories from her 20 years of experience working with both Hispanics and the Anglo American community. She described the main differences between these two cultures regarding their funeral practices as well as their expression of grief:

[There is a difference] with Hispanics, definitely. The families are used to the long hours of visitation because they used to do it in their homes, and now they do it at a funeral home and they want to stay as many hours as possible with the deceased, and many of them do not want to go home. They don't want to part with the deceased since these are the last hours they'll spend with their loved one, and may stay through until morning when they leave for the cemetery. Most of the Hispanic families we service are still Catholic. Some are more church-goers than others, so for those that are pretty orthodox or [attend] Mass on a regular basis, we would go to a Catholic church on the day of the burial and from there we leave for the cemetery. Those families that are not as religious or church-going would have a clergy, or a priest, come here the night of the viewing, and then moments before we leave for the cemetery. But everything is done at the funeral home. . . . [If the family wants it] we can have the mariachis. Normally, we would do that at the cemetery. We have done it here in Miami. The mariachis would play a favorite song of the deceased.

Diana also focused on the differences in funeral customs between Hispanics and Anglos:

Hispanics hold tight to their customs, to how they were raised. They want to honor that, don't want to break away from it. If you knew your grandmother wanted a 24-hour viewing, you would go ahead and [do] a 24-hour viewing. You wouldn't change your mind or do something different. You honor the traditions. And that's what the Hispanic funeral homes are trying to do, honor whatever customs they have that other places will not honor: the 24-hour viewings, very large [floral] pieces, lots of flowers at the viewing. . . . traditionally they're very large pieces—they're called *coronas*. On the other hand, Anglos have a wreath [that is] smaller in size.

Diana also explained that Hispanics give out prayer cards at the funeral, which are usually religious, but that Anglos

[often] have a different kind, usually like a service folder that has details of the service, like an agenda. This is more like a keepsake for people, Hispanics tend to keep [prayer cards] in their wallets, to remember the deceased with their name, date of birth, date of death, and a prayer.

Finally, regarding the casket, Diana observed, "The Hispanic client leans sometimes more toward a Catholic motif than the other families. They will require a crucifix for inside the casket, they'll want rosary beads in the hands of the deceased."

Diana's words can help counselors appreciate the central role that religion plays in the lives, and at the end of the lives, of many Hispanics and their families.

Fajardo (2009), a therapist and a certified thanatologist of Mexican descent, observed that Hispanics express their feelings in different ways, such as with "poetry, story-telling, and song. . . . An understanding of the Latino perspective toward death and dying may be obtained by reviewing music frequently played at Latino wakes or rituals" (p. 11).

Regarding the choice of burial, María Gómez, a licensed social worker employed by a hospice provider in Florida, shared the following:

There has been a big change in Latin culture regarding the funeral. When I started 14 years ago, most of the families chose burial; now many choose cremation. I have found two reasons for this: one is the hope to be taken back to their homeland and the other has to do with finances.

Psychologist Dr. Alex Fiuza added the following:

> There are some differences that have to do with practicality, au-
> tomation, [the] life cycle. Most countries don't have as many
> choices as there are here. Here . . . you can drive down the street
> and see a sign for cremation for $899. In Latino countries you
> do not see that; it's kind of a very private thing. They don't ad-
> vertise death like selling a car. In Latin American countries it's
> very sacred. In the United States you have an array of choices
> of how you're going to go, whereas in Hispanic countries that
> is not the case. It is a sacred moment, and we will usually view
> the body and grieve at home, which is unheard of in the United
> States. The rapidness of the way things take place in this country
> as compared to Latin American ones is also a big difference. Also
> the way we value the human body, not to say [North] Americans
> don't . . . ; they do, but it's almost as if here (in the United States)
> once the person dies they are not here anymore. In Latin coun-
> tries you still honor the mother, father, the loved one, and you
> still value that bond.

DIVERSITY BASED ON COUNTRY OF ORIGIN

In this section I present examples of rituals used in different Latin
American countries. Keep in mind that my purpose is to illustrate not only
the diversity of these rituals but also, at the same time, the similarities. As I
have noted at the beginning of the chapter, I want to emphasize that many
variables influence the funeral and mourning rites followed by Hispanics.
My purpose in offering these examples is to give readers a better understanding of how Hispanics cope with death and dying.

Mexico

Maria Imelda, age 54, from La Yerbabuena, Michoacán, explained mourning rituals in her region:

> In my village when someone dies, whether it is a person from my
> village or news of someone from my village that died in the United
> States, they will ring the church bells. The whole village will know
> that someone has died. We just await news of who it was that
> died. If the person died in the United States, then the body will be

brought back to our village. [Pauses and begins crying.] My son . . . died 24 years ago . . . I was already living in the United States. He was 7 months old. He was asphyxiated in his crib. He turned over and became tangled in the blanket between the bed and the wall. We brought him back to Mexico to bury him there. . . . We arrived in the middle of the night. People met us out in the street to receive the body. People come and don't leave the family alone. Women will bring food. Even people from surrounding villages will come and stay with the family. The body is still viewed at home in my village. In the capital of Mexico the body is viewed in a funeral home. I think a lot has to do with your economic status as well. If you are poor you hold [the viewing] at home. . . . in my youth we would [observe formal mourning practices]. I remember that we would not even turn the radio on because we were in mourning, but nowadays not so much. In my youth even other people would mourn with you out of respect for the family who was grieving.

If it is an adult [who died] then you would do a viewing. Depending if they had family who would be flying in from the United States, then they would prepare the body to give the family some time to get there. But if there is no family flying in then they will view the body overnight and the next day the burial would take place. People go to Mass and then to *el campo santo* [the cemetery] . . . [people] still wear black. We still pray the *novenario* [nine days of praying]. We also pray to the rosary for nine days. . . . I think that many of us Latinos have a hard time letting go of the dead. We hold on to our departed loved ones out of fear that they will be forgotten.

Adriana, also from La Yerbabuena and 27 years old, shared the following about their traditions when there is a death in the community:

The [U.S.] Yerbabuena community is large and divided between California and Florida. In California there are special cities (i.e., where people from Yerbabuena live), as well as in Florida, and a special network exists. For instance, if someone dies, I will call my siblings, my aunts and uncles, my cousins, other relatives and friends in California, and all of the community will become aware that same day. . . . If they can, those that live in Florida, in cities like Ft. Myers, LaBelle, Ft. Pierce—and depending where the Mass, wake, and burial will be held—everyone comes out. The community gathers to show solidarity and support. Let me give you an example—there was a woman who used to drive a tractor and she had an accident and died. The funeral was full of family members, friends and family members that came from California and Mexico. This was the reason why my mother would prepare an herbal tea, to calm the nerves.

El Día de los Muertos [The Day of the Dead], the most popular holiday in Mexico, is celebrated from October 31 to November 2. This celebration "is the Mexican version of a pan-Roman Catholic holiday, All Saints' and All Souls' Days, observed on November 1 and November 2, respectively" (Brandes, 2006, p. 6). One of the most salient elements of this celebration is the display of art and poetry. The art is displayed in candies in the shapes of skulls or caskets, or in breads and plastic toys decorated with death symbols. During these days Mexicans clean graves and decorate them with flowers and candles. It is also a common practice to watch over the graves of one's relatives. Although it is said that this celebration belongs only to the Mexicans, it is also celebrated in Guatemala, with decorated altars and kite contests (Brandes, 2006), and in other Latin American countries as well. In my country of Nicaragua we celebrated *El Día de los Muertos* on November 2 in a very solemn manner. We go to Mass and then to the cemetery to visit our loved ones. We will take flowers to the graves but will not have any music or colorful celebration. People would wear black clothing and cry, remembering the deceased.

Maria Imelda shared how The Day of the Dead is celebrated in her hometown of La Yerbabuena:

I believe *El Día de los Muertos* is celebrated differently in different parts of the country, but where I am from, all day long people go back and forth and bring wreaths of flowers to visit the dead at the *campo santo*. There is a place near where I am from that they bring a mariachi [band]. They bring food and spend the whole day over there celebrating. We would go see the priest and attend Mass.

Well [as with another custom], there are people who buy the candy and those that make [the candies] and name them. Those that buy [the candies] will buy them with the name already on them. They are offerings to those that have departed. There are people who will make the favorite dish of the person who died and bring it to them as an offering as well. They hold a party for the dead at [the] *campo santo*.

Lucia, a bereaved mother, also shared a tradition regarding The Day of the Dead:

> On November 1st they put together a domestic altar at home to honor their loved ones (they believe the souls of the dead are wandering since they died). They prepare it with great care and use a special tablecloth (a *mantel picado*, which is a type of tablecloth that one can cut, e.g., in a skeleton shape). If one does not have this type of tablecloth they can use a pretty white one. They prepare the altar with great care. It is a special ritual. Then they place *veladoras* [votive candles] and pictures of the loved ones who have passed (if there are many, the most important are chosen). Their favorite food is placed on the altar, like *tamales* [a dish made of corn dough typically wrapped in banana leaves] sweet pastry, cheese, whiskey . . . and if the person smoked, they place a cigarette with an ashtray. Family visits the house, gets around the altar and prays the rosary.

Lucia shared that although her son died 7 years ago, When she visited Mexico last year she performed this ritual for the first time, and also for her aunt, who had recently died. Her sisters do this ritual every year. Lucia said that many Mexicans continue this tradition in the United States.

The Caribbean Islands

Cuba

Barbie is 42 and arrived in Miami 12 years ago. She described the great differences between funerals held in the United States and funerals in Cuba:

> In Miami people express their grief differently. Back in Cuba the pain is almost touchable. Here [in the United States it] is colder, even among Cubans. Here the funerals are like social events. I don't understand why [people want] to express it in public. I understand people want to be with you, but maybe you want to be alone. The visitation or wake has changed. Before it was at home and people would stay with the family all night long. People would suffer from *ataque de nervios* [nerve attack], and some even lost consciousness. In rural areas, it was customary to kill a bull or cow and prepare food for everybody. It would depend on the province; for example,

in Matanza, people wouldn't eat, and the deceased would be in the house for some days. They would also pray the novena or *el Rosario a la Virgen* [the rosary to the Virgin Mary]. All neighbors showed solidarity keeping silence for some days and the house of the bereaved family kept its door closed.

The Dominican Republic

Pablo is 29 and left the Dominican Republic when he was 3 years old. He explained how funerals are done in his home country:

> When someone dies in the Dominican Republic, they don't see it as a celebration; they see it as a grieving time. The last time somebody died was my great-great-grandmother, and she lived to 102, and that was awhile ago in a small town in the Dominican Republic. The town where my great-grandmother lived, people are very curious. When somebody dies, they take them home and they have [the body] there in the house for sometimes even a week. People are mourning the person in the house during that time. They do get embalmed but you . . . have the body there. It is an open casket, but as far as I remember, it was a box. It didn't have a lid; it was an open box. . . . After that, they take them to church. There are flowers; sometimes . . . it's just a simple carnation on their chest with the hands clasped around them, but [other times] there [usually] are . . . no flowers, just a bunch of candles around them. . . . It's not like how we see here in Miami, where you send the flowers from *Trías* [a flower shop] and you have all these beautiful flower arrangements that get thrown out the following day. [In Miami], it's just more people surrounding the body and people are just so curious, you have everyone from the community coming by, peeking in and wanting to see a dead person. They want to see, they really want to be close to the dead person. Here, some people consider that macabre, oh there's a dead person right there. [In the Dominican Republic], it's like wow, there's a dead person I'm looking at. After they leave the house, they take them to the church, they have their procession for them and they take them to the cemetery. They do have a Mass and it's open to the public and you do get a lot of people. The most interesting thing is the caravan that forms when they're taking the person from the church to the cemetery. They have a wake at the house,

there are no funeral homes; probably now there are some funeral homes but [likely not many] with the limited resources they have.

My great-grandmother died back in [19]90, about twenty years [ago]. Tradition still stays the same. . . . The only thing that's changed is the number of days that people are keeping the [body] at their house. Back then, it was a week-long thing; nowadays, they're probably shortening it to three days. They're modernizing it a little bit more, there's still not a funeral home setup but it's more of inside the person's house, typically dressed how they were when they passed away, it's just a very casual approach to it. It depends on the social status of the person whether they put a suit or not because suits are not commonly used unless you're a businessman; families might not have it, sometimes they may wear a *guayabera*-type shirt (a popular male shirt in Latin America).

The very close family keeps *luto* [mourning] for a year, dressed in the darker shades of gray or black and they follow that really well, they really do abstain themselves from loud music or things like that and they typically keep it for that whole year.

South America

Perú

Lucy, age 39, offered the following description of funeral practices in her home country of Perú:

About funerals, we can't generalize in these times because . . . there's been a lot of immigration [to the capital, Lima], so there are many country people in the capital. There's such a mixture now, so nowadays you won't see just one version of funerals but many. Now, if you look by region, let's say the rural sector versus the urban sector, there are tremendous differences. I'm going to tell you about the general things. In the provinces, [the funeral process] can take up to days, depending if you are well known or not. Let's say if you are the mayor of the town or his son or the father of the main church. There's going to be the viewing. There won't be any sleep at all, but people will take shifts. They can even hire *lloronas* [wailers] or people who will pray the novenas, depending on how well known or how loved the person was. If he or she was from a small town, for example, they can then hire a folklore band and have a procession for the deceased, leading to the cemetery. The father (priest) offers a few words, a mini-ceremony, and they leave. The majority are Catholics, in Perú, like 95%. Then, you can then go to a dinner, again depending on the region, but that's in the provinces. You can also have drinks. Mourning in provinces can take 3 months. The closed casket is traditional, but there's a viewing window [in the lid of the casket through which] you can see the deceased. There are many flowers, flower wreaths, crosses in abundance. In the capital, from what I've heard now, you can do the viewing in the living room of your home. All the furniture is removed. However, I haven't heard much of that lately in my family and there have been a few deaths—they actually go to a salon in the hospital or of a chapel or church. There are funeral homes. Maybe they have salons, but I couldn't say. The last deaths that have occurred have been held in a salon specially made for viewings, usually in the churches. The body is placed there, the viewing is held, and they try to make it an all-night affair, and the transition is very fast. For example, there was a death in the morning and by the evening, they were having the viewing and then burying the deceased the next day. It's very fast. The shock of the news, the handling of the paperwork, the doctor, what needs to be signed, then we're all at the viewing that evening passing coffee and cookies around. You don't make a huge meal. No one feels like eating. The men will say, that's life, the shock has worn off, and they'll tell you that we will all get to that point someday. There's plenty of conversation, maybe a little wine and some laughs, but not in mockery, and you reincorporate yourself, but it's very fast. You don't have time to process anything. You only have three days. If you want to see a comparison, the first truly devastating death for me was my father-in-law's, and to me it was agony. On the third day, it was a feeling of disbelief, but life has to go on. . . . You spend the first week in complete agony, like dying while living. The first time I went to an open casket viewing was appalling and scary and horrible. You see half the person and it's quite shocking, but in Lima you can approach the deceased if you want. There's even a footstool that's been placed at the edge of the casket so you can [sit there and] pray or cry for the deceased. There's no procession or music. Mourning, for those who wish to do it, nowadays is rare. It depends on the generation. You [dress] in navy blue or black, and if you were very close, then you wear black from head to toe. Others can go with dark clothing. You can sit around with the family members and you maintain mourning for those days. There's a monthly or yearly Mass. You can also do a half-year Mass, but the yearly one is more common. Also, [people often commemorate] the deceased's birthday. In my family, we make a lunch and we bring a priest, if it's possible, if you know him well since it's not easy, and he performs a ceremony. Cremation exists in the country, but it's not very accepted, more than likely for religious reasons.

This ritual of *las lloronas*—professional wailers—exists in other Latin American countries as well as Perú. For example, Martha shared that in her native country, Colombia (as well as in Mexico and some other countries), they are called *plenideras*. Furthermore, when a person chooses the service at the funeral home, different kinds of wailers are offered, from very dramatic to more subdued in their crying. They attend the funeral dressed in mourning clothing (black or black and white), and they perform their act with great emotion.

Colombia

Adriana, age 46, explained funeral rituals in her home country of Colombia:

> I am from Medellín. It is the second [largest] city in Colombia; the first one is Bogotá. When a person dies, whether it is an accident or a violent death, it's basically the same as [in some states] here (the United States)—they do an autopsy. The body cannot be cremated. They have to leave the body untouched for five years in case it has to be exhumed. It cannot be cremated, but it can be buried. That's [the case] in all of Colombia. There are some differences in burials between big cities and villages, and between people in high society and poor people. When someone from the high class dies, they do a viewing the day before they are buried. It's usually just one night. In Colombia, burials are usually very quick. It's not a long, drawn-out process. It is not a process that takes weeks. Usually everything is taken care of very quickly and set up so that the funeral home takes the body to prepare it to either be buried or [be] cremated. I also want to point out a difference [in] how things used to be as to the way they are now. In the past the family would stay and view the body overnight. People, loved ones, other family members, friends would come and go. However, now due to all the problems Colombia has had with security, the funeral homes do not stay open overnight.

Once [the funeral home] is closed, everyone has to leave. So this has changed the ritual somewhat. People leave at night and come back in the morning. When it comes to actual burials, in the provinces, you can attend the ceremony [wearing] colors. [You do] not have to [wear] dark colors in order to show grief. They also leave the casket open so you can see the body. The first thing a person does is go see the body. In the higher classes they do not do this. The casket is closed. In the higher classes, it used to be customary to dress in black for a year or so, but now not so much. People will go dressed in dark colors now, not necessarily black, and dress conservatively. People will grieve for a few days, weeks, some people a month. It all depends on the family. [In the funerals] they usually give out black coffee or coffee with milk or an aromatic tea. There is no food. I think there are some parts of the country where they do, maybe in the coast. I think it depends on the family. In the funeral home they don't give food. In the lower classes you see a lot of crying and wailing. You don't see that in the higher classes. There is something in common, though. Everyone gets together, says their hellos, and it ends with a visit. They pray . . . the rosary at times. You'll see a lot of scenes of people who are praying . . . the rosary while others are outside talking. Also, during the viewing, if it is at home, which actually I am not too sure of because the ones I have attended are the ones in funeral homes, not in homes, . . . it is probable that at the viewings done at home they may give food, more visits because you see more people you haven't seen in a while. There is something curious in the coastal part of Colombia. They hire people who cry at funerals. They're called *pleñideras*.

Argentina

Cecilia, age 30, shared the following about funerals in Argentina:

The only death I experienced in Argentina was my grandfather's. My grandmother, for a long time, could not talk about him. She even removed his pictures. He was very sick for years, practically in a vegetative state, and my grandmother would take care of everything for him, from feeding him his daily meals to changing his clothes to dealing with his doctor. She became his world, and that's the only reason he lived for so many years. We were all speculating when his time would come and when it happened, it was a very difficult moment. My sister Pinta made a painting of him, and she had it hidden away for years since she couldn't bear to look at images of him. In my father's case, from the moment he died, precisely the opposite happened. She put a smiling picture of him on her desk from before he fell sick. The typical male tends not to express his emotions the way a woman would. I've only been to two funerals in Argentina (not counting my grandfather's) and for the most part, everything's pretty calm. There are conversations; there isn't any food; it's a very solemn occasion. The wakes I've attended were not in homes nor [sic] in funeral homes—which do exist, by the way—they were in salons . . . in churches. Protestant churches. The pastor speaks a few words, a prayer, and there aren't any flowers. Normally, it's an open casket viewing but I've heard of cases where it's a closed casket viewing due to the deceased being very sick. I have the memory during my childhood of a friend's grandmother's funeral, and for me, it was a very strong experience since I loved this lady very much and knew her well. She was a neighbor and I was always over at her house. Seeing her in the casket, in a table, I think, was such a strange moment for me, and on top of that I saw a group of young boys running around her casket, betting with one another to see who could kiss her. I felt so offended at actually seeing them do it and thought, how could they do such a thing. They thought it was a game and despite the behavior, children were often taken to funerals, at least in my family. I don't know whether it was just in my family or if it was a cultural thing.

For my grandfather's funeral, my grandmother dressed in black, but didn't remain in mourning for a period of time afterward. . . . On his birthday, she remembers him and we call her to speak of him, and she tells of memories that she had with him. I always call her. It doesn't matter how many years have passed, and his birthday happens to fall the day after [my own birthday], so I always remember and so does she. I always knew him as a sickly man, and I never saw him as she knew him before that time, and for her, it's very important that we know him in that manner. I've gone to a couple of funerals here, and to me, they're more like events. One funeral was Anglo and the other Hispanic, one of an Argentine lady, but there were people from . . . many countries, being [that this is] Miami. After the funeral, there was a dinner. In Argentina, everybody doesn't go to eat together. This was a lot more elaborate, with many flowers and people bringing poems on scraps of paper and photos. Many people spoke, not just the family members, during the viewing, almost like an open mic, which was not just for the family. In Argentina, the pastor will speak and maybe the husband or wife of the deceased, but that's about it. Not much is said. People remain for a longer period of time here.

As burial practices, we have in Buenos Aires *La Recoleta*, a very expensive cemetery for those who can afford it, where they have their own mausoleums and it becomes almost a museum. The coffins slide, because of the space, into drawers. Now in Argentina cremation is accepted. We have niches in a columbarium. In my grandfather's case, his remains were sent to La Plata, where he was born. In the case of my grandmother's family, they are buried in Córdoba, in a niche. We went one time and I saw they were cremated.

Central America

Nicaragua

Here I, a 50-year-old Nicaraguan woman, share my story, which was published in my book *Transform Your Loss: Your Guide to Strength and Hope* (Houben, 2009). In this story you will find cultural and religious elements that were present when my father died in 1971. With time, some of these customs, such as having the viewing at a funeral home, and having a more relaxed mourning period, have changed.

> We went to the house where we held a wake with the body present. I remember that I did not leave the head of my father. I could feel his stiff cold face in my hands, and although my tears covered his face, I was unable to warm it. I was there for a long time, in a state of total bewilderment. I looked around and amid all the flowers that surrounded the casket, one arrangement stuck out; it represented a golf course with a white ball in the center. The flower arrangement had a banner across it with the following words, "The Wednesday Group." As my father was a golfer, he met every Wednesday with a group of friends to play golf. This same group was present at his funeral, accompanying him with camaraderie and care.
>
> After the wake we went to the funeral Mass, where the priest gave us words of consolation and hope. (p. xxx)

El Salvador

Maria, age 46, provided the following description of funerals in El Salvador:

I'm from Morazán, [El] Salvador, which is not a too small city but it's not so large either. The small towns are where I've seen funerals the most because in the capital, it's totally different. . . . When someone passes away, you have to wait 24 hours. You can't bury the person before the 24 hours have passed. All the surrounding neighbors will attend the funeral and go to the wake, which takes place at the deceased's home. From the first moment someone has been declared dead, the wake begins. The body is prepared, [and] people start showing up little by little as the day progresses, then it's customary to start killing chickens to make food for the visitors, usually *tamales*, so people can eat throughout the night. After 24 hours, the deceased will be taken to the cemetery to be buried, and after the burial what is known as *los nueve días* [the nine days] will take place, where people pray every day from the first day the person died until that ninth day, *el novenario*. People dress in black almost for a year, and that's pretty much what I've seen. It is a very emotional situation and that's one of the reasons why I didn't like to attend funerals, especially for the children because I feel the children suffer greatly when they go to funerals, as . . . in my case. Adults tend to take [all the children,] from the youngest one to the oldest, and that's complicated because the family, in their pain, will forget the children, in the funerals and wakes I've attended. The children are roaming around unattended because it's so painful, and besides that, there's no psychological help anywhere whatsoever. There you live by God's will and mercy.

HISPANICS AND SUICIDE

Suicide, the taking of one's own life, is one of the most painful deaths to deal with because to talk about it openly "is difficult or even taboo for many people" (DeSpelder & Strickland, 2007, p. 411). A person's real or imagined reasons for suicide may be diverse, but according to Klimo and Heath (2006), they include the following:

[People who commit suicide] feel they have reached a point in their lives where they: (1) have no other option, (2) are exhausted from the constant pain and struggle in life, (3) believe it will garner them sympathy or emotion from those left behind, and/or (4) think they have nothing to live for. (p. 31)

Suicide is the 11th highest ranked cause of death in the United States and is the third leading cause of death among 15 to 24-year-olds, with nearly 30,000 people committing suicide yearly in the United States (DeSpelder & Strickland, 2005). Duarte-Velez and Bernal (2007) suggested that Latinos are at a greater risk of contemplating and/or committing suicide because they have "less access to mental health services . . . and are less likely to received [sic] needed care"; the most at risk are Latino youth/young adults (p. 81).

Hispanic youth at a greater risk of suicide than any other ethnic group: It is the third leading cause of death among Latinos aged 10–24 in the United States (Duarte-Velez & Bernal, 2007). Duarte-Velez and Bernal (2007) cited National Institutes of Mental Health studies showing that Hispanic females demonstrate "a higher prevalence of depression, suicide ideation, and suicide attempts than males, even though males are more apt to actually kill themselves" (p. 82).

Pablo, from the Dominican Republic, shared the reaction of his family when his cousin committed suicide:

> It was very difficult for our family because we felt we hadn't been there for her. The family wouldn't say she killed herself, but said she died because she was sick. What happened is that she had cancer and couldn't cope with it any more. My family hardly talked about it and also felt guilty for not being able to be there for her.

Funeral home manager Diana de Armas described how Hispanic families respond to suicide:

> It's very upsetting to the family because they always feel like they weren't there for their loved one, because Hispanic families tend to resolve everything amongst themselves, both with their immediate and extended families, so when there's a suicide, they feel that they let that individual down because they didn't resolve whatever problem was ailing them or bothering them, that that person didn't come to them for it. Suicide is tragic in any respect, but I think more so for Hispanics because we're used to resolving each other's problems; more so than a friend, you go to your family first. . . . Maybe years

ago they may have been more ashamed to [talk about it] but I think over time now in more modern times, they accept mentioning it but still feel that they should have been there. But they're not afraid to [talk about it] and they immediately want to see the remains as soon as possible, so we don't postpone the funerals two or three days. As soon as the death occurs, or as soon as is humanly possible, if there are legal problems, as soon as all of that is settled, we go ahead with the viewing as soon as possible. I don't like waiting days to start visitation.

Sexual and/or gender identity may also be a factor in suicide among Hispanics. As they grow up, Latino males and females are taught different "processes of gender role socialization," rules, and roles (Duarte-Velez & Bernal, 2007, p. 85), which may influence how men react to their sexual identity. Consider, for example, the *machismo* value of encouraging overt sexuality for men but not for women. Female traits are viewed as weaker, and male displays of effeminate characteristics are frowned upon. Another prevalent value in Latino culture is tied to religion, which for most Hispanics is Roman Catholic. Religious values are "the predominant moral parameters that represent a continuum of very conservative-traditional to liberal" (Duarte-Velez & Bernal, 2007, p. 86). They tie in to the patriarchal society often seen in Latino cultures. As a consequence, homosexuality may be rejected by the family members. Sexuality is essential in the development of any human being, and Latino adolescents who are forced to compromise their sexual identity because of the values with which they were instilled tend to fall into a deep depression and desperation, leading some to contemplate suicide.

The Congregational Health Bereavement Program of South Florida uses the following case example in its training:

José Luis, 48, is suffering the death of his partner Héctor, who died of AIDS. He is grieving in silence due to the shame he feels. He has never shared that he is homosexual, nor [sic] that he just lost his partner. Due to this situation, he has been admitted twice to the hospital with [chest pain], which has been diagnosed by the [emergency room] doctors as panic attacks. José Luis is Colombian, and his family constantly asks him what is wrong with him, but he doesn't dare to share. Sometimes he thinks that maybe it would be better to [end] his own life, because out of fear, he hasn't had the HIV test done, and he doesn't know if he will have the same destiny as Héctor. He needs support but is unable to ask for help because it would be a dishonor to the family to know he is homosexual. His father always told him to be *muy macho* [very manly].

BEREAVEMENT SUPPORT GROUPS

Bereavement support groups have the power to help and heal the bereaved (Bissler, 2005) because they give people the opportunity to express what they are feeling and realize they are not alone. The following are some of the activities that counselors can include when conducting support groups:

- Written activities (e.g., writing a letter, poems, journaling, or scrapbooking)
- Sharing experiences in group or in dyads
- Having a guest speaker, either a professional or a bereaved person, tell his or her story to help serve as an inspiration
- Conducting rituals, such as lighting a candle
- Playing music that evokes memories
- Reading religious/spiritual material
- Engaging in visualization or meditation

In all the trainings and groups I have facilitated I include most of these activities. I have come to realize that for Hispanics writing in a journal may be challenging, but once they are introduced to the benefits, they respond in a positive way.

I recently co-facilitated a training workshop for the Congregational Health Bereavement Program on how to establish bereavement support groups in churches. This training is conducted in Spanish, and each time my colleagues and I offer it, we have people from different countries who share their experiences about bereavement and their mourning rituals. In the last training session we conducted, we had people from Perú, Chile, Argentina, Puerto Rico, Cuba, and Nicaragua.

The following is the story of María, a Salvadoran who lost her son. She transformed her grief into action and established a support group in her church after completing the Congregational Health training program.

To have a support group was an idea I thought was impossible for me. Although many people asked me, it was not something I saw myself doing at first. I didn't see myself saying, "Well, I'm going to take a hold of this pain and do this with it." I feel that it was something that God was pushing me little by little to do. I always say that if it weren't for God pushing me along the way to do this and [putting] many things in front of me to do I wouldn't have done it. The news of [my son's] death really put us on the map, and it got to the point where it was so public I couldn't even go out without being recognized. But I had to go out. Something really curious happened to me when I was in public, whether it was at a restaurant where I was eating or just about anywhere else I would go, people would come up to me and say, "I know you, I've seen you on television and I feel that this person I know who just passed away, I feel that you could really help out their loved ones who are going through this tragedy." And I would wonder, how could I help them while I'm still suffering with my loss? The first time I went to a funeral [after my son's death] was six months later. And people would continue to tell me that my merely being present would really help the persons that were suffering at that moment, that they would identify with me and feel better. I was meeting up with about 15 women in public to go have a coffee since they were telling me they had all suffered the loss of a child, and they kept telling me I should start a bereavement group. I felt that wasn't for me, and during that time, I took a friend to a Catholic group since at that time she didn't want to go to an English[-speaking] church, so then she told me she wanted to go to a Catholic one, and so I took her to Good Shepherd and she said, "You are ready to start a group." She told me to go take the necessary classes and to go ahead and start a bereavement group, and I thought, "I can't do that, it's for more studious people; that's not for me and I'm not ready to go through that," and she said, "Yes, you are ready," and she said, "Well, then at least come to help yourself out." Honestly, creating the group was not my idea. I did the course and then I decided if these 15 women wanted to keep getting together with me, then I might as well have a place for us to meet. The pastor kept telling me I could do it, despite my doubts. I feel that that group of people was the tool God used to push me. That's how I see it now. The pastor kept telling me that if God wanted me to do this then he would provide me with the necessary people to help me along the way, given that I didn't know computers or how to make flyers or any of these things. God puts these things in your path.

> At this time there are about 30 people in the group, and we meet once a month. They don't always come at once. Sometimes it's zero people, sometimes more, but generally [it] is between 8 and 12.

In the Preface I mentioned the bereavement support group *Personas Unidas en el Dolor y la Esperanza* [People United by Grief and Hope] and how this group was born out of an educational seminar I facilitated on how to handle grief, and the inspiration of a bereaved mother. I believe that one of the most vital elements to presenting the concept of a support group to Hispanics is through education. Throughout my work as an individual trainer, or when I train others through Congregational Health programs, I have witnessed that once Hispanics are informed about the benefits of a support group and how such a group can be established, the positive response is tremendous. Grief is universal, and the need for support is also universal.

Counselors need to make sure they are open to different rituals concerning death and dying. If we want to understand other cultures, we need to be certain we understand our own. Death and bereavement are issues we rarely explored in U.S. society, but if we take a moment to reflect on how we relate to this experience, we could develop more insight and understanding about other cultures. Remember that each culture is unique and that at the same time there are individual differences within the same culture. Grief and bereavement are universal processes, but they also differ across cultures and among individuals.

TWO CASE EXAMPLES

As I end this chapter, I present two cases with elements that pertain to Hispanics and grief. You can then answer the questions that follow each case.

Juan Carlos

> At 87 years of age, Juan Carlos, a Venezuelan man, lives by himself in a small apartment. He can hardly walk and spends his days sitting on a recliner next to a table where he has a picture of his deceased wife, Perla. Next to the picture is the image of the Virgin Mary and a *veladora* that he lights every morning. Juan Carlos and Perla left their country more than 30 years ago, and Perla died in the United States. Neither could he bury her in her country of origin, as she always

wanted, nor could he have the funeral he wanted for her. Juan Carlos knows his wife was very religious, and he had wanted to buy to her a casket with the image of the Virgin on it, but it was too expensive. Against his own beliefs he had to cremate Perla, and now every day he lives with guilt and regrets [for] ever leaving Venezuela. He thinks he doesn't have anything to live for. They never had children, and now he has to deal with his grief and guilt by himself. He has heard there are support groups for widowers, but doesn't believe in these groups or in moving to an assisted living facility. He wants to remain in the house he lived in with his wife.

- What are the main losses in this story?
- What are the predominant feelings?
- What is the most salient reason for Juan's grieving?

María del Carmen

This is María del Carmen's story, told in her own words, after her grandmother died:

Although the days were distracted by so many friends and relatives keeping me company, the nights were long and scary. I remembered my grandmother telling me she would "appear" to me if I didn't take her to Nicaragua and bury her there. How could I? I couldn't travel out of the country because of my visa. I tried to explain this to her at the hospital just before she passed, but it was impossible. She made me swear to her I would take her back home. My mother didn't know about this[;] . . . it was a "pact" between [my grandmother and me] because we were very close. Actually, she raised me because my mother had to work in another city. I used to call her *mamita*, and she is the one who taught me how to pray. She always prayed with me in Spanish because she didn't speak English. She came to Miami when she was already 70 years old and never learned the language. Actually, she never wanted to learn it. She loved being Nicaraguan. She never wanted to leave the country, but my mother brought her here in order to take care of me, so she would be able to work. She was never happy here. She missed her country. Every night she cried, longing to be in her small ranch in the outskirts of Managua. In 8 years she never went back. Now, I feel I have the [obligation] to carry on her last wishes.

- What are the main losses in this story?
- What are the predominant feelings?
- What is the most salient reason for María del Carmen's grieving?

HELPFUL SUGGESTIONS

- Be knowledgeable regarding the bereavement rituals of various cultures, including the Hispanic culture, and be aware of the richness of their traditions and the variety of their customs, depending on the country of origin.
- Remember that *El Día de Los Muertos* [The Day of the Dead] is a Mexican celebration. Although other Latin American countries honor their deceased on November 2, *El Día de Los Muertos* is a unique way that Mexicans honor the dead.
- Be aware that, despite differences in customs, all Hispanics mainly share their emotions with their families and are not ordinarily open to joining a support group, their attitudes have been changing. Bereavement support groups are becoming more and more accepted in Hispanic culture.

PERSONAL REFLECTIONS FOR THE COUNSELOR

- Do you accept the way Hispanics experience their grief during funerals and their mourning rites?
- Are you comfortable talking about rituals, including funeral rites, that differ from your own?
- Do you think you would be able to conduct a bereavement support group for Hispanics?

CHAPTER 8

Grief Counseling: Different Approaches

Grief and bereavement are normal experiences that are very personal and are accompanied by pain, and often hopelessness, in individuals across cultures. Because we as human beings are each unique, our grief is also unique. People express their feelings of sadness and loss in highly individual ways; thus, the care of grieving patients in any health care setting must be considered and implemented in such a way as to be sensitive to each person's specific needs (Bougere, 2008). In this chapter, I cover different techniques that mental health professionals can use when working with Hispanic clients according to the type of loss they encounter and taking into account the kind of perspective that will work best to help them process their grief. It is my hope that we as counselors can inspire our clients to use the resources they already possess to achieve a positive outcome in their lives. Furthermore, in chapter 9, I explore different techniques to be used in *grief counseling*, a process that differs from *grief therapy*, which, according to Worden (2009), comprises "those specialized techniques, . . . that are used to help people with abnormal or complicated grief reactions" (p. 83).

Understanding the influence of culture on the way bereaved clients express their grief is a vital aspect for providing counseling from a culturally sensitive perspective. Every client's story is unique, just as his or her grief is unique. Furthermore, this uniqueness supports the fact that Hispanics, although they belong to the same culture, are a heterogeneous group whose members have differences as well as commonalities.

UNDERSTANDING GRIEF

Grief is the combination of thoughts and feelings a person experiences when he or she experiences a loss. Grief is not a disease; it is the way an expression of our humanity, although many people experiencing grief may feel they are losing control (Giddens & Giddens, 2003). Grief is such an overwhelming feeling that it can paralyze and cripple the bereaved. Moreover, it is not static; it comes and goes, much like waves in an ocean (Del Rosario, 2004; Houben, 2009). If one defines grief as "the natural reaction we experience when we suffer a significant loss in our lives" (Houben, 2009, p. 37) and takes into account the losses Hispanics living in the United States may face, it is reasonable to expect that many of them suffer from tremendous grief, despair, and hopelessness. So, how can we—health care professionals—help Hispanic clients who have encountered multiple losses, who do not speak English, and who do not feel comfortable talking about their pain or sorrow? How can we guide them through particular losses and know which technique would work best in certain cases but not in others? Counselors must take into account the thoughts, feelings, and behaviors of bereaved Hispanic persons as a frame of reference that gives them the insights they need to use the proper theoretical orientations and counseling techniques to help these clients.

In my work with Hispanic clients, I have learned never to expect a certain behavior or way of expressing grief. Some of them cry without reservation, others do not even talk about the fact that the loved one has died. I have come to realize that my Hispanic clients' individual reactions have to do more with the dynamic of the family than with the Hispanic culture itself. For example, when one client, Diana, came to see me she was totally devastated. She had lost her husband in a plane crash, but she didn't talk about it at home. Her children, two boys, ages 9 and 7, never mentioned the father's name and acted like nothing had happened. After talking with Diana about her communication style, I found out that women in her family didn't talk much about sad issues with their children in order to protect them. It is important to keep in mind that bereavement has more than one dimension and that not everyone experiences it the same way (Houben, 2009). Grief can be short-lived, or it can become a longer, more complicated process. When people feel totally overwhelmed by the pain and are unable to function in their daily routines, they may be suffering from complicated grief, which may persist for years, especially if they do not have the opportunity to do grief work.

THE DYNAMICS OF THE GRIEVING PROCESS

Individuals respond to significant losses in diverse ways. Some may experience great distress from which they cannot recover, others experience grief in a lesser manner and for a shorter time, whereas others may seem to recover quickly. Bonanno (2004) asserted that many people demonstrate resilience and a stable equilibrium after experiencing a loss, a situation that is more prevalent than assumed. Some individuals, especially the most vulnerable ones, such as those who face a particularly traumatic loss or find themselves emotionally paralyzed, may benefit from grief counseling (Boss, 2006). If the person can function in society in a reasonable manner, then others tend to believe that person is showing signs of being resilient. However, the question here is this: Is this perceived equilibrium internal or external? In other words, does this apparently normal functioning reflect the way the person truly feels inside or is it simply the way he wants to project himself to others? Counselors can better answer these questions after considering the topics discussed in the next section.

HUMAN DIMENSIONS AND MANIFESTATIONS OF GRIEF

When working with clients in general, I apply a holistic approach in which I assess all four dimensions of the human being: (a) emotional, (b) physical, (c) social, and (d) spiritual. I believe that for a person to be complete, it is of vital importance that all these dimensions be balanced.

Grief is a multidimensional process that can be expressed in all four of these dimensions. Many people think that grief can be expressed only in the emotional dimension, through crying or being depressed. If you tell a person, for example, that a backache can be a sign of grief, he or she may find it difficult to believe, but prolonged grief can indeed manifest itself physically.

Each time I see a client, I conduct an evaluation that involves specific components of the four dimensions. If a client complains of any physical manifestation, I suggest he or she see a doctor, to rule out any physiological problem (Houben, 2009). You can use the following checklist as part of your assessment of your clients (Houben, 2009):

Physical

- Headache
- Stomachache
- Dizziness and nausea
- Back pain
- Chest pain
- Lack of appetite
- Excessive eating
- Lack of sleep (insomnia)
- Too much sleep

Emotional

- Depression
- Anxiety
- Fear
- Hyperactivity
- Lethargy
- Mistrust
- Despair
- Shock
- Numbness

Social

- Isolation
- Poor communication
- Excessive social activity
- Overwork
- Excessive shopping

Spiritual

- Lack of faith
- Inability to forgive
- Lack of hope
- Anger toward God
- Anger toward life

I want to stress that the social and spiritual dimensions can also be evaluated in regular conversation with the client as well as when taking the client's history. I have especially found the spiritual dimension to be a challenging one for clients to share.

Rosario is a Cuban mother whose son completed suicide. She had a difficult time even stating the cause of his death. She explained to me how guilty she felt:

> I am Catholic, you know, and the way my son died is a sin. I am afraid he is not in Heaven. However, also, I don't understand; if God sees everything, how did He allow this to happen? I feel so angry, but know this is also a sin. I shouldn't feel this way. Whenever I have these feelings, I try to forget them.

I allowed her to cry, telling her it was safe to express her anger. I handed her a soft pillow I have in my office, and she squeezed it, allowing all the anger she had kept in her heart to come out. Sometimes it is difficult for our clients to express these feelings, because they think they are not supposed to feel this way. Once they let go of their anger, they can deal with their grief. Not too long ago, a woman brought me her grandson.

He was very angry that his mother had committed suicide and said he couldn't cry. I asked him if he wanted to do an exercise with me. He agreed, so I asked him to sit on the recliner in my office, and I played some soft music. Then I asked him to close his eyes and gave him a small ceramic heart. I told him to move the heart in his hands and tell me what he felt, whether he had memories that came to his mind. As he did the exercise he said, "It is rough on one side and soft on the other just like love," and he started crying. He then recounted the whole story of when he found his mother in the shower and how painful it had been to lose her. It was not until he expressed his pain that he could let go of his anger.

TYPES OF GRIEF

There are different ways of expressing grief, and they have to do with the kind of loss the person is facing, when and how the loss occurred, and the coping skills the person is using to deal with the loss. The three specific types of grief I discuss in the following sections are (a) anticipatory grief, (b) disenfranchised grief, and (c) complicated grief.

Anticipatory Grief

Many times when we expect a loss to occur we can experience pain as we imagine it will be when the situation arises. This type of grief is called *anticipatory grief*, and it is more prevalent than most people assume (Hodgson & Krahn, 2005). Although the concept of anticipatory grief may be associated mostly to the death of a loved one, it may also occur when a person is planning to leave his or her homeland, seeking new horizons: "We leave our homeland with enthusiasm, awaiting our new life, but at the same time we leave behind our family, friends and traditions. This can cause us great sorrow and produce a sense of anticipated mourning" (Houben, 2009, p. 50). Clients who are grieving the loss of their homeland may have actually started the grieving process even before they moved to the United States or another country.

How can the counselor be of help in such cases? One of the best techniques I have found to validate one's life and traditions is what is known as a *life review*. This activity can be done either individually or in a group. You can ask clients to write a story about their lives in their home country. Ask them to name the school they went to; the names of their teachers and their friends; and (if their family was religious) their memories of religious traditions, such as First Communion or a bar or bat mitzvah. They can continue writing about their years as teenagers, their first love, and their adult years, describing their favorite places to go and what made their country so special. Perhaps clients can create a collage of photos. The idea is that they share with you what they love from their country and at the same time revise the past losses related to their homeland that they haven't been able to share or process.

Disenfranchised Grief

Renowned American sociologist Kennetth Doka developed the concept of *disenfranchised grief*, which is experienced when losses of any kind are not socially acknowledged or accepted. The person may be experiencing pain for a loss, but because that loss is not validated by society (e.g., deaths owing to suicide, death of a same-sex partner) it is not acknowledged. As a result, "The person does not have a 'right' to grieve that loss since no one else recognizes a legitimate cause of grief" (Doka, 2002, p. 160).

Although the term *disenfranchised grief* has been applied to losses owing to death, there are other losses associated with disenfranchised grief, such as when a relationship is not recognized by others. For example, Rosaura had maintained an extramarital relationship with Jose Antonio for more than 2 years. One day, a friend called her to let her know Jose Antonio had had a heart attack and died. Rosaura did not know what to say. Automatically, she got dressed and went to the funeral home to see Jose Antonio for the last time. When she arrived there were many family members, and she couldn't cry the way she wanted. She had to conceal her grief.

One of the greatest challenges faced by a person suffering from disenfranchised grief is that health care and social service providers may lack awareness of the loss and thus do not formally recognize it. The grieving person may also suffer because of the absence of social support and lack of validation among relatives (Thornton & Zanich, 2002).

Complicated Grief

For most Hispanics, bereavement is a meaningful event involving family, community, and culture-specific practices. Clinical professionals who ignore or negate these practices, including personal and communal rituals, can emotionally harm the bereaved family, impede grief resolution, and cause the family to regard the care provided negatively.

It is now known that bereavement can take the form of a disorder called *complicated grief* (Houben, 2009), which manifests as an intense longing for the dead person, often without signs of depression. This disorder goes beyond the normal appearance of a grief response and has the potential to cause later problems at the physical, emotional, social, and/or spiritual level. One can observe a difference between complicated grief and *bereavement*, the latter of which has been completed, according to Cutcliffe (2004). This difference has to do with the bereaved person's sense of hope. When the person is able to embrace hope again in his or her life, it shows that the bereavement is complete. However, if the client maintains a sense of hopelessness, it can be linked to "a complicated bereavement process" (Cutcliffe, 2004, p. 13).

Furthermore, as Stroebe, Stroebe and Hansson (2001) pointed out, it can be a challenge to distinguish complicated or pathological grief because of many factors, such as differentiating complicated grief from related disorders; distinguishing whether the grief is normal or not, based on cultural manifestations; and because "grief is not a single syndrome with clear diagnostic criteria" (p. 6). In my discussion of different counseling perspectives for facilitating a client's processing of grief later in chapter 9, I introduce *cognitive behavioral therapy* (CBT), which targets the cognition, emotions, and behavior of the person, as being one of the most promising approaches in terms of positive outcomes. For example, the therapist may work with a client on the client's thinking process (cognition) to discern what types of thoughts he or she is having. Then the therapist and client focus on the emotions these thoughts elicit and how the person consequently behaves. The premise underlying CBT is that if clients learn how to reframe their thoughts, they can change their emotions and, therefore, their actions. The purpose is to empower clients as they take charge of their thinking and behavior (O'Donohue & Fisher, 2009). I use CBT techniques with clients who tend to dwell on painful thoughts or live in the past, limiting their ability to move forward.

HISPANICS' EXPRESSIONS OF GRIEF

As human beings we experience not only losses that are visible or known to others, such as the death of a loved one, the loss of health, or loss through divorce, but also subtler losses, such as the loss of one's homeland and cultural traditions, that often go unacknowledged or invalidated. Because a thorough discussion of all the losses Hispanics can experience is beyond the scope of this book, I include here only the more relevant losses, especially those experienced by immigrants as they move to the United States. I want to emphasize the word *immigrants* as referring to first-generation immigrants, because second-generation Hispanics born in the United States may already have acculturated and appropriated the customs, rituals, and lifestyle of their adopted country. They may not have experienced any of the cultural losses that their parents or grandparents endured as first-generation immigrants. (These cultural losses are more fully discussed in chapter 10.) It is vital to keep in mind that the experience of grief is influenced by many variables, including the type of loss the person has experienced and the circumstances surrounding the loss. In my work with Hispanic clients I also consider the personality, support, and spirituality of the bereaved individual as vital factors in the grieving process.

As the U.S. population continues to grow, so does its racial, ethnic, and cultural makeup. Growing in tandem with this phenomenon is the need for more culturally sensitive grief educators and counselors who can expand their awareness of the many ways that culturally diverse persons grieve and of the various causes of their grief. Many Hispanics leave their homeland because of a crisis, such as war, political unrest, or a natural disaster. The counselor can help them to see their loss of homeland as an opportunity for personal transformation rather than a cause for extended grief. This may be difficult in the context of a new culture and new environment. In experiencing the world, people need to feel a congruency between their values and reality. If there is dissonance, they may experience unease, conflict, or even a sense of loss or crisis. This dissonance can be resolved if a person has good coping skills to deal with the new situation, but if the situation involves changes that are greater than a person's inner resources, such as adapting to a new country or culture, a crisis may occur. Maldonado (2003) described a crisis as follows:

A temporary state of disruption and disorganization characterized by 1) the inability of the person or the family to resolve problems with their normal methods and strategies, and 2) the potential to produce results that are radically positive or radically negative. (p. 13)

A common therapeutic response among mental health professionals is to treat the client's grief symptoms with tranquilizers and antidepressants. Many clients have shared with me the prevalence of antidepressant medication taken by bereaved people. Such was the case in Lucia's situation after her husband's death. She came to counseling after reading my book *Transform Your Loss: Your Guide to Strength and Loss* (Houben, 2009). Her purpose was to follow each of my Eleven Principles of Transformation (discussed in detail in chapter 9), by performing the guided meditations at my office. Her description of her response to her husband's death illustrates the principle of living your grief:

> I felt like screaming when I heard the news Jaime had had a car accident and died. I collapsed to the floor crying out loud his name. Rosaura, my best friend, handed me a Xanax, saying it would calm me down. I remember being really upset with the idea of taking a pill, but felt out of control. With the passing of time, I still felt very anxious, crying and suffering from severe migraines. Rosaura called me one day and suggested I ask my doctor for a Xanax prescription. I didn't. I wanted to experience my pain. As you say in your second principle, "live your grief." I didn't want to mask it.

In this case, a counselor could recommend that Lucia keep a journal, in which she can write how she feels everyday and how she is coping with her grief. Many times clients have difficulty naming the emotion or emotions they are experiencing. The following questions could help them in this endeavor:

Which of these emotions do you feel on a regular basis?

- Sadness
- Anger
- Fear
- Anxiety
- Nervousness
- Hopelessness

Next, you can ask your client to write a sentence about a situation when they experience the emotion. Example:

I feel anxious when _____.

Bereaved individuals are not passive agents. I believe that participation in one's recovery is more effective than simply letting time heal all wounds. *Tasks* and *grief work* are words that indicate action is the essential ingredient in getting to the other side of a difficult process. Unfinished grief work may in some cases result in pathology. In fact, grief that one is avoiding is often referred to as *pathological, unreleased, repressed,* or *disguised* and requires grief counseling (Leick & Davidsen-Nielsen, 1991).

Grief work can cause some people, even those with solid social support networks, to isolate themselves and miss the benefits of their support system out of a fear of seeming weak or vulnerable in front of others. It is best for mourners to be flexible, spending time both alone and with others. Those living in an unfamiliar cultural or religious context may become especially isolated in times of crisis or grief (Leick & Davidsen-Nielsen, 1991). Social class also has a big influence on people, including their lifestyles, values, where they live and where they are to be buried, and whom they marry and the number of children they have (Doka, 1998). Class may have a great influence on Latinos who have a lower socioeconomic status because of the jobs they have, because they don't speak the language, or because they are in the country illegally. All of these factors may influence their grieving process.

Many Hispanics who have left their country because of the sociopolitical situation, including living through war and/or oppression, may have suffered trauma that manifests itself in their behavior. McGoldrick et al. (2005, p. 57) found that the following symptoms are common in people who have experienced a traumatic event:

- Psychic numbing
- Hypervigilance
- Dissociation
- Intense fear, free-floating anxiety
- Survivor guilt
- Fixation on the trauma
- Victim identity, death identity, and identification with the dead
- Low self-esteem
- Anger
- Self-destructive behavior
- Weakened immune system and chronic disease processes
- Depression
- Substance abuse

These responses could offer the counselor a valid resource when working with Hispanic clients:

> When starting working with the client and in order to resolve any grief or trauma, treatment must provide for cathartic release of affect during the initial process . . . [it] must provide an emotional container so that the client feels safe and competent to handle the feelings that emerge . . . therapists must guard against judgmental statements and affect and should cultivate nonjudgmental acceptance. (McGoldrick et al., 2005, p. 62)

INTEGRATING ALTERNATIVE APPROACHES TO HEALING

According to their cultural traditions, some Hispanics rely on an alternative form of healing instead of, or in addition to, the conventional health care system, to deal with their losses or grief. These are generally viewed by mainstream culture as folk healing practices. Oftentimes, Hispanics use both approaches, sometimes turning to culturally traditional ways when conventional care does not meet their needs.

Folk Healing

Padilla and Salgado De Snyder (1985) observed that a common assumption about Hispanics is that when "suffering from emotional distress [they] use folk-healing practitioners (curanderismo, santería, espiritismo)" (p. 159). Although some Latinos may use folk healers, it is not the norm. On the other hand, *espiritismo* among Puerto Ricans can be seen primarily as "a crisis-healing cult that attracts people in times of interpersonal stress and substitutes in many cases for professional mental-health care" (Padilla & Salgado De Snyder, 1985, p. 160). However, a therapist should embrace diversity when working with Hispanics and try to understand their worldview. Therapists who operate only from their worldview may misinterpret as pathological an approach that is a vital component of the client's culture.

Therefore, it is crucial that alternative healing modalities ingrained in the client's culture be taken into consideration. Merluzzi and Hegde (2003) observed that "there are many culturally distinct folk disorders, and indigenous healers administering folk remedies for all of these cultures" (p. 426). For example, Merluzzi and Hegde indicated that Mexicans believe that hot or cold air may influence the wellness and health of a person. In my home country of Nicaragua, if one stays out late it is common to hear a mother tell her child to come in the house because *Te vas a serenar* [The cold air will hit you]. Nicaraguans also believe that if you drink cold water after ironing you could catch a cold.

Even though many Hispanics do not rely on folk healing (or *superstition*, as some people may call it), I share the case of Susana, a 49-year-old Cuban woman. She was laid off 3 months ago from a job she had held for 19 years, and she felt very anxious. For as long as Susana could remember, she had gone to *santeras* [spiritual healers] to have *los caracoles* [seashells] read to see what the future will bring. She also believes *los santos* [the saints] send messages to her, and she bases many of her decisions on these messages. One day she was feeling particularly anxious and went for a reading. The *santera* told her she needed *una limpieza con un huevo* [a cleaning with an egg around the body], because somebody had placed a spell on her to deter her from succeeding (*te hicieron un trabajo, no te quieren ver que levantes cabeza*).

When Susana shared her story with me, I respected her beliefs and worked with her to deal with her job loss. Although she believed *alguien le había hecho un trabajo* [someone had done a job on her] that caused her to lose her job, she wanted to talk to someone about her loss.

I worked with Susana on her feelings of anxiety, which were a product of the grief she was experiencing after losing her job of 19 years. I asked her to keep a journal of her feelings and to determine what thoughts she had when she experienced anxiety. For the most part, she had catastrophic thoughts, such as "I won't be able to find a job," "This was the best job ever," and "I don't have the skills to get a new job." Using an approach called *dialectical behavior therapy*, discussed in more detail later in this chapter, I taught her how to reframe these thoughts with affirmations such as "I can find a new job" or "I have the necessary skills to succeed," and consequently her emotions changed.

THE ROLE OF EMOTIONS IN LOSS

When facing a loss, we can experience an array of emotions—anger, fear, guilt, stress—which, if not expressed appropriately, can manifest in the human dimensions previously mentioned (i.e., physical, spiritual, social, and emotional; Houben, 2009). Counselors can work with their clients to release painful emotions and stimulate them to embrace hope when evaluating their future (Cutcliffe, 2004). Because of the kinds of losses many Hispanics experience, their grief can include resentment, uncertainty, hopelessness, helplessness, and/or an inferiority complex.

During a counseling session with me, Laura, a Colombian who for her personal safety had to leave her homeland, started to cry while expressing her guilt about her attitude toward living in the United States:

> I am sorry. I shouldn't be crying. I should be grateful for being able to be in this country and to have my family with me, but . . . I really miss Colombia. I wish I could go back in time. I pretend in front of my children I am happy, because I don't want them to see me sad, but . . . it is so difficult for me to adapt to this country.

Obviously Laura pretends she is happy about living in this country even though she feels guilt and despair over leaving her homeland. If she could openly express her feelings, such as through keeping a journal, and be guided by a counselor to focus on the benefits of being with her family and of having the freedom she did not have in her home country of Colombia, she might be able to develop a more positive perspective, one of gratitude. For cases such as Laura's, journaling can be extremely helpful. Using CBT, I taught her how to evaluate her thoughts and be able to elicit different emotions and behavior.

This table is an example of her journal:

Thought	Emotion	Behavior
I cannot adapt to this country	Anxious	Drinking and complaining
I miss Colombia so much!	Sad	Crying
Why did I have to leave Colombia!	Angry	Snapping at her husband
English is so difficult to learn	Afraid	Quitting school
I am so lonely here	Sad	Being isolated

After the client has been recording his or her thoughts in a journal for some time, I ask him or her to reflect on his or her behaviors. For example, when Laura felt anxious about thinking she couldn't adapt to the United States, she complained or drank. Obviously, these behaviors did not help her to solve her situation and do not empower her. Once she started keeping a journal, Laura realized how much she complained and was a victim of her own limiting way of thinking. She changed her thoughts and consequently acted in a more empowering manner.

Another kind of journal I ask my clients to keep is a journal of feelings. Sometimes we are not in touch with how we feel, just with what we think. By recording his or her feelings, a person can develop greater awareness of the predominant emotions he or she experiences throughout the week. The best way to proceed is to record the emotion one is experiencing several times a day for a week and to record the thought that originated the emotion or write down what was happening at that moment that elicited the emotion. This is helpful in two ways. First, clients evaluate the influence of their thoughts on how they feel and begin to notice the events that produce certain emotions. Second, they can then do something about it, such as reframing their thoughts or avoiding events that elicit negative emotions but are under their control.

The following is an example of a chart a person could use to help record these thoughts, emotions, and events:

	Monday	Tuesday	Wednesday	Thursday	Friday	Saturday	Sunday
8:00 a.m.							
11:00 a.m.							
2:00 p.m.							
5:00 p.m.							
8:00 p.m.							

Journaling also helps clients see that people do not experience only one emotion. If a client comes to you and says, "I am sad all day long," she may not be aware that perhaps she was happy when a friend called or that she was able to talk to a store clerk in English. People experience many emotions during the course of a normal day, but when a person is grieving, he or she tends to filter the whole experience through a sad or negative lens. However, when people are grieving, it is important that they allow themselves a time to experience those emotions as well.

Frijda (1994) noted that there is a connection among a person's emotions and his or her appraisal of an event, the capacity of the individual to deal with it, and the individual's cultural background. In an event such as loss, the person's appraisal of the event also depends on the codes and values that the person uses to evaluate the loss as a threat. Frijda asserted that there exist universal elicitors that provoke certain emotions in individuals; for example, personal loss is one that universally causes grief.

When considering how to counsel Hispanics who are experiencing different kinds of grief or are in different stages of grief owing to their loss, it is important to understand the prevalence and overt expression of deep emotions in their culture:

> Emotions are part of culture and of strategic importance to our understanding of the ways in which people shape and are shaped by their world . . . emotions are discourse; they are constructed and produced in language and in human interaction. They cannot be understood outside of the cultures that produce them. (Scheper-Hughes, 1993, p. 431)

For many Hispanics, especially men, to admit that they suffer from depression is a sign of a character failure. However, if you ask them about the signs of depression they are having, such as losing their appetite or having problems sleeping, they will not hesitate to answer affirmatively (Avila & Parker, 2000).

One of my clients Rodrigo, who was from Venezuela, told me the following:

> I couldn't cry or show how I really felt. In our culture men don't cry. I still remember my uncle telling me, when I was 10 years old and lost my mother, "You are brave. Men don't cry!" Now I am 57 years old, have lost a daughter, and am being tough for my family. Although I want to cry, tears cannot come out of my eyes.

According to Wunnenberg (2000), as a person experiences a loss he or she may feel "shock, disbelief, numbness, confusion" (p. 21). However, emotions that are considered negative (e.g., anger, despair, sadness) are not dysfunctional in and of themselves. What can be problematic is that these emotions may *become* dysfunctional and may remain so for a long time.

One of the salient behaviors of a grieving person is apathy; he or she does not feel like doing anything. As a way of helping your clients experience emotions, one technique is to provide them with three pieces of poster board and suggest that they create three different pictures of (a) apathy, (b) sadness, and (c) peace. They can do this with a pencil, or with markers, or they could even cut and paste figures or images from magazines that symbolize or represent the subject of the drawing. The title of each drawing can be written on it, but they can also write any thoughts that come to mind among the images.

Once a client has created the three pictures, ask him or her to bring to you the first picture. You and the client can talk about the feeling of apathy, and you can put that first picture through a paper shredder. (I suggest you have a paper shredder in your office; it is really helpful when doing rituals such as this with your clients.) Next, ask the client to bring in the second picture and tell you the story behind his or her drawing of sadness, and ask the client whether he or she has ever experienced that emotion. It may take a couple of sessions for the client to express his or her feelings. Once they have gone through this exercise with you, they can put the drawing of sadness through the paper shredder. Finally, tell the client to bring the third drawing, of peace, and ask how he or she feels about the picture. If you want the client to be able to experience peace right then and there, you can do a guided imagery exercise.

If you have never worked with any guided imagery techniques, I encourage you to give them a try. You may be surprised with the effect it has both on you and your client. You can start by asking the client to get into a comfortable position and close his or her eyes. Then, speaking in a very slow and calm manner, ask the client to take a couple of deep breaths in and out. Ask the client to visualize an image in his or her mind, and allow him or her time to be with that image. You can guide the client through the imagery, or you can tell him or her to visualize the image he or she wants. The following is an example:

> Close your eyes and let yourself go. . . . Take a deep breath, and then let it out. One more time take a deep breath and then let it out. . . . Now, as you take another deep breath, allow yourself to relax even more. That's right. . . . As you focus on your breathing, imagine the picture that symbolizes peace to you. In your mind, see this place clearly and breathe in a sensation of peace. That's right. . . . Now imagine you are in that place and are able to surround yourself with this feeling of peace and calmness. . . . You feel totally relaxed and at peace. . . . In this place you find yourself walking slowly and appreciating your surroundings. Every little thing that comes to your perception brings you peace, calmness, and serenity. . . . Feel how your heart fills up with this sensation of serenity. . . . That's right. . . . Allow this sensation of peace and serenity to expand to every cell of your body, producing a sense of calmness from inside out. . . . Now your whole body is filled up with a wonderful sensation of peace, serenity, and calmness. . . . Enjoy the moment. . . . And now, in a moment you will come back to

the room, bringing with you the same sensation of calmness, serenity, and peace. . . . When you are ready you can slowly open your eyes.

This is just one example of the many kinds of guided imagery I use with my clients. The sense of well-being it brings to them always amazes me. I had a client who was experiencing high levels of anxiety, and I asked him what produced in him a sense of calmness. He said that walking on the beach was very soothing for him, so in our session I invited him to picture the image of a white beach.

In traditional grief work theory, the acceptance of the presence of positive emotions during bereavement has been rather ignored because some professionals view them as a form of denial that is not beneficial when dealing with a person's mourning. However, the inclusion of positive emotions, including laughter, is linked to better adjustment to losses, including the loss of a spouse. Moreover, laughter seems to influence, and even reduce, the time people grieve (Bonanno, 2004). I find this perspective especially valuable in that the bereaved can remember funny stories, jokes, or even silly things about their deceased loved one and thus lighten up the situation they have to face. One of my clients, Sandra, was grieving the death of her husband in Iraq. When I asked her about the strengths she had, she started to laugh, and with a warm expression on her face, said:

> Well, you might say that stubbornness is not a strength, the same as Carlos. He would get so annoyed by it. I drove him crazy. I remember the day he wanted to deter me from riding a motorcycle. I really wanted to do it and despite his fear I went ahead and did it. I fell. He said, "You are so stubborn . . . you don't listen." I was hysterical with his comments, because he knew me so well.

Apparently Sandra got momentary relief from her grief when laughing about this instant, which struck her as humorous, even though she was feeling the loss of her husband deeply.

What makes emotions positive or negative is the way one expresses them or act them out. Even in times of despair a person cannot grieve all the time. As Juana, who had lost her daughter, said one day at my office when I asked how she was occupying her days, "I need to do other things. I cannot be grieving all the time."

The objective of grief counseling is to find ways to help clients deal with the emotions produced by complicated grief. In treating a client's depression, anger, or anxiety, Selligman (2007) integrates the modalities of relaxation, cognitive therapy, and meditation. Anxiety has been strongly related to complicated grief and, if overlooked, could develop "into a full-blown anxiety disorder" (Rando, 2000, p. 168). According to Selligman, these emotions can be handled through disciplined effort. Despite self-help books and psychotherapy, we cannot become perfect individuals; however, we can learn how to control our moods. Earlier in this chapter I introduced an example of guided imagery, which is a wonderful technique for teaching clients how to control their moods. For example if they are angry, take them to a place of calmness. If they are frustrated, take them to a place of empowerment.

In the final part of this section, I want to share the thoughts of Van Heck and De Ridder (2001), who emphasized the value of helping clients integrate positive emotions into the grieving process: "It is recommended that positive aspects of emotions associated with loss events should be considered" (p. 462). Helping your clients realize that there can be positive aspects to painful emotions, such as love, may help them realize that, despite their grief, they can still experience some other, happier emotions.

REFRAMING THE PERSPECTIVE OF
DIFFERENT TYPES OF LOSS

In this section, I discuss three of the most salient losses many Hispanics face as they move to the United States: (a) the loss of their homeland, (b) the loss of their language, and (c) the loss of their self-esteem. I also address how counselors can help their Hispanic clients reframe their perspective on their losses. In the preceding section, I described the role emotions play in how people behave and deal with their situations of loss. Many clients have difficulty expressing their feelings because they are embarrassed or do not know how to describe them, so they operate mainly at a cognitive level. Consider the example of Paula, a Venezuelan woman, who described how she was dealing with her loss of self-esteem:

> I think I won't be able to find a job because of my dark skin. They always tell me "you look so Latina." ¿Qué creen ellos? Para empezar hay muchas Latinas que son rubias y ojos azules [What do they think? For starters, there are many Latin women who are blond with blue eyes]. I don't know how to deal with these remarks. I believe people will pay more attention to how I look than to what I can do. I wish

I was blond like my Aunt Carlita. On my mother's side they are all light skin[ed]. They are so beautiful.

An empathic and observant counselor may notice that Paula used only phrases pertaining to her thoughts, such as "I think," "I don't know," and "I believe." She does not use any words to describe how she feels. As the counselor to such a client, you can be a role model and guide her to identify her emotions. For example, you could ask a client to complete the following sentences:

- I feel _____ when someone does not appreciate me.
- I feel _____ when I think about getting a job.
- I feel _____ when someone tells me I look "so" Latina.

With this approach, you can show clients how to be in touch with the feelings they are experiencing and how to work on appreciating their circumstances in relation to their feelings. When people work only from their thoughts, they are unable to process their emotions.

When working with clients it is important for them to believe three things regarding the outcomes they wish to achieve: (a) It is *possible* to achieve them, (b) they are *able* to achieve them, and (c) they *deserve* to achieve them (O'Connor, 2001). As O'Connor (2001) noted, in U.S. society we tend to focus too much on the problems or the crises we face, instead of looking for the outcomes we want. If clients are inspired to reframe their perspective, from being reactive to being proactive—that is, to ownership of the problem (or crisis) and starting to move toward a solution—then they can become empowered and ready to make the necessary changes in their lives. This approach can help clients work through losses of their language, homeland, and self-esteem, as the following cases illustrate.

Loss of Language

Juan thinks he lost his job in the United States because he speaks English with a strong accent. He assumes he will never be able to find a qualified position like the one he had in Venezuela. Each time he has to do a presentation during a job interview he suffers from anxiety and starts to stutter. He says he misses his role as the chief director of a marketing company in his former country. There, he was able to set up marketing campaigns that covered the whole of Caracas. Here in the United States Juan thinks of himself as just another employee and feels that, because of his accent, he is the subject of jokes and laughter.

How can a counselor help Juan reframe his experience? First, a counselor could help him recognize and accept the loss he has experienced and to realize that he is not living in Venezuela anymore. It is also important for Juan to acknowledge the feelings he may be experiencing and to keep a journal in which he records when those feelings occur and how he can work with them. As long as Juan has an idealized perception of what had been before, in contrast to what he needs now, he likely will not be able to move on. The counselor could also suggest that he focus on the benefits of living in the United States and to remember why he decided to leave Venezuela in the first place. What was the purpose behind his emigration? Furthermore, with respect to Juan's lack of proficiency in English, the counselor could work with him on not focusing on "I have an accent" or "I cannot speak English" and guide him toward finding solutions and setting achievable goals, such as enrolling in a class or listening to television and radio in English to improve his language skills.

On the other hand, consider the case of Ileana, a Colombian woman who works as a cleaning woman in Miami, Florida, and decided to shift her perspective:

> I work cleaning this gym from 8:00 a.m. to 2:00 p.m. Then I go to my English classes. I decided to learn English because *me da mucha pena no hablar el idioma despues de ocho años viviendo en Miami* [I am embarrassed for not being able to speak English after eight years living in Miami]. I want to better myself in order to get a better job. I feel much better now! I know I may always have an accent, but at least I will be able to speak another language. Who said one needs to speak a foreign language without an accent?

This shows how one person facing the loss of her language is taking action and doing something about it. If a client shows resistance to take action, the counselor can use visualization or guided imagery to help the client see himself or herself already speaking the language. I have used this technique extensively with both Hispanic and non-Hispanic clients regarding different kinds of losses or challenges, and the results have been very rewarding.

Loss of Homeland

When people are separated from their native country they experience a sense of loss and nostalgia, and small details often elicit memories, grief, or hope. Gisela, a Venezuelan woman who loves and misses her country but has found ways to remain connected to her roots, sent me the following e-mail with a picture and description attached:

> Those are my own orchids. The plant has been with me for the last three years, and every year she gave me those beautiful flowers with fragrance, color and . . . do you know it is a "Venezuelan Catleya"? She even gives me good energy from my far country.

As Gisela's counselor, I worked with her and coached her to accept her new circumstances. She had a very difficult time accepting the loss of her homeland because she thought emigrating meant she would lose her native country completely. When we discussed the fact that by accepting her living situation she was taking the first step in the transformation of her loss, she could see the bigger picture, reframe her perspective, and get involved in local Venezuelan organizations in Miami. She aims to write a book on her experience as an immigrant— transforming the "loss" of her beloved Venezuela.

Following is the case of my client Miguel, a Peruvian who decided to move to the United States 17 years ago:

> I was not planning to come to the United States, but a wealthy man from my country needed my help in some business and because I had my passport I traveled with him by car to go to Los Angeles, California. We traveled for a couple of months, visiting different Central American countries like Costa Rica, Nicaragua, and Honduras. When we finally reached our destination, Los Angeles, I was almost ready to go back to Peru. I missed my wife and child [who is] 2 years of age. Because the need for workers was high, I looked for a job to put together some money to take back to Peru, and with that idea I stayed month after month until my visa expired and I had to make a decision either to stay in this country or go back to Peru. My wife and I talked every week on the phone and she would tell me the pretty things she was buying my child. She sounded happy and my daughter had things I could never have given her in Peru. I made the decision then to stay and be able to give them a better life. Since then 17 years have passed. My wife and I got divorced and I haven't seen my daughter in all this time. I loved my wife but understood she needed to rebuild her life. I have had several relationships, but nothing serious.

In the case of Miguel, although he missed his daughter tremendously, he focused on the benefits of being able to give her an education and made plans to bring her to visit him. He actually learned to be grateful for having given her a good future by remaining in the United States and supporting his daughter and wife.

Loss of Self-Esteem

If a client complains about being rejected, or treated unfairly, because he or she is Hispanic, it is a good idea to evaluate the situation for him or her and ask for examples of situations in which he or she felt that a bias or prejudice was indeed a factor. It would also be helpful to bring to the client's awareness that we are all subject to rejection or hurt by others; as Burns (1999) asserted, "Being rejected and failing are universal human experiences" (p. 69). It is natural for a person to feel disappointed if he or she has failed to achieve a goal; however, clients who consider themselves worthless and disgraceful and give themselves such messages (e.g., through negative self-talk) may destroy their self-esteem (Burns, 1999). Intercultural relationships also can hurt Hispanics' self-esteem. They may find themselves caught between two cultures and at times embarrassed by their culture. If their traditions are not validated, some may experience a sense of loss as well as guilt, especially if the family complains about their absence. Such is the story of Laura, a Salvadoran woman who was dating an Anglo-American:

> I love spending time with him and knowing his friends, but I want to bring him into my world because family for me is very important. He doesn't understand it. He doesn't want to be included in my Latino atmosphere, and that hurts me. My family has started questioning me about his concerns with our culture. He says he loves me but doesn't understand the enmeshment in my family. Now, I feel embarrassed that my family is so clinging. He makes fun of the way I say some things in English. I wish I were not Latina.

Many of my Hispanic clients who are facing the loss of their self-esteem or identity have developed the attitude of the victim, or have become defensive, even aggressive. Their sense of inadequacy is so great that they develop filters to process others' comments, actions, and behaviors. In return, they respond by criticizing "the system," the people around them, and by saying that they are not understood or respected. In some cases this may be true, but the client's responses to these situations will reflect either a proactive or reactive attitude. Counselors who are cognizant of the feelings of grief that a loss of self-esteem may bring about can help their clients assess their loss, focus on their strengths, and reframe their perspective. Every person has valuable skills and qualities. If clients are led to focus on these instead of only being conscious of what they do not have, they will be able to use these strengths as they reevaluate their situation and begin to build a better life for themselves. If they do not learn to refocus on their strengths, it will be very difficult for them to rise from their place of pain, distrust, and grief.

Clients who find themselves responding defensively, or even condemning the person who is hurting them, may be trying to get something positive out of their negative thoughts or comments. A helpful way for your clients to become aware of the feelings arising from their thoughts is to develop the skill of self-observation. Rizzetto (2005) provided insight into what being present in the moment is, with the following example of self-observation: "[A] student reported that he felt as if he had put up a shield of armor around himself. He observed rigidity, anger, and hardness whenever he sensed his self-image threatened" (p. 42). If clients can share these feelings with their therapist, the therapist can work in a more efficient manner, because he or she will know the root cause of the client's anger or grief.

A person with low self-esteem may feel imperfect, worthless, or inept. Some may be unaware of their strengths and may maximize their weaknesses and, possibly, suffer from depression and sadness. One of the negative outcomes of low self-esteem is that the person does not set goals for himself or herself out of a belief that he or she will be unable to reach them (McKay, Davis, & Fanning, 2007). How can you as a counselor work with clients who have low self-esteem? According to McKay, Wood, and Brantley (2007), counselors can work on the following:

- Helping clients discover their automatic thoughts (i.e., what is the first thought that comes to their mind?)
- Changing patterns of thinking that limit them
- Changing hot thoughts
- Testing their core beliefs
- Changing their core beliefs through visualization.

These techniques are part of an approach called dialectical behavior therapy that is linked to CBT. I find this approach very useful because it helps my clients to handle overwhelming emotions by showing them how to use their ability to handle stress and difficulties in an empowering manner.

Another technique that has worked well with my clients to elevate their self-esteem is to focus on their strengths. I like to challenge them with the following statements and question:

- Name three difficult situations you have overcome in your life.
- Name a quality or strength you have that helped you in this situation.
- How could you use that strength in your present situation?

Gloria is a client who came to the United States from Cuba. She came to therapy to share the loss of her marriage. Once she and her husband arrived in Miami, her husband left her. She felt devastated and hopeless, thinking she could not make it on her own. When I asked her to name a quality or strength she has that helped her in past difficult situations, she immediately answered "courage." Then we focused on her courage and how she had been able to overcome difficulties in the past. With some personal work and self-assessment, Gloria decided she would stay in the United States by herself and continue with her plans of starting a new life. She didn't speak English, but she didn't care. She enrolled in English classes and got a job as a cashier at a local market. She empowered herself. Counselors' should aim to help clients to work with the strengths they have, and not to focus on what they are missing.

HELPFUL SUGGESTIONS

- As you do the initial assessment of your Hispanic client remember to include the history of their losses. This will give you an idea of the different transitions they have experienced and how they have processed (or not processed) their grief.
- Your client can give you valuable information about their perception of the different transitions and how they feel about them. If they only talk about their losses at an intellectual level you can be help them to process their losses at an emotional level.
- If your client is a man, ask him how he feels about expressing his grief through tears. If you notice him holding back the tears you can remind him he is in a safe place and that it is OK to cry. He may just need that reassurance to cry and open his heart without reservations.

PERSONAL REFLECTIONS FOR THE COUNSELOR

- Do you understand the different issues that could lower the self-esteem of your Hispanic client?
- What modality do you find most useful when dealing with the loss of homeland. Do you think this loss can be transformed into an occasion to be grateful?
- How can you empower your client to overcome the loss of language? Do you have available resources to suggest to them?

CHAPTER 9

Different Perspectives Through Various Counseling Techniques

Although many people facing a loss are able to cope with the situation, others need a therapist's help to process their grief and handle the emotions provoked by their distress. Therapists use many different perspectives and techniques to help clients go through the grieving process, depending on the training and theoretical orientation. The techniques used depend on the type of loss the client has suffered, his or her personality, and the desired outcome. In this section, I cover some of the most empowering and effective methods for dealing with crisis, emotions, and well-being. You may choose to use one of these different approaches or a combination of one or more.

There are many modalities that can be used in counseling. Kumar (2005) observed that among these one can find "cognitive behavioral, existential, humanistic, psychoanalytical, interpersonal, eclectic, integrative, and so on." Of these, "cognitive behavioral tends to be the most strongly supported empirically" (p. 109). Using this modality, I explore in the following sections different techniques that counselors can use with clients experiencing a loss.

COUNSELING TECHNIQUES

Cognitive Behavioral Therapy

Cognitive behavioral therapy (CBT) is based on three elements: one's (a) thoughts, (b) behaviors, and (c) feelings. According to CBT theorists, people behave or feel according to their thinking. Therefore, if they have negative thoughts, they will likely experience negative emotions. Burns (1999) stated that feelings of sadness and depression result when a person thinks about his or her loss; however, if that person learns to have more positive thoughts, he or she may experience more positive emotions. There are different ways that CBT can be applied to grief counseling. The value of this kind of therapy is that it does not ignore the grieving process but addresses how not to perpetuate thoughts that could foster negative feelings or cause catastrophic thinking. CBT as applied to grief focuses more on helping the client move forward. Schupp (2007) cited behavioral theorists such as Albert Ellis and Aaron Beck as pioneers of this theory that has been primarily used with depressed people and those suffering from posttraumatic stress disorder.

There are different ways to keep track of our emotions and understand how they may be a product of our thinking. In this section I include a technique I use with some of my clients that has helped them see how their thinking process can cause negative emotions. If they can learn to shift their thoughts or perceptions, they can be in a better emotional space. Consider the case of Juana, a Cuban woman who came to see me after the loss of her husband, Manuel. She felt constant guilt after his death because although he had made her promise that she would take his ashes to Cuba to bury them, she did not. I asked her to describe on paper what had happened (the event), what her thoughts were, how she felt about the event, and what actions she took. After this process, I asked her to reframe her perspective as an observer and recount her story.

The event
    Juana's husband was buried in Miami, Florida.

Thoughts about the event
    I failed Manuel. I promised to take him to Cuba and did not keep my
        promise.
    I failed him as a wife.

What emotions did you experience?
    I feel guilty I didn't carry out my promise. I feel I failed him.

Now, recount the story as an outsider.

    Juana was married 58 years with Manuel and had a wonderful life with him. Manuel was a gentle and hard-working man. They were just 10 years married when they came to Miami, Florida, owing to the situation in Cuba with the revolution. However, Manuel always had the desire to go back. He always told Juana that when he died, she had to take his ashes to Cuba. Juana told him she would do it because she didn't want to upset him. Manuel recently died of lung cancer and his last words were, "Remember to take my ashes back to Cuba." Juana did not have any other option than agreeing with him, but in reality she is too old to travel and this would be a very difficult task for her. She is 88 years old and [it is not possible] to go to Cuba. She doesn't have family there or the resources to go. Manuel knows that deep in her heart she wishes she could honor his wishes, but it is just impossible for her. She is sure he can forgive her because for 58 years she was totally devoted to him and made him very happy.

As you can see, Juana's perception of her situation and herself changed from thinking she was not a good wife to recognizing that she had been a good wife even though she could not honor Manuel's wishes, despite her desire to do so. She found value in her steadfast love for him for 58 years and found peace in her heart by accepting that she could not carry out his wishes.

The main focus of CBT is on the correlation of problematic beliefs and behaviors and the resulting psychological issues. Moreover, CBT reveals how these psychological difficulties are maintained. The purpose of this therapy is to change eventually a person's beliefs to produce a more positive outcome (Ledley et al., 2005). CBT helps clients accept that the way they perceive and interpret some of their experiences may be detrimental to their mental health.

In defining CBT I offer the following sequence:

- The person ascribes meaning to an event according to his or her own perception of reality.
- Cognition has an influence on emotions and behaviors.
- Our thoughts (or cognition) can be accessed (and therefore altered).
- Changing our thoughts is key to changing ourselves.

When using CBT with a client, Ledley et al. (2005, p. 105) proposed that therapists do the following:

- Collaboratively set the session agenda.
- Review homework.

- Conduct the main session content based on a specified treatment plan.
- Assign new homework (usually based on the main session content).
- Summarize the session with the client (ask the client what he or she learned).
- Check in with the client (does he or she have any issues, concerns, or other issues to discuss?).

I use a very similar approach and find that this agenda works very well with clients going through a loss. I always provide homework (I call them *reflective exercises*) for clients in between sessions. In general, these exercises include journaling, keeping a record of their emotions, writing letters and poems, or scrapbooking.

Although some therapists and clients believe that CBT does not take into consideration the client's past, this is not accurate. As Ledley et al. (2005) observed, "Clinicians who do CBT are most definitely interested in the connection between past experiences and current beliefs and behaviors" (p. 132). Therefore, as we have seen, CBT is an exceptionally useful tool for empowering your clients because it offers hope: Just as certain beliefs and behaviors can be learned, they can also be unlearned.

Positive Psychology

In 1954, Abraham Maslow introduced the term *positive psychology*. His focus was on giving more importance to the strengths of human beings than to their weaknesses (Lopez & Snyder, 2009). Hence, to value and enhance strengths, and not focus on weaknesses, has been the approach of many professionals in positive psychology, including "visionaries in psychiatry such as Karl Menninger, and business gurus, notably Peter Drucker" (Lopez & Snyder, 2009, p. 4). The purpose in positive psychology has been to help people utilize all aspects of themselves and develop to their full potential, even in the midst of loss and grief, as Lopez and Snyder (2009) argued:

> Prolonged negative situations like bereavement or joblessness evoke negative emotions but often cannot be solved by the kind of immediately, narrowly defined action that negative emotions encourage. Consistent with this view, studies have shown that grieving individuals who experienced some level of positive emotions alongside their negative ones showed greater psychological well-being a year or more later and that this occurs partly because positive emotions were

associated with the ability to take a longer view and develop plans and goals for the future. (p. 18)

If you share with your clients different ways to cope with their losses and help them focus more on what they have instead of what they are missing, you can help them find some joy in their lives, even in the midst of a crisis or loss. One of the suggestions I give to my clients is that each night, just before going to bed, they write a list of three things they were grateful for that day. In the case of the death of a loved one, I ask them to write a list of things they have in their lives, or experiences they have lived, because the deceased person was in their lives. Their loved one may not be with them physically, but their memory will always be in their hearts, and for this the client can be grateful.

Some clients respond that, because of the loss they are experiencing, they don't have anything to feel grateful for. They may respond this way at first, which is fine. The idea is not to rush them but to make them aware that just being alive, or having a roof over their head, or having someone who loves them, are reasons enough to be grateful. Then, I ask them to expand the list of things they are grateful for. Little by little, as they go through their grieving process, they find strength and inspiration from what they still have in their lives after their loss.

Family Systems Therapy

In defining family systems theory, Rosenblatt (2009) stated that rules exist in families and that these rules are played out when a loss of great importance occurs. I find this kind of therapy very valuable, mainly because *familismo* is one of the salient characteristics of Hispanic culture. As Conoley and Conoley (2009) suggested, it is a good idea to let the family know that family systems therapy could help them when a family member is going through a loss:

> Family therapy is a way to help each person in the family reach his or her goals using the strength of the family. Family therapy helps the family help the person or more than one person who is having problems. (p. 116)

Family is one of the strongest resources Hispanics have in their lives; therefore, a specific therapy that is helpful in working with this population is *positive family therapy* (Conoley & Conoley, 2009), which combines "systems theory and positive psychology to derive an approach that builds upon the strengths of a family to enhance the growth of each individual member" (p. 1). This is a useful and meaningful approach to use with this cultural group. Hispanics depend very much on the interaction of their family members and on the family system. Because Hispanics tend to have larger families, with 19% having three or more children living at home and almost two-thirds having two parents in the home, the entire family system may be influenced and altered after a loss (Sullivan, 2002).

Part of the initial counseling assessment should include a section dedicated just to the family. The following questions may be included in the initial assessment:

- Who is the head of your family?
- Are you close to your mother? To your father?
- Do you live with your family or by yourself?
- Do you make decisions independently, or do you consult with your family?
- Do you share your problems with your family?
- Do you feel your family supports you?
- What is the most important value for your family?
- Do you share the same value?

When a family experiences a loss, the family members interact in ways that can bring meaning to their common experience. For example, if the family thinks that death could have been prevented, much of their energy will be invested in figuring out how they could have prevented the death (Nadeau, 2002). I recently had the opportunity to work with a family who had experienced the loss of a loved one. Each member was processing the grief in a different manner, and consequently, instead of growing closer they were growing apart. Each one of them was hiding their real emotions from the other family members because they didn't want to cause anyone more grief. Their way of grieving was based on protecting one another. When I presented to them the value of expressing their emotions and grieving together as a family, sharing their experience to find meaning in their grief, their reaction was quite different. Their behavior changed. They were more relaxed and natural. They cried together and laughed together. Moreover, we explored other occasions when they had easily overcome losses and how they had used their strengths as a family to deal with the situation and grow stronger.

In one sense this type of process involves a *life review*, which I discuss in more detail later in this chapter. Garland and Garland (2001) found the life review, which "draws on autobiographical memory and focuses on reminiscence to maintain or modify coping strategies" (p. 3), to be a valuable tool in therapy. In doing a life review, the counselor can gain a better idea of the history of the family and how the family dynamic works as well as what has been meaningful to the family members, what losses they have experienced, and other relevant information, such as how long they have lived in the United States.

Another valuable tool for family therapy is the *genogram*, a graphic representation of the members of a family, using a family tree format. This technique can clarify the dynamic of the family relationships and show how to engage the family in therapy. It is used as a "graphic way of organizing the mass of information gathered during a family assessment and finding patterns in the family system for more targeted treatment" (McGoldrick, Gerson, & Petry, 2008, p. 388). Counselors can use a life review and/or a genogram in conjunction with the traditional approach to assist in the healing process.

One of the main concepts to be considered when doing family therapy is the rules by which the members play. In the case of Hispanic immigrants, many times the family separates from the children, with the mother emigrating first, and then the father. What is the effect on the family when the father is the head of the family and the teenage children pay attention to him? What if the mother never worked in her country of origin and finds herself in the United States functioning as both father and mother, and supporting her children? Who sets the rules to follow?

The therapist must understand this aspect of the client's family dynamic to work effectively with the strengths of the family unit in the bereavement process.

SPECIAL FACTORS TO CONSIDER WHEN COUNSELING GRIEVING HISPANICS

Grandparent–Grandchild Relationships

The presence of the grandparents is very common in the everyday lives of Hispanics—to the extent that many times they live in the same household. In many instances the grandparents leave their country of origin and move to the United States to take care of their grandchildren while the parents work. In other cases, according to De Vries, Blieszner, and Blando (2002), grandparents in the United States may not be "integrally involved in the daily lives of their grandchildren, [but] they are available and on call when the need arises" (p. 230). A grandmother reported such a situation to me in one session:

> When I was told Carlitos (her grandson) had leukemia, I immediately took the plane and moved to Miami. I had a small business in El Salvador, but I didn't care. My daughter needed me. They were long months sitting next to the child's deathbed, until he died. Someone mentioned to us a service called hospice, but we didn't know what it was. We heard that some people would come home and take care of Carlitos, but we didn't want strangers in our house. On the other hand, I was worried for Josefina, my daughter, because she wouldn't eat. I even made *pupusas* [a kind of pastry] for her because she loved to eat them as a child. But it was futile. She just wanted to die with her son. I couldn't see her going through that pain. I wished I could take it all inside of me. It is the worst to see your child suffering. At times I wanted to take her back to El Salvador with me. At least she would have the rest of the family there. Here it was only the two of us. It made it worse. There is nothing like family. I regret I didn't oppose Josefina's decision to come to the United States. Maybe this wouldn't have happened.

Hispanics depend very much on the interaction of their family members, and they are deeply affected when something happens to a member of the family. It is common that everybody gets involved and wants to help. Consider the case of Manuel, an 18-year-old man who comes from a large Mexican family and recently lost his job. He is totally at a loss and doesn't know what to do. He is embarrassed to let his mother know about his job loss because it would be shameful. He is complaining of anxiety attacks and a sensation of lethargy. Manuel is thinking of leaving his home and joining *una ganga* [a gang]. Coming from the perspective of the family as a unit, the counselor could explore doing family therapy and ask the members of the family to work together using their strengths to support Manuel. On one occasion Manuel mentioned his grandfather, Julio, who lives in Mexico City. Although Julio is not with him physically, he is respected and included in many of the family decisions. Now, with the technological advances of computer communication such as Skype, Julio can be included in family systems therapy.

Counselors need to remember the role family has in most Hispanics' lives, including the extended family, because the nuclear and extended family are sources "of identity, cohesiveness and support . . . and are generally viewed as increasing relational resources, and therefore better for psychological well-being" (Scharwzbaum, 2008, p. 68).

Consider the case of Lucia. Despite many good things happening in her life, she misses her family and the traditions of her country, Perú. When her husband, Carlos, told Lucia he had been promoted, she was extremely happy. She assumed his new position was in the new building outside Lima. But when Carlos announced the new job was in Manhattan, New York, she felt as though her world had shattered. Although it was an incredible opportunity, she didn't want to leave Perú. Her mother was 90 years old and fragile and needed her help. Her two sisters worked, and it was Lucia who took care of her mother. Lucia explained her dilemma to her husband, but Carlos wanted to embrace this opportunity and promised her she would be able to travel back to Perú any time she wanted. Because Lucia was a loyal wife and wanted to support her husband, she agreed and left with Carlos for New York. As she embarked on the plane she started feeling nauseated but assumed it was because of her fear of flying. When they arrived in New York she went through a frenzy looking for an apartment and furniture and getting settled in their new home. Throughout this time she had some episodes of dizziness but didn't pay attention. She was too busy. However, Lucia started complaining about headaches and dizziness on a regular basis. She went to different doctors, but couldn't find any physical reason for her complaints. She spent her days in her beautiful apartment, by herself, while her husband worked until late at night. He wanted to demonstrate to his superiors that he was a loyal employee and an asset to the company. Lucia, on the other hand would have preferred to share more time with her husband and have a sense of family, as she used to have in her beloved Perú. This case is a perfect example where the counselor can apply any of the techniques mentioned in this chapter to help Lucia process her grief and reframe her perspective.

Reflections for the Counselor

What is the counselor to do in Lucia's case?
Which of the techniques proposed in this chapter would help Lucia process her grief and reframe her perspective?

Social Support

Social support has been studied in many cultures and ethnic groups. Close personal relationships are quite beneficial, and engaging such support when one is dealing with a stressful event is a very helpful coping strategy.

Friendships and sources of social support seem to be strengthened when a person is experiencing grief if he or she shares his emotions and feels understood by others. However, expressions of social support may differ in "well-functioning families across ethnic groups and acculturation experiences" (Chaos, 1994, 2001, as cited in Conoley & Conoley, 2009, p. 65). Hispanics usually get much of their social support from their family members because they have a great sense of interdependence and family values, which become more pertinent in a loss or crisis. However, they also value the presence and support of friends and others who can understand them.

As Murphy and Price (1998) stated, "All people who experience significant loss should have support and practical assistance" (p. 120). One of the greatest services counselors can provide to their Hispanic clients is to inform them of resources that can be helpful for their situation, such as support groups in Spanish, immigration lawyers, schools that offer continuing education, and vocational schools. In cases of domestic violence, counselors can provide information about shelters or victim centers. These social resources can bring more quality to clients' lives as they face or go through a loss. Sometimes clients do not take action because they do not know that they have options and therefore may sink deeper into their sense of loss and despair. A good counselor works as a coach to help his or her clients become the best individuals they can be and guide them in how to achieve their goals by using their inner resources and the services that are available to them.

MEANING RECONSTRUCTION: TECHNIQUES TO HELP CLIENTS WORK THROUGH THEIR LOSS

One of the most compelling ways to work with the bereaved is the approach introduced by Robert Neimeyer, the pioneer of the meaning-making perspective. I especially share his philosophy of the value for the bereaved of making sense of their loss. When one faces a loss owing to death or illness, for example, he or she may begin a search for meaning, for making sense, so they can find "a way to restore order to the universe or accept that there is no order" (Godfrey, 2006, p. 7). Neimeyer (2001) suggested that to understand the personal narrative of the grieving individual, therapists need to pay attention to the language clients use as they tell their stories. Stories tell who we are, where we come from, and how we make sense of what has happened to us. Counselors who pay close attention to their clients' narratives can understand better their worldview. Neimeyer drew on the constructivist approach to psychology to evaluate how "it views the human effort after meaning, how it understands the complications introduced into this quest by profound loss, and how psychotherapists might intervene to assist grieving people with this essential struggle" (p. 262). In discussing grief related to death, and how survivors must relearn the world by continuing to live in it without the lost loved one, Thomas Attig stated that the search of the bereaved for meaning is multidimensional in that it involves "simultaneously finding and making meaning on many levels" (Corr et al., 2008, p. 231). Therefore, as people grieve, they can find meaning in their actions and suffering and thus can relearn the world.

Some of the tools your clients can use when telling their stories and searching for the meaning of their loss include a narrative essay, life review, history of losses, scrapbooking, and journals. In the following sections I discuss each of these techniques.

Narrative Essay

When using the narrative essay technique, you can ask your client to write a story about the loss he or she is experiencing. As the client writes the story, ask him or her to focus on what he or she experienced. In this narrative essay the client could also include the family's experience—what was expected of the family members. The client can also describe what it has been like to experience this loss in a country that is not his or her homeland. He or she could also rewrite the story as if he or she had experienced it in his or her homeland.

Life Review

With the life review technique, one tries to revisit one's life since childhood. The client recalls happy and sad memories and the most important life events. You could use color codes to identify the emotions linked to various life events. As the client sees the different colors, he or she will realize that in life people encounter many situations that provoke different feelings. The purpose of using color in the life review technique is to help the client realize that life is a mosaic of hues.

History of Losses

I find the history-of-losses exercise very valuable when I conduct the first assessment of a client. In this history, clients basically revisit the losses they have experienced since they were children. Many clients assume that losses refer only to death of a loved one, but I explain to them that loss also includes other events, such as natural disasters, moving, loss of a pet, illnesses, and divorce of one's parents. Besides stating the loss, I ask them to write how they felt about the experience, who was with them, and how they coped with it. Many times clients can find a pattern regarding how they have coped with losses and, if the coping has been dysfunctional, they learn to handle it in a more meaningful way.

The following are examples on how to do a history of losses. You can show these to your clients and see which one resonates most with them. Some clients are more visual than others, and in this case the graphic is more appealing to them.

History of losses

	Yes	No
• Loss of a loved one		
• Loss of health		
• Loss of a job		
• Divorce		
• Loss of freedom to return to country of origin		
• Loss of identity		
• Loss of self-esteem		
• Loss of language		
• Loss of traditions		
• Loss of homeland		

Scrapbooking

Scrapbooking is a technique that works beautifully with families, but many Hispanics are not familiar with this activity. Therefore, I keep a scrapbook in my office, and I show clients how they can do one individually or as a family activity. They can paste pictures in a scrapbook, write their thoughts about the pictures, write poems, or even paste stickers. Many of my clients enjoy this activity very much.

Journals

At the beginning of this chapter, I described how to keep a journal. You can suggest to clients to write how they feel in the journal to express their emotions.

THE BODY–MIND–SPIRIT PERSPECTIVE

The body is a vehicle with which we express emotions. If we are tense or uptight, we may suffer from headaches, stomachaches, or rising blood pressure. The body is very sensitive to the way we are feeling inside, which is what the term *somatization* refers to (*soma* means "body" in Greek). Linda Hartley, in her book *Somatic Psychology: Body, Mind and Meaning* (2004), gave a well-rounded definition of *somatics*:

> The term somatics was introduced in modern psychology by Thomas Hanna with his book *Bodies in Revolt*. The Greek word soma is defined as "the body experienced from within" and reflects the efforts of modern bodywork practitioners and somatic movements' therapists to move away from the dualistic splitting of mind from body, towards a model of integrated functioning of the whole person, psyche and soma. (p. 11)

Many mental health practitioners, including myself, use yoga in their professional practices as a way to help clients relax and get in touch with their bodies. Whittington (2009) said she finds in yoga a medium through which the bereaved can become aware of the emotions they experience and reduce their suffering through "awareness and compassion for the grieving body" (p. 15).

In my work with clients I incorporate a holistic approach that embodies body, mind, and spirit because spirituality is a vital aspect of many people's well-being, providing them with a sense of balance in their lives and helping to keep them centered. Lee, Ng, Leung, and Chan (2009) observed the benefit of integrating the values of their clients: "Individuals have a greater ability to endure hardships and persevere through difficult moments in life when they are reconnected with their values and their spirituality" (p. 117). For example, asking clients and their families about their values and whether they act on them can really help them to feel empowered and to focus on their strength. Lee et al. offered the following example:

> We ask them, "What are some of the things that you have done that greatly energized you? What happened at that time . . . What values underlie these actions? What do you anticipate will happen when you engage in these activities or behaviors again? Is there anything that you can think of right now that will help you to reconnect with those values?" (p. 117)

Meditation

Meditation is a valuable technique to bring peace and harmony to oneself, including as one experiences grief. It involves special breathing techniques that help us be aware of our thinking and our emotions. These techniques can be used when one feels afraid or is experiencing negative emotions: "They are designed to help people develop physiological awareness, positive habitual thoughts, and appropriate emotion regulation" (Peterson & Seligman, 2004, p. 227). I like to use breathing techniques with clients as they rest on a recliner. I ask them to inhale positive emotions, such as feelings of peace, calm, and love, for a count of seven; hold the breath for a count of four; and then exhale negative feelings produced by grief, such as anxiety, sadness, or depression, for a count of eight. After they do this for three or four times, I remind them that they can do this exercise at home—or anywhere—when they feel especially stressed or anxious. I have also done this technique in groups, including with a group of elderly Hispanic women, and I always receive a positive response. The clients feel a tremendous relief and sense of well-being.

I also use with my clients guided meditation for different kinds of losses, including the loss of loved ones. I share the case of Alex, a 44-year-old Cuban man who lost his 15-year-old son. After one of the visualizations he experienced during my guided meditation, he wrote the following in his journal:

9/2/2009

Today's meditation was much like many others [in] that while the scene was familiar, the events are always different. Slipping into a meditative state I was drawn to a lake surrounded by a green valley and in the distance was a castle-like structure made of a brilliant shiny substance that I am unfamiliar with. As I walked along a golden path that led me to the castle the lake was on my right side. The doors of the castle were well over twenty feet high and seemed to be made of silver. As I entered into an open space I saw my son, Andrew, on the third floor, and he came running down excitedly yelling, "Dad, you're here!" We met on the second floor, hugged, and we both gazed out a window into the distance at the edge of the lake. In an instant we were transported and were swimming together in the lake. Andy turned to me and said, "Dad go under water, you can breathe."

We swam for a short while but suddenly we were transported to the edge of the lake, and we began to walk along the golden path in a direction away from the castle. As we approached a forest my Lord, Jesus, stood there waiting for us. He stood well over nine feet tall, [and] wore a marvelous long white tunic. His skin was light bronze and his face long and slender; it resembled my brother's when he was younger. His hair was a perfect wavy golden brown and was parted at the center. On this day I couldn't make out what he was saying to me, but I felt an overwhelming peace that encompassed the area and an aura of love that was breathtaking. He was there to show me my son, as if to say, "See how wonderful he is." I do recall his saying to me on this day, "We wait for you eagerly but first you must still finish your mission." There was not much my Lord had to say to me this day because he had already said it all to me in the morning.

I had gone to bed with a heavy heart and had awoken with the same grieving pain that seemed to not be letting up. Andrew had passed away on April 15th and I was still going through all the pain that someone should experience when your son or daughter had gone home so young and unexpectedly. Last night I was on my knees crying over my son's picture in the family room, and the pain hadn't subsided. For some reason the pain was troubling me on this morning and my mind was full of doubt. I specifically remember saying to God this morning, "My Lord, please don't leave me now, please don't forsake me." His answer came quickly and directly because as I walked into the bathroom to use the restroom I noticed a daily meditation booklet that was handed to me at church that Sunday. It was thrown to the back of the toilet. I bent down to pick it up and opened it to September 2nd and there was God's immediate and impactful answer to my pleading. The verse for the day was Hebrews 13:5 and the book stated: God has said, "Never will I leave you, never will I forsake you."

All I could do was smile in amazement, look up to the ceiling with my eyes in tears and a heart of gratitude and say, "Lord, you are amazing." He has robed me with his Grace, is filling me with his love, reassuring me with his word, all to relieve me from the pain and anguish of the loss of my son Andrew. How special must I be to him! How special must we all be! But most incredible, how special must he be that though we have turned our backs on him a thousand times he has always been there, in the wings, waiting to reassure us and restore us.

Alex has kept a journal with the meditations he has done at my office. When he is by himself at home, he finds great solace and comfort in this activity and uses it as a complement to prayer. You can incorporate meditation with your clients in different ways, whether through guided meditation, breathing techniques (e.g., belly breathing), or just repeating a mantra, such as "Om, peace. . . ." or visualizing a white light to bring peace.

In my book *Transform Your Loss: Your Guide to Strength and Hope* (Houben, 2009) I have included meditations and affirmations for each of my Eleven Principles of Transformation. In addition, the guided meditation CD, "Momentos de Reflexión" [Moments of Reflection], contains all these meditations so that the reader can use it as a guiding companion.

Mindfulness

Grief is experienced not only after the death of a loved one but also after other losses, such as careers, relationships, or physical activities. In an 8-week program, David Sagula and Kenneth G. Rice used mindfulness meditation to determine whether this technique was helpful in the grieving process of 39 patients who suffered from chronic pain. The results showed that the treatment group versus the comparison group moved faster through the initial stages of the grieving process, and the treatment group showed greater reduction in anxiety and depression (Sagula & Rice, 2004).

As we start cultivating and practicing mindfulness, we can really see a difference in our lives, as Jon Kabat-Zinn (1990) observed:

> Mindfulness can serve as a doorway into a profound way of knowing ourselves better and for mobilizing the inner resources we all have, no matter what our situation and our condition, for learning, for growing, for healing, and for transformation across the life span, starting from where we find ourselves, no matter where or how that is. (p. xxvviii)

Prayer

Larry Dossey, MD, in *Healing Words: The Power of Prayer and the Practice of Medicine* (1993), expanded on the power of acceptance as one confronts a disease, including cancer, to the point of not being worried about any outcome. Dossey referred to the power of prayerfulness in acceptance, which he said is

> [a] kind of action that bears little resemblance to the showy activity to which we are accustomed. This quiet, inner-directed action is acknowledged in many spiritual traditions as the highest form of activity in which humans can engage, and is almost identical with some forms of prayer. Prayerfulness . . . is accepting without being passive, is grateful without giving up. (p. 24)

THE ELEVEN PRINCIPLES OF TRANSFORMATION

Using a body–mind–spirit perspective and inspired by the works of Worden (2002), Kumar (2005), Neimeyer (1998), and Burns (1999), I created a system for people experiencing a loss called The Eleven Principles of Transformation—a strategy for moving beyond grief. The purpose of these principles is to offer a guide to growth through the grieving process that can bring about personal transformation. In working with bereaved persons facing various life transitions, I have found empowerment to be an essential component to help clients continue to live a meaningful, fulfilling life after their loss. This can be a lengthy process, depending on the kind of loss and the person's inner resources, but with care, empathy, and compassion it is possible to transform a person's loss and change him or her. I had introduced these principles in my book *Transform your Loss: Your Guide to Strength and Hope* (Houben, 2009). The Eleven Principles of Transformation™ are applicable to any kind of loss and can be used individually or in group settings. This system has already been used for bereavement support groups (e.g., in Nicaragua) as well as in a group of retired women, for adult children grieving the aging of their parents, and people going through divorce. Furthermore, many immigrants who are grieving the loss of their homeland are using these principles on a personal level, with meaningful results. The following is the testimony of Carla, a Venezuelan who has greatly suffered the loss of her homeland and who found it difficult to express her grief:

> Here I am, crying a pain I discovered I haven't processed before. I wrote a letter, as you recommended, and it certainly helps a lot. What an interesting experience when one thinks she knows everything . . . and doesn't know anything. Thank you. Really . . . The Eleven Principles work.

Kessler (2004) used the image of a map to describe the course of grief. First, she said, is the protection stage, in which the person may experience shock and denial. Then the person may experience emotions such as anger, fear, guilt/shame, or sadness. Then comes a stage of healing, in which the person experiences acceptance and hope and knows the ups and downs of the grieving process (Kessler described this as the *landscape* of the map). The person understands that time by itself will not heal grief and that he or she can make a transformation from grief to personal growth. I find this last part to be the core essence of the process because I believe that, with the appropriate resources and tools, the bereaved can transform their loss into personal and spiritual growth and change their lives. Kessler found that expressing one's feelings is essential for the transformation process. I also consider this to be essential for transformation to occur. However, there is a slight difference in our approaches, Kessler thinks that acceptance occurs after the expression of the feelings, whereas I find acceptance to be the first step for transformation to occur. This is why I placed acceptance as Principle I. In the following sections I describe each of the Eleven Principles of Transformation.

Principle I: Accept Your Loss

When facing a severe loss, people can use several strategies to maintain a sense of control in their lives. These strategies, according to Harvey and Miller (2000), include the following:

> Acceptance, changing to reachable goals, finding and creating control, and using humor . . . acceptance or secondary control involves being satisfied with one's situation as it is and accommodating oneself to the loss. Finding benefits and meaning in the loss and in one's current life situation make it easier to accept one's current circumstances. (p. 139)

To transform any loss or transition, we need to recognize what has happened to us, embrace it, and make it our reality. For Hispanics this can be a challenge when they miss their home country and need to adjust to their new cultural environment. Some may still hold on to the idea of the homeland they remember and long to be back there. At times, they do not assimilate to their new society because they still have the illusion or hope of going back home, and thus they do not develop a sense of identity in the new culture. Some people have a problem with the word *acceptance* because they consider it to be like conformity, and so they take a passive position. I believe, however, that making the decision to accept one's situation is indeed taking action. A person who simply continues to complain and dwell on the past may prevent growth from taking place. According to McKay et al. (2007), the term *radical acceptance* in dialectical behavioral therapy means accepting "something completely, without judging it" (p. 51). Kamet (2005), in *Grieving Mindfully: A Compassionate and Spiritual Guide to Coping With Loss*, also tapped into the spiritual dimension in regard to dealing with loss and stated that the more one practices mindfulness, the better one can understand the concept of radical acceptance. McKay et al. also contended that this does not mean that a person should just give up and accept everything that happens to him or her but emphasized that it gives the person the "opportunity to respond to that situation in a new way that's less painful" (p. 51) for himself or herself and others. McKay et al. included the Serenity Prayer, written by Reinhold Niebuhr and widely known, as an example of acceptance. I include it here because it is truly an excellent example of real acceptance: "Grant me the serenity to accept the things I cannot change, the courage to change the things I can, and the wisdom to know the difference."

In my book *Transform Your Loss: Your Guide to Strength and Hope* (Houben, 2009) I include a meditation for each principle. This is the meditation for Principle I:

> By confronting my loss and accepting that I am starting a new stage in my life, I have been able to acknowledge that I have the capacity to keep loving and to transform my life. I understand that I have painful memories and moments of doubt; however, I do not fear them. They are not easy to confront, but I will embrace them and make them mine. They are a part of the process of accepting this new dimension in my life. I have realized that I suffer such pain because I have a great ability to love and feel. (p. 265)

Principle II: Live Your Grief

We as humans are unique; therefore, our experience of grief is unique. We cannot expect our clients to go through the process of grieving by experiencing the same emotions or reacting the same way when dealing with those emotions. However, we can offer our guidance to help them work through some of their feelings. Clients need to be assured that their emotions are normal and that they can change. At times, clients may be numb, not feeling anything. At other times, they may feel angry and become sad afterward. Grief can be like a rollercoaster, but it is only when one goes through the *gate of grief*, as Dale Young called it (Bereavement Training, 2010), that a person will be able to come to terms with his or her loss. Some people may prevent themselves from walking through this gate because of alcohol abuse, withdrawal, isolation, excess work or recreation, or other reasons.

I find it essential for bereaved clients to be able to name their emotions and describe how they feel about them and how they express them. For example, anger may be expressed by screaming or hitting; anxiety by an uneasy feeling in the stomach, cold sweats, or a fast heart rate; and sadness by crying (Spradlin, 2003). As mentioned earlier, it is valuable for clients to be aware of their thought processes and how these affect their sense of loss. For example, with the loss of their homeland, clients may talk about their native country, what they remember, what made it so special, and how they miss it. They could use the narrative essay as a valuable tool to express what they miss the most. If a person can write or talk about his or her loss, he or she can face it and embrace the new situation.

It is important to realize that what is ignored does not go away. However, some clients, like in the case of Rosa, who lost her husband, may avoid situations in order to repress their painful emotions. She shared the following with me one day as we started our session:

> At times I fear to come here because I will have to face the death of Ramiro and will have to feel the pain. I don't want to feel it! I don't want to talk about him or think he is not alive! I prefer to stay at home and have a glass of wine. At least with the wine I get relaxed and forget about it.

Rosa's comments are not unusual, and the best we can do as therapists is to allow clients to share how they feel. That is a way for them to express their emotion. In my self-help book, *Transform Your Loss: Your Guide to Strength and Hope*, I offered the following suggestion:

> It is common that when you are dealing with a loss, you avoid confronting or experiencing your feelings, as they can be too painful or even ambivalent. To deal with your emotions may be so painful that you avoid talking about your pain. But it is necessary to search deep

within yourself until you are somehow able to experience your real feelings. (p. 269)

To help bereaved clients deal with their emotions you might ask them to answer the following questions in their journal (Houben, 2009, p. 273):

- What am I feeling at this moment, physically, spiritually, and emotionally?
- What made me feel this way?
- How do I try to hide my feelings:
  - with alcohol or drugs?
  - with excessive work or exercise?
  - by sitting in front of the television or computer for hours?
  - or by just not talking about the loss?

Principle III: Go Deeper Into the Spiritual Dimension

The spiritual aspect of the individual is a special source of strength and hope when that person experiences a loss or crisis. In chapter 4, I discussed how prevalent religion is in the lives of many Hispanics. In this principle I suggest, besides religiosity, some spiritual tools that may help the bereaved in their process of transformation.

With this principle, the therapist and the client explore the benefits of integrating positive elements into the grieving process. Among the emotions I find to be especially helpful are hope, love, forgiveness, and gratitude. Hope is what moves us to find new ways and means of coping after a loss or transition. I like to work with clients on their personal strengths and resources and see how they can apply them and start to live again with purpose. Hope may mean different things for your clients, according to their personal situation of loss, and it changes as the situation changes. Explore with your clients how they would like to see themselves in the future, and use some visualization techniques with them. For example, if a client tells you that he or she wants to be happy again, you can take the client through the following journey:

Close your eyes and imagine yourself a year from now. You find yourself in a wonderful place and you are experiencing a complete sense of joy. Where are you? Imagine the place in your mind very vividly. What are the predominant colors, the smell, the sounds you hear?

Now, make the colors brighter, the smells stronger, and the sounds louder, but still pleasant to the ear. You feel tremendous joy inside. You feel centered. You feel happy. Get into that emotion. Allow this happiness to envelop you like a cloud of white light, and know that nothing can disturb your happiness now. Take a deep breath and inhale that sensation of happiness into your being. Now, slowly, take another deep breath and slowly open your eyes.

When I talk about forgiveness, I mean not only forgiving others but also ourselves. Some clients may recriminate themselves for acting in a certain way, even if it's not their fault. Consider the case of Marisol, a woman who felt guilty for leaving her mother in Perú:

I moved to the United States when I was very young, despite my mother's advice. She didn't want me to come here, but I wanted to have a better life. A whole year passed before we talked on the phone. She was really upset with me, but finally she forgave me and we rebuilt our mother–daughter relationship. Each week my mother asked me to go back to Perú and visit her because she was not feeling too well. With the demands of school and work I couldn't plan to go before Christmas. One night, at 11:48 p.m., the phone rang. It was my brother, to let me know my mother had passed away. I didn't get to see her before she died. She knew. . . . she knew!!! I will never be able to forgive myself!

Counselors can work with their clients as they experience feelings of guilt. One of the most meaningful resources I have found for doing so is writing a letter of forgiveness to oneself. Such a letter can be very healing; clients can let go of the negative emotions that may hinder their grieving process and at the same time allow feelings of gratitude to emerge.

For some people, finding a reason to be grateful may be challenging, but as the bereaved work through their feelings of grief while appreciating what they still have in their lives, they can generate positive feelings. This may be beneficial in the healing process.

The following meditation may help your clients expand their spiritual dimension:

In my times of distress I just need to close my eyes and look inside myself. I seek the deepest part of my being, to charge myself with the spiritual gifts that I possess. Within me reside pure feelings that provide me with peace and hope. I let God penetrate my life and deliver me from my sorrow. I know that my faith in Him will help me move forward, step by step, along the path of my grief. (Houben, 2009, pp. 281–282)

Principle IV: Express Your Feelings

Once clients are able to get in touch with their feelings, they can learn how to express them in a useful manner. Some of your clients may have been reared in an environment where expressing one's feelings was not appropriate. In the Hispanic culture women tend to be more expressive than men, possibly because from a young age boys receive the message that "Men don't cry." During counseling they may have difficulty talking about their emotions, but the therapist can find ways to help the client talk about their loss with the help of questions such as the following:

In the case of loss of a loss of homeland:
    Tell me about your country? How was it?
In the case of loss of a loved one:
    How did you meet your husband (or wife)?
In the case of loss of identity:
    How was your life in your native country? How is it different here?

When people have problems facing their grief, they may prefer to talk about other things to divert attention away from the grief. If the counselor can find a way to start by discussing other things and then slowly guide clients into their real feelings, the opportunity for discussion can occur in a natural and safe manner. This reminds me of the case of Pablo, a Salvadoran who lost his wife. Each time he attended the support group he wanted to talk about only happy memories, because he was afraid to get into his more negative feelings of grief. It was only when another widower from El Salvador started sharing how he missed the *pupusas* [a type of pastry] his wife used to cook for him that Pablo felt strong enough to talk openly.

Principle V: Share With Others

One of the social manifestations of grief may be self-isolation. The person does not want to share how he or she feels and can become detached or immersed in solitary activities such as working to excess, watching television, or spending time at the computer. The more isolated the person is, the less he or she can share with others, perpetuating the problem. This may happen to Hispanics who have not yet established a social network in their new country or whose families are still living in their country of origin. This isolation by itself may be a source of grief and despair. In some instances, family or friends do not want to continue listening to the story of a person's loss. In this case the role of a support group can be of great help for the grieving person because as the client participates in a support group he or she can identify with the loss of another person and find that he or she is not alone. It is common for people facing a loss to believe that they are the only ones experiencing their feelings. A support group helps to normalize these feelings. There are different types of support groups, depending on the loss (Houben, 2009). With so many immigrants in the United States, I strongly suggest the establishment of specific support groups for individuals from the same homeland. However, these should be transformative groups. By this I mean that the purpose behind the group members' sharing of their feelings should be to focus on the strengths they all have to embrace their new situation and start a new life with hope and gratitude and not to simply reminisce about the lost homeland.

Principle VI: Take Care of Yourself

As I explore this principle, I want to call your attention to the process of this system of the 11 principles. They are intended to take the person to an experience of transformation gradually. Although it takes time, it gives the person the opportunity to take an active stand instead of a passive position. The more engaged a person is in the process, the greater will be his or her well-being. Principle VI emphasizes the body–mind–spirit perspective. The counselor can have a positive influence on how clients take care of these three dimensions to find more balance in their lives. They may be too depressed or sad to pay attention to their eating, sleeping, or exercise habits. As a counselor, you can remind them to go to their doctor for a physical checkup or to engage in an exercise routine with the purpose of feeling better physically and emotionally. Yoga is an activity that I highly recommend, as is taking long walks. These activities can also give the bereaved an opportunity to engage in meditation and relaxation exercises. More and more, these types of activities are being embraced by the Hispanic community once they are brought to their attention.

The following affirmations support Principle VI (Houben, 2009, p. 298):

- My body is my temple, which I lovingly care for.
- I feed my body with healthy, nutritious food.
- I participate in physical activities for the health of my body and mind.

- I feel healthy and full of energy.
- I want to grow spiritually.

Principle VII: Use Rituals

Rituals have been used since the beginning of time to bring meaning to our lives. We engage in different types of rituals, such as birthdays, religious festivals, holidays, and the ultimate ritual: the funeral. In my book I provided the following explanation:

> A ritual is a ceremony that holds some special personal or community meaning . . . they generally have one common element in terms of meaning and purpose: to make us feel good, and in many cases, to maintain family traditions. (Houben, 2009, p. 299)

Rituals may mean different things to different people, especially if they belong to a particular culture. Counselors who take a multicultural perspective may want to learn about common Hispanic rituals and what they mean at a personal and communal level.

Clients may want to perform a ritual to let go of negative emotions, embracing new situations, or honoring their loved ones. I suggest the following ritual for the loss of a loved one. It can bring a sense of connection and love to the bereaved:

> Take a picture of your loved one and place it on a small table with a white candle. When you light the candle, say a prayer or intention on behalf of your loved one (e.g., for peace or release from suffering), give thanks for the love you had and the eternal love you will always feel for them. If you are religious, you can make the following request:
>
> > Dear God, I ask You to fill me with white light and let my whole soul be in communion with my loved one. Give me the peace that I need and may this feeling of peace stay forever in my life. (Houben, 2009, p. 302)

There are other types of rituals, such as journaling, writing a letter, or releasing balloons. Once when I did a seminar with a group of people who had lost their jobs and were fearful of the future, each of them held a balloon in their hands and said the following:

> As I release this balloon, I let go of my fear. I feel lighter and lighter, and the fear goes higher and higher, until I can no longer see it. I am able to face this new stage of my life with hope and confidence.

As they said these words, they all gathered in a circle, holding hands, and did some breathing exercises. They shared how empowered and free they felt.

Counselors can be very creative with their clients in performing rituals that resonate with them. It is important to suggest ideas that are congruent with clients' own values and desires, because rituals are symbolic and the more they reflect what the client expects, the more they will represent their healing process.

Principle VIII: Live the Present

People tend to use different mechanisms to cope with loss. One of these mechanisms is to either dwell on the past or think about the future. The impact of losing someone or something dear to you is at times difficult to assimilate into your present life. Consider, for example, a person who had to leave his homeland owing to war. The situation the person was living in was probably unbearable and traumatic, filled with horrific incidents of persecution, fear, and insecurity. As the person longs to be in his homeland because of his intense feelings of grief, he may just remember the good things of the country, such as how nice it was to share with family, to enjoy his native food, and to have a more relaxed lifestyle. This effectively deletes the difficult experiences from the person's memories. People tend to apply what is known as a "mental filter" (Burns, 1999) in relation to their past. When they think about their future, they may see it as black, doomed, and hopeless, with no way out. Instead of focusing on what they have in the present moment, they waste their energy longing for what they had and worrying about what the future will bring. How can you as a therapist help such clients? In the case of missing one's homeland, you can work with these clients in helping them remember the reasons for their departure from their homeland and to be mindful of all the problems they had, and not to remember *only* the happy memories. You can also help them appreciate their present situation and work on ways they can make the best of it. You can teach clients mindfulness, discussed earlier in this chapter, and how to live moment by moment. By writing this I do not mean to imply that clients shouldn't plan for the future, but it is one thing to plan and another to worry. If there are valid issues to worry about, then it is important to face them and take action. You can also work as a coach to help clients find meaning and put together an action plan that will tie in beautifully with the remaining principles.

The following meditation was included in Principle VIII of my book:

> Learning to live in the present is not easy, but it helps me to live fully. I have discovered that I have a source of wisdom and strength not known to me before. I appreciate every experience of every day. I listen to my inner self. My worries and intrusive thoughts are allowed to escape. Living to the fullest each day makes me feel alive. (Houben, 2009, p. 311)

Principle IX: Modify Your Thoughts

When clients find themselves considering this principle, it is expected that they have gone through the previous eight principles, including living their grief. The purpose of this principle is not to avoid the pain produced by the loss (it has already been processed) but to work on how clients' thoughts can empower them to embark again on the journey of life, renewed with hope and possibilities. As I discussed in the "Cognitive Behavioral Therapy" section, our thoughts influence our emotions, which determine our actions. If the client can learn to apply these techniques by stimulating positive emotions based on the messages of their self-talk, they will be more prepared to face their loss in a new light.

You can teach your clients to reframe their thoughts with the following sentences:

- If your client is continually saying, "I cannot live without my beloved." Ask them to repeat the following:
  I will learn to live with my loved one.
- If the client is repeating this phrase, "I cannot move on." Ask them to say the opposite with conviction:
  I can move on!
- If they think the following, "Life is no longer worth anything." Ask them to state with conviction:
  Life is a great gift!

Principle X: Rebuild Your World

At this point, the clients have nearly completed the principles of transformation. They have accepted their loss, lived their grief, developed their spirituality, and learned to express their feelings and communicate with others. They are paying attention to themselves, performing rituals to help them cope, living in the moment, and modifying their thoughts to their benefit and growth. Now is the time to pick up the pieces of their shattered world and rebuild it from scratch. As they have gone through this grief and growth work, clients have developed a strong foundation on which to build a new world after their loss. This means not that the loss has ceased to exist but that the clients have learned how to accommodate it in their new situation; they have learned to live with their loss. This is a process that may vary from person to person, because each of us has our own personality, history of losses, coping skills, and desire to take action.

I believe that as clients rebuild their world the greatest inspiration is to find meaning and purpose. You can work with your clients to help them find their real purpose in life. It is probable that, after facing a loss, some of their values have changed and they have found new things that matter to them. In Appendix B, I have included a list of values that you can use with your clients in rebuilding their world.

Principle XI: Visualize the Life You Want

Earlier in this chapter, I discussed the value of visualization. In our minds, everything is possible. What about your clients? Can they imagine the life they want to live once they have rebuilt their world? It is vital that you remind them that they have choices. As one of my clients, Julia, said to me once: "Ligia, each time I hesitate about something I hear your words saying 'Julia, remember; you have choices,' and then I act on what I think is best for me."

Clients need to feel that you believe in them, that you trust their ability to live a life with purpose and meaning after facing a loss or transition. Grief is the logical response to loss, but it should not be interminable. There is a time to grieve and a time to rejoice. Pain should neither be avoided, nor be perpetuated. As Robert Gary Lee said, "Wisdom is nothing more than healed pain." You want your clients to heal, to enjoy life again after a loss. Work with them. Provide them with tools that will make their path smoother, with more meaning and purpose. We all can transform through a loss. As you witness the transformation of your clients, you too will be transformed.

I leave you with the last meditation of my book:

> My life is a gift and it has great meaning. I understand that my happiness is the result of my decisions and how I relate to myself and others. Therefore, I choose to be happy. By transforming my loss I have acquired the ability to build a life with a greater purpose.

I thank God for my life and for giving me the ability to love and feel. (Houben, 2009, p. 326)

In the following section I include a sample of a holistic assessment that will give you a comprehensive idea of your clients' situation regarding the losses they have endured, the connection they have with their homeland, and how they cope with their losses or transitions.

History of Assessments and Evaluations

Name:
Age:
Country of origin:
Years living in the United States:
Do you have family in the United States?
Do you visit your country of origin?
What do you miss the most from your country?

Coping Mechanisms

	Yes	No
Talking about it		
Praying		
Not thinking about it		
Withdrawing		
Overworking		
Religion		
Family support		
Friends		
Support group		
Aggressiveness		
Drug/alcohol abuse		

Which has been your greatest loss while living in the United States? What has helped you to cope? What hasn't helped you? What would have helped you?

_____

_____

_____

_____

continued

continued

Please describe in a paragraph your loss and the way you handled it.

_____

_____

_____

_____

_____

The following evaluations/techniques could be part of your assessment of the client, and you can have them ready for use based on the loss the person is experiencing or the therapy being used:

- History of losses
- Coping skills
- Strength
- Values
- Social support
- Religious beliefs/spirituality
- Examples of techniques:
  - Exercises in gratitude
  - Exercises in forgiveness
  - Writing in a journal
  - Writing a Letter
  - Making a collage
  - Scrapbooking
  - Life review

HELPFUL SUGGESTIONS

- Depending on the type of loss your clients have experienced, you can use a technique that will be the most meaningful for them. Find a perspective that you find comfortable and use it with your clients. Your clients will perceive whether you feel you can help them and believe in their capacity to heal and grow.
- Be adventurous and try new things. Ask your clients what would make them feel most comfortable in therapy, and be open to integrating innovative systems into your repertoire of techniques. You can only

grow more as a professional by doing so. The more versatile you are in your approach, the more you can accommodate your clients' needs.

- Learn about new modalities; for example, if you are not familiar with the body–mind–spirit approach, read about it, attend seminars, and share with colleagues who are using it. You may be surprised how clients can grow, with your help, as they surpass the acute stage of grief and develop into a person who has been transformed by their loss.

PERSONAL REFLECTIONS FOR THE COUNSELOR

- Do you believe that transformation is possible even in the midst of pain or loss?
- What modalities presented in this chapter resonate with your philosophy?
- How can you use your clients' resources to go through the grieving process and grow because of their experience of loss?

PART III

Hispanic Immigrants:
Are They All the Same?

CHAPTER 10

Assessing Loss Within Hispanic Immigrant Populations

Although space limitations prevent me from providing an in-depth exploration of immigration, it is nevertheless a significant factor in bringing a sense of loss to many Hispanics living in the United States and thus deserves mention. Immigrants from any country can experience many of the losses I discuss in this chapter, but I focus on the Latino perspective. I limit myself to the emotional and spiritual impact of these losses, abstaining from other realms, such as politics, economics, or social services, because it deviates from the purpose of this book. However, compassionate counselors can provide clients with information about other services, in addition to therapy, that could enhance the quality of their lives.

The fact that immigrants go through hardships causing them to grieve-many times in silence-is often ignored. It is in these moments when they need to tell their story, as María Gómez, a social worker employed in hospice care, reminds us:

> There has been too much trauma and loss in the lives of the Hispanics: immigration, losing what they had in their homeland, rebuilding a new life in the adopted country, and at the end of their life, realizing they haven't talked much about death. They were too busy surviving. So, it is very important to ask the Hispanic to share his or her story.

With hope for a better life, or because their current living situation was too difficult to withstand, many people have left their homelands and moved to unknown territories. People from different countries and cultures have come to the United States with the idea of living the "American Dream."

Even though immigration is not a new phenomenon in the United States, newer immigrants face a different situation than those who arrived more than two centuries ago. Now, the United States is worried with the availability of resources even for its own people; therefore, "newcomers are often unwelcome" (Cafferty & Engstrom, 2000, p. xiv). When migrating to another country one may experience many losses, such as "the loss of personal, social, and cultural identity, as well as the loss of familiarity, place, safety, connectedness, and shared history" (Humphrey, 2009, p. 20). Close to one-third of immigrants find it so difficult to adapt to the new culture, or to find what they are looking for, that they move back to their country of origin or to another country (Massey, Alarcon, Durand, & Gonzalez, 1987). A particular challenge in gaining accurate statistics regarding the U.S. Hispanic population is the fact that illegal immigrants do not participate in formal studies or surveys.

Uprooting (i.e., from one culture to a completely different one), according to the World Health Organization, is "the common factor in a number of high-risk stressors such as migration, urbanization, resettlement, and rapid social change" (Falicov, 1998, p. 43). Counselors and health care professionals should be aware of the implications such stress has on the lives of individuals at multiple levels. It is not surprising that uprooting, as Falicov (1998) observed, is related to "substance abuse, depression, crime and delinquency, family conflict and violence, school dropout, and other forms of individual and family breakout" (p. 43).

Many Central and South Americans have left their countries because of unstable political situations and/or issues with safety and civil wars. Many have faced serious challenges in obtaining legal status or asylum in the United States. One of the misconceptions regarding immigrants is that all of them want to stay in the United States. Although this is the case with many immigrants, it is not true of all of them. One of the reasons Hispanics come to the United States is to work, to make some money to send back home to their families, and to save money so that they can eventually go back to their country of origin and start a business. Amparo, a woman from Honduras, worked as a cashier at Publix, the supermarket chain. After more than 20 years of saving every month, she went back to Honduras to establish a business with her family. As she told me, "I never expected to stay here. I miss [Honduras] too much. . . . I especially regret not being present when my mother died. At that time I didn't have my papers ready."

Immigrants who cannot travel back to their home country when a loved one dies experience an extremely difficult loss. Among the feelings they may experience are guilt, anger, sadness, and regret. The counselor's ability to help clients share these feelings and explore each of them helps to bring in them a sense of relief. Some immigrants may not be able to share their feelings with their family members, who may be experiencing the same emotions. Some people may cope with their loss by abusing alcohol or using drugs. Counselors who notice any substance abuse behaviors should suggest that the client attend an Alcoholics Anonymous or Narcotics Anonymous meeting. These are valuable resources, and the counselor should have information on hand in both English and Spanish.

Amparo's story reveals her longing to go back to her native country. Is there a sense of hope in her words? What if an immigrant is not able to return to his or her country of origin eventually? What losses does that person experience? The following are some of the questions a counselor could pose to their Hispanic clients to evaluate their worldview in reference to their long-term goals:

- How long have you been in the United States?
- What was the reason you left your country?
- Do you have a close attachment to your country?
- Are you planning to go back?
- What makes you want to go back?
- How are you coping with your current situation?

In some cases, a first-generation immigrant who chose to move to the United States starts missing his or her country, family, and traditions. The problem is not the decision the person originally made but the nostalgia for what he or she left behind. Lucy, who came to the United States from Perú, explained:

When I came to this country, I came with an illusion but I built a shell of courage around me and started to think that in this country, none of that existed, that the sadness I felt did not exist and would dissipate and of course, is merely momentary. The storm comes and it, too, passes, and tomorrow would be another day and I would move on. OK, well, I've enjoyed it immensely but all this bravado that I had built to give myself courage had started to crumble once my kids were born. Now my homeland calls out to me, my family calls out to me desperately, and the longing to have that family relationship, of which I have none here. I had my husband's family's support, good yet different, very German, and even so, the pillar of that family (that has held us together) and I have remained in contact, and when my father-in-law passed away, it just crumbled. If I had to sign somewhere so I could leave tomorrow to Perú, then I would do it in a heartbeat . . . Maybe I'm going through a mid-life crisis, but almost at my forties, I would like to reinvent my life but do it the right way.

HISPANIC SUBGROUPS AND THE EXPERIENCE OF LOSS AND GRIEF

In the following sections I present different cases of immigration-related loss. Readers will be able to identify the different losses this population may be facing, such as loss of a loved one, loss of homeland, loss of traditions, loss of language, and loss of family connectedness. You can refer to Chapter 5, which focuses on losses in more detail, to be able to identify the losses experienced by the individuals in the case examples provided.

I focus on three main groups: (a) Hispanic older adults; (b) refugees, exiles, and immigrants, including illegal immigrants; and (c) second-generation immigrants. I present the cases of several different individuals, in their words, experiencing various types of loss.

Hispanic Older Adults

In the lives of older adults, because with old age physical, emotional, and social losses can become common events that may provoke grief and bereavement (Houben, 2009). In the case of an older Hispanic immigrant, adapting to his or her losses is exacerbated by having to deal with traditions, language, and a lifestyle that is different than those of his or her homeland. A compassionate and caring counselor will be able to appreciate these clients' perspective and enter their worldview. When dealing with Hispanic older adults, it is important to talk to them in their native language. Because most of them moved to the United States as adults, they may not be able to speak English fluently. Counselors who address their older Hispanic clients in Spanish will give them the opportunity to express their feelings and needs. Communication is thus easier and the counselor–client bond can be strengthened.

In addition, older Hispanic immigrants may face economic struggles, or live in poverty. Statistics indicate that "nearly 30 percent of older Hispanic immigrants live in households with incomes in the bottom 20 percent (less than approximately $15,000 per year) . . . Among older Hispanic immigrants, nearly one in four lives in poverty (22.7 percent)." (Burr, Gerst, Kwan, & Mutchler, 2008, p. 55)

Adapting to a new culture, especially at older ages, is not easy, as Grisel Ibarra, a Cuban lawyer specializing in immigration, observed:

> Older Hispanics never really integrate or adapt themselves because, as the saying goes, *A un perro viejo no le puedes enseñar trucos nuevos* [you cannot teach new tricks to an old dog]. The older the immigrant is, the less likely they are to let go of their own traditions or to accept new traditions, no matter how much they speak English.

In the group of elders I work with at an adult day care center, we do a game of sharing memories from your country of origin, with questions such as "How did you celebrate?" and "What were your favorite foods?" You can even share recipes.

Furthermore, when doing guided imagery with older Hispanic clients, you can ask them to imagine a place they love and where they feel totally at peace (see Chapter 8, this volume, for more details on guided imagery techniques). Many of them mention a special beach or farm in their homeland.

For older first-generation immigrants, as I discussed in Chapter 5, acquiring a new language may be challenging and thus a source of stress, frustration, and fear. Lack of proficiency in the new language creates dependency on others, keeping the person in a place of hopelessness and inadequacy. The following is an example of the hardships many older Hispanics confront as they need to adapt to a new lifestyle.

Beatriz, Age 90

> I moved permanently to Miami, Florida, in 1995. For many years I continuously traveled between Miami and my homeland, Nicaragua. I had a business in my country and had a small apartment in Miami, where my children lived. It wasn't until the war came to my country and destroyed my business that I was forced to

leave Nicaragua and moved [sic] to Miami. I had to put my papers in order and sell the house where I had lived with my husband and raised my four children. It had always been my desire to die in my house, but this was not going to be possible. I continuously wrestled between staying in my homeland and being with my children, because I missed them too much. Also, I was getting too old to travel and was getting too tired. One day I decided to make the move, and despite the pain I felt in my heart when I said goodbye to my sister, my nieces, close friends, and even [our] maid for over 30 years, I moved to Miami.

At the beginning I didn't feel much difference. I thought it was just like before, when I would come for 3 months and then go back. This time it was for good. I was almost 80 years old and had to adapt to a total new lifestyle. My children were going to [help me get my U.S. citizenship] and I would not be able to travel for some time. I had to make many decisions and found myself in the need of speaking English. In the past, my children would do the different things for me, [but] now they were busy working, and I had to do things by myself. How would I communicate? Even though in Miami many people speak Spanish, in most governmental places, offices, etc., people speak in English. I would cry out of frustration when I couldn't communicate. I remember one day that I had to call the pharmacy to see if my prescription was ready. The pharmacist didn't speak Spanish and was not able to understand me. She became very impatient to the point that she hung up on me.

During the last 10 years I learned to live depending on my children, especially because of the language. All my life I tried to learn English but [it] was very difficult. I learned to speak Italian, but English . . . I just couldn't. I remember one time that I was in the hospital. My children asked for a nurse who spoke Spanish, but it was not easy . . . I couldn't communicate with [the English-speaking staff]. I am glad I had always someone from my family with me, so they could translate what I was asking or what the nurse was saying to me. I also missed having people come visit. In Nicaragua I used to have friends and family to spend time with me. I never felt alone. Here it is different. People are always in a hurry. I still have a relationship with some relatives in Nicaragua who asked me when will I go and visit. I wish I could go, but now I have to use a walker and it is very difficult. *¡Me hace tanta falta* *mi Nicaragua!* [I miss so much my Nicaragua!]. Although I feel sad at times, I have great faith and that helps me. I pray everyday the rosary and listen to Radio Paz, where they transmit the Holy Mass everyday. I feel my religion is what has given me hope and resignation. It is not easy to live away from one's homeland and I am sad that when I die I won't be buried next to my husband, in Nicaragua, but I want my children to visit me at the cemetery, so I will be buried here in Miami.

Beatriz's Losses

- Loss of tradition
- Loss of language
- Loss of self-identity
- Loss of family connectedness
- Loss of appropriate health care
- Loss of status

Because Beatriz had been an independent woman, part of my sessions with her focused on her strengths, one of them being her religion, and the traits that helped her run the business in Nicaragua after her husband died. We did this through storytelling and going through photographs. As she saw herself making decisions, she felt empowered and decided she wanted to learn the language and that age was not going to be an obstacle for her.

One technique I like to use with clients that produces great results is for them to write the list of things they are grateful for. Beatriz was especially grateful for being close to her four children, and even though she didn't see them as often as she wanted to, she liked the fact that they celebrated special occasions as a family.

Counselors should be careful to pay attention to unspoken words and the behaviors or emotions they may indicate. I remember that on one occasion, Beatriz was looking at a picture of her husband at his business, and her eyes welled up. I asked what made her so emotional, and she shared with me the guilt she experienced for selling the business and letting go of her husband's legacy. I worked with her in finding meaning in that decision; we talked about how the situation in her country had been getting difficult and that she had fought for many years by herself. She was getting older, and he would have liked her to enjoy her last years with her children instead of staying alone in her country.

The Value of Family and Traditions

Many older adults live by themselves and cannot see their children or grandchildren as often as they would like. Eighty-four-year-old Carolina, for example, complained of spending too much time by herself:

> In my country, Venezuela, I lived with my daughter and her husband. I always had dinner with the family. After dinner we sat in the living room and told stories about my youth or how their day had been. Now I find myself living in a small apartment, all by myself. If it [weren't for the] adult day care center [where I can] spend time with my friends, my life would be very, very sad.

As Carolina's comments demonstrate, elders from other cultures may miss things they are used to in their country of origin. When working with older adults in a group it would be a great idea to give them the opportunity to talk about their own culture, traditions, and values.

The following are some examples of questions counselors can use when facilitating groups with elders from different countries and cultures:

- Where were you born?
- What were your parents like when you were a child?
- Who lived in your house with you?
- How did you celebrate the holidays?
- How did you celebrate your birthday?
- What was your favorite dish?

Religion

As I noted in Chapter 4, almost 70% of Hispanics living in the United States are Catholic (Pew Forum on Religion & Public Life, 2007), and 28% "claim to be evangelical or 'born again'" (Oklobdzija, 2006). Remember that religion plays an important role in how one deals with transitions, and it can be a powerful tool for the older adults. In the case of Catholics, for example, devotion to the Virgin Mary is a source of comfort and hope (Martinez-Houben, 2004). Other vital elements of the Catholic faith are respect for priests and the concepts of hell and heaven.

Counselors should allow their older adult clients to express their concerns and make the necessary arrangements if they want to speak with a priest and make a confession, which is one of the pillars of the Catholic faith

(Weigel, 2001). I remember a time when I conducted a focus group at a nursing home to assess the needs of the residents. One of the women, who was from Spain, held my arm in a desperate manner and told me, "*Diles que me traigan un sacerdote Hispano, yo necesito hablar con un sacerdote*" [Tell them to bring me a Hispanic priest; I need to talk to a priest]. She was afraid to die without making her confession.

Refugees, Exiles, and Immigrants

It is important to notice that refugees and other types of immigrants are treated differently in the United States. Immigrants who are not refugees do not have access to many welfare and support programs that the refugees are entitled to (Van Hook & Bean, 1999).

Gabriel, age 66, one of my Cuban clients shared the pain he experienced when he left his father, his homeland, and his life:

> The greatest loss I have experienced in my life is possibly not being able to return to Cuba, the place where I grew up and enjoyed my youth, because I cannot go back. I left in 1972 because it was then that I had the right to leave legally. Previously my departure had been suspended for 13 years. I tried to get out the first time in 1960, but I finally managed it in January 1972 as a civil servant. . . . I made the necessary arrangements for my departure from Cuba. I left by plane when I was 31 years old. I left with my mother, my wife, and my wife's aunt. I still vividly remember the moment of departure. The international airport in Havana is 25 minutes from the city. My father drove very slowly, contrary to usual; it was the only time I saw him driving slower than everyone else. I realized he was trying to stretch out the time for as long as possible; it was the last time we were going to be together. I understood this, but did not talk about it.
>
> I said, "I'm going. . . . I'm never coming back! This is the last time!"
>
> Now, we grew up in a very rigid emotional environment. . . . Things were experienced, but not mentioned. My parents were divorced, and my father had remarried and was staying in Cuba with his wife. We had to be at the airport at 6:20 a.m. Sitting in the car, despite all the enthusiasm of leaving, I felt I had no right to tell my

father to rush and that we were going to be late. Upon arrival at the airport at 7 o'clock, we were moved to the "fishbowl," a room surrounded by glass, where we were given back our passports and our luggage. The only things we were allowed to take were one suitcase, 11 inches long, 8 inches wide, and 8 inches high, and whatever fit into it, but no more. This meant one pair of tights, one pair of underwear, a shirt, and if it fit, a pair of trousers.

We left the "fishbowl" at 2:45 p.m. without even a sip of water. We got on the plane and took off at three in the afternoon. I said goodbye to my father by a glass door, and I remember stopping, not knowing what to say and with a lump in my throat, both perfectly aware that it was likely that we would never see each other again. Speaking by telephone, perhaps, but meeting, never! We were both very aware of that. He put his hands on my shoulders and said,

"I want to ask you a favor."

"What will the old man say now?" I wondered.

"The only thing I ask is that you never come back as a tourist."

"As a tourist?"

"No! Never come back as a tourist," he said.

I knew what he was saying. I could return, but not as a visitor. I could only return to live. I knew that he would not have received me in his house. I remember taking off at three in the afternoon on January 9th and arriving in Madrid the next day. At that time there were only three places where one could go: Jamaica, Mexico, or Spain. I did not know where we were going. I knew I had bought tickets for a round trip, because we left on a tourist visa and on arrival in Spain we had to seek political refugee status. I understood that I had left my country when the landing gear went up. I cried nonstop until we passed over Puerto Rico. I was not hysterical, but it was something like uncontrollable laughter. I had collected everything I had bought and known for 31 years, put it in a box, and thrown it into the sea. I was leaving Cuba with only the clothes on my back. . . . In those moments I did not consider my memories, only I was not happy because I was leaving. I did not want to go. But things were complicated and I had to seize the opportunity.

My mother at 71 was in bad health and died a year after leaving Cuba. She is now buried in Spain. When we arrived in Spain, my wife's sister had booked us two rooms in a hostel. The pain was so great that it was like carrying a scar on my face.

I remember when I arrived in Madrid; it was one of the saddest days that I had lived. Immediately we asked for permission to stay, not as political refugees; that was an administrative thing you did later. After 2 years and 9 months we went to New Jersey, as we could enter the United States through a cousin of mine who lived there. In those days you had to live where the person [sponsoring] you lived. . . . Then I came to Miami.

If there is something that I want to communicate to people who are in situations like [this], it is that while you are away from home, never forget where you came from, because it is the only way to know where you are going.

Note: This story was originally published in my book *Transform Your Loss: Your Guide to Strength and Hope*.

Gabriel's Losses

- Loss of tradition
- Loss of language
- Loss of self-identity
- Loss of family connectedness
- Loss of appropriate health care

Gabriel's story shows the underlying losses he has experienced in his life. Some of them were never processed, and he may carry them in his heart. Doing a history of losses with him would be helpful and give him the opportunity to grieve past losses (see Chapter 8, this volume, for a discussion of the history of losses technique). The experience of bereaved emigrants, as they face multiple losses may greatly affect the rest of their lives. Hispanic male emigrants may feel compelled to show a stoic response to their situation and suppress their grief. On the other hand, Gabriel has a message to people, like him, who have emigrated: Have an identity; value your roots and be proud of who you are.

In some cases people do not like to write or do not know how to tell their story. You can use various assessments to help clients identify their losses as they start telling you their story. Your role as a counselor is to help them deal with any unresolved issues they may still be experiencing.

You can do this by helping them explore their feelings with direct questions such as the following:

- What is the most prevalent emotion you felt when you left your homeland?
- Did you have the opportunity to say goodbye to your relatives?
- What would you have liked to say to them?

Reina, Age 63

I came to the United States in 2003, because of the situation in Cuba. I had to leave because there, either you adapt to the control that exists in the country or you leave—it's one or the other. If you rebel then you may find yourself in hot water. In reality, I never wanted to come here—or to have to go anywhere else, for that matter. I wanted to stay in my country. I'm a *regionalista* [regionalist]; . . . I've always been in my same area. I was born in Matanza but then quickly moved to the city, to La Havana, and that's where I stayed and carried out my life, but then my life started to fall apart. My husband left the country, then my son left on a boat, and so it was just me and my daughter. Everybody was making their own decision as to what they were going to do and so I had to do the same. I decided to come here to see if I could get my daughter out of there and I'm still in that process, to date.

I was able to leave Cuba because I won a raffle. In this raffle you fill out a form and send it along with your picture. If you win the raffle you win [a] visa to come to the United States. A group of 15 of us came here. Originally I was not planning to come to Miami. I was going to go to Boston, but I found a sense of solidarity and community here, as well as my son living here. Also, I was told the winters are brutal up north and I wouldn't get used to them at my age, so I decided to stay, and a short time [later] I married a Cuban gentleman. But besides the fact that I came to an area that was surrounded by Latin people, the change was horrible. I was very depressed and lonely and I don't wish it upon anyone. Despite the fact that I didn't have any financial needs, thankfully, the depression took over me. Not having my family around and being in a strange environment deeply affects you. The laws are different, the customs, and even the way people treat each other is different. One comes from a country where we all regard ourselves as equals and there's a deeply rooted connection with family and that doesn't exist here. That's the reason why I keep away from the people who don't seem to have a heart, because I know I will never get anything from them. Back [in Cuba] even your neighbors are treated like family, and here not even your own family stays together, so it's very frustrating for me. But hey, we have to adapt to the situation. I have tried to learn the English language but there's too much going on in my head and it doesn't stick and I can't remember. Also, there's a lack of motivation due to emotional conflict. The emotional issues were so strong that I decided that I needed help, I went to see doctors. It seems I have been around doctors my whole life. . . . It's . . . helped me to take notice of other people's pain and to realize that my problems are not so terrible, and it keeps things in perspective. In terms of advancement, I think I'm doing just fine since I already have my citizenship, and that's not an easy thing to attain for most people. I actually like this country for the freedom it affords its people, and that's something I never experienced before. My entire life and youth . . . [I was] oppressed and couldn't express myself. That's something that you don't see here.

When I had counseling it helped me to look for the silver lining in my life, so to speak, to look at the positive side of things, especially when they seemed negative. I started to spread my wings and I studied several things—English and computers among them—and while it didn't lead to anything, I feel good that I did it. During those studies, I was able to meet many people from all different countries, and I just love seeing the differences between the different cultures. I have many friends from many places, and I'm a very social person.

But I have realized that the immigrants need to be told to strive for what they want, to fight for their objectives. If you left your country for a reason then you can't come here and not do anything—you have to carry out your vision and follow through with the decision that you made and to try to leave that sentimentalism behind and take things in a more detached manner, calmly, in order to move forward, little by little. If you don't do that then you can't get ahead. As far as mental [health] professionals, I am not in agreement with utilizing medication to resolve emotional issues. Let me tell you something, sincerely, from my experience of going to see these professionals. They would ask me how I was doing . . . [but] all they wanted was to prescribe me something based on what I would tell them. That is not the way to resolve issues. The psychiatrist seems to take a more personal approach and I prefer him over a mental counselor, who only wants to prescribe me something and send me on my way. You can even forge a friendship of sorts with a psychiatrist, once you pass the negative stage in your life. The way I see it, if you feel depressed, then do something to get rid of that feeling, like take a walk, [or] go to the store like I do—or read books and seek spiritual means. Those who are religious can follow the guidelines that God has denoted in the Bible, as we all should, and therefore bypass the need to seek counselors.

Reina's Losses

- Loss of tradition
- Loss of language
- Loss of self-identity
- Loss of family connectedness
- Loss of appropriate care

In her story, Reina offers advice on what Hispanics or immigrants in general need to succeed. First, they need to feel validated, empowered, and hopeful for the future. The counselor's task is to work with clients to find the resources that can help them transform their situation into an opportunity for growing and developing as a person. If you have clients who are resistant and choose to dwell in the past—on the things they had, on what they are missing—help them resolve this grief and let go of what is holding them down. For example—you can ask them to write down on pieces of paper all the things they do not have and place them into a little box. Then, after some time, while they work on finding resources and on recognizing what they have now, you can perform a ritual of burning those papers to let go of regrets from the past and start focusing on the present they have and the future they want to build.

The following story shows how a person who experienced the loss of his homeland, Venezuela, and focused on the positive transform it into a growth experience.

Baldo, Age 51

My greatest loss, which I am currently suffering, is the loss of my homeland's future. This loss initially started legally through the presidential elections in Venezuela. I never thought, as did the large majority, that things could get worse. I realized that life is a state of perpetual change, so things are always going to change for the better or worse, depending on factors and results of decisions or positions taken. When the new situation arose, I was [uncomfortable], annoyed, and frustrated, and I shared this with my family. I felt a lot of tension and nervousness at the same time. On the spiritual and religious side, I was shocked to see that the strong values and principles that I consider sacred, such as freedom, came into open conflict with the practices of the new regime. This caused me deep sadness and made me feel a sense of loss and emptiness.

But I understand that one learns to live with these moods day by day as [if] they are only chapters of an unfinished book. What has helped me through this loss was keeping up to date with the developments and to discuss and talk about alternatives for the future. I realized that I was going over the same things in my mind and investing time in analyzing and understanding why things happen, but yet I had no control over them.

I have learned that when and how one faces things will determine, to a greater or lesser extent, the learning that one receives from them.

Baldo's Losses

- Loss of tradition
- Loss of hope
- Loss of self-identity

In sharing his story, Baldo reconstructed his reality through connecting with his inner self. He did this through a cognitive restructure, spiritual awareness, and sharing with others. These three elements are essential to integrate as the person shares his or her story. In the case of loss of homeland, the story of the person's life that he expected to write has been interrupted. The scenario, plot, and characters have all changed. Your job, as a counselor, is to help your clients rewrite their story in another scenario, create a new plot, and transform the characters. This exercise could be done by asking them to collect pictures of their homeland and then to write, in chronological order, the memories they have that are related to the pictures. If they do not have pictures, ask them to elaborate on people, places, and traditions of their homeland. Then, once they have written their story in an objective manner—including the day they left their home country and started a new life in the United States have them write another story; this time focusing on their new reality and the good things that have happened to them because of this move. Help them identify what they have in their lives now that is beneficial and that they can be grateful for.

Nubia, Age 38

I am from Nicaragua and have lived in the United States for 30 years. I left my country due to the civil war with the Sandinistas [a political party]. When they came into Managua, we were living at home; my brother and father were in the Guatemalan embassy in Nicaragua [under conditions of] asylum due to my father's work with several important government groups. For example, when there was an earthquake in Nicaragua, my father was involved with the team that was in charge of providing relief to victims. That being said, the Sandinistas were after him; so, my mom, knowing the ambassador to Guatemala, got him asylum granted—for him and my brother. We were all supposed to leave together, but when [my father's and brother's] . . . plane [from Guatemala] was trying to land, they started to shoot at it and so they had to turn around and go back to the embassy. I was with my mother and grandmother and bombs started to fall not too far from us, bullets started to shower around the house, and we would hear the screams of victims. It was just horrible. I remember hearing the sign over the radio from the guards asking for help. We lived like that for a month, but when the Sandinistas finally took over Managua, that's when we went to the embassy where my father and brother were. We were there for about a month and that's when they allowed women and children to leave. They took us to the airport so that we could go to El Salvador, but the airport turned us around [sic] because they weren't letting people leave. We tried leaving again and the second time they let us. The thing I remember very much was having to leave my father behind at the embassy . . . he and I were so close. When we got to the airport, they stripped us of all our belongings—they even wanted to take my medications [we had brought along] since I was sick at that time. My mom fought for us to keep the medications. That whole time we were in a bus when all this happened. The only things they didn't take from us where [sic] the things my mother was able to hide, and my parents, not thinking that this situation was going to escalate the way it did, they never took out their money from the bank and they ended up losing everything, the properties, the money, and so we came like that. We were [put on] a cargo plane and sent to Honduras like that. In Honduras, we took a bus to a convent and there we stayed for a while, thanks to my mother having obtained a letter for the convent from a nun in Nicaragua, until we were able to fix up the papers to obtain visas to come to the United States. We went to the American embassy in Guatemala and presented our story of what had happened, I spoke to the gentleman and told him of the bombings, the shootings, and thank God that they gave us the OK because they weren't giving visas to everyone. We had an aunt who lived here in Little Havana and that's where we came to live. I can remember all the people who were living there since she was trying to help as many as possible who were arriving in the States for this reason. My mother, not knowing a stitch of English, told me how now she had to find work, no matter what, and she did find it in a factory, so she went from being a professional, a director of personnel at a hospital in Nicaragua, to a factory worker. My father was a CPA [certified public accountant]. When we left Nicaragua my mother didn't share anything with us because she had to be strong for us, but now she's told me that it was horrible, that she couldn't share her story with other people because of the way people would embarrass her, so she learned quickly enough to keep it to herself. We didn't have a car at the time so we had to take the bus at six in the morning. She would drop me off and leave right away to catch three other buses, since I think the factory was in Opa-locka, and then back the same way in the afternoon. Anyway, this went on for 3 months, for the three of us.

My grandmother stayed behind in Nicaragua, but my elder brother came with us. He's 7 years older than I am; so he was 15 at the time. Eventually, we left that crowded house we were in to look for a small apartment there in Little Havana, but let me tell you, an apartment of the worst kind and I think there was a rat there, my mother says, but she didn't want to tell us. We shared that apartment with a cousin of mine and let me tell you, I believe we were sleeping in the closets because the moment you would open the little door, you would hit the bed and that's where the three of us would sleep. It was a second floor [apartment] and on the first floor, you would hear this old man complaining, and that's how we would sleep, suffering through that all night. When we moved to Little Havana, we had a ton of help from many Cubans, and we even spent our first Thanksgiving and our first Christmas with this Cuban family. Obviously, it was a completely different world from Nicaragua, where I went from being in a Catholic private, all-girls school to Douglas Elementary, where no one knew Spanish and I didn't know English, and that hit me about as badly as not having my father around and I would throw up, perhaps from the nerves, and it would happen often. That's how I spent months and that was my ritual, to throw up, because again, it was totally strange and I couldn't communicate. But it was a blessing in disguise for me because even though I didn't spend more than a year there, I came out of there speaking English perfectly, never having had to take an [English as a second language] class. My mom would get many phone calls because I refused to eat the cafeteria food—that's not what I was used to. We used to get [free/reduced-price school lunches] and overall, it was not like home cooking and so my mother kept telling the [lunch] lady to leave me alone, that I would slowly start to accept the ways of the school, and it happened. She would also get calls because I was too chatty—go figure, not even knowing the language—and they wanted her to come in to talk to her and she would tell them that she couldn't even miss one day of work.

When my father finally came over, after 3 or 4 months—that's when we moved to another house. But the same thing that happened to my mom, happened to him—he came here without knowing the language and went from being a CPA to looking for the first job he could find. Of course, my parents didn't want us to worry about anything and wanted to provide it all for us but I can definitely say we never had the life here that we would have had in Nicaragua.

I stayed in public schools. After school, the bus would drop me off and I became a latchkey kid because there was no one home at that hour, and that's what I would do at 8 years of age. I cannot imagine my daughter having to do that. I would come in, make myself something to eat, especially since my brother would go to Jackson High School, which was really far away, and he was able to make a small group of friends who were also from Nicaragua, and when we moved he wanted to stay in the school since he only had a couple more years to go 'til graduation. So I would always get there before him. We both had to clean the house, do the laundry, everything, because both our parents had jobs, and we wouldn't see them until close to midnight. Thank God, my brother was always a calm person. Nowadays, I try to give my children everything [that] I couldn't have back then, not because my parents didn't want it but because it couldn't happen out of circumstance, and it changed us. I think because of all the things I had to do since such an early age, I ended up becoming stronger and much more mature, like on the day that [I] arrived at my new school—alone—not knowing where to go, and I said to myself, *OK, now go figure it out!* Of course, it's not the same for everyone, but I do believe it made me much better suited to adapting to situations. Despite all these difficulties I have completely assimilated [sic] into the United States. I think it's because I came at such an early age . . . of course, I will be from Nicaragua until the day I die, but when I hear the Star Spangled Banner, I cry, because I am from here now. I consider myself a part of this country. When I go to Nicaragua, I get super-emotional, even though I don't have as many memories there as I have here. I went over there after 20 years of being here but I went as a tourist because my mom was not into keeping up with people so we had to go look for somebody to take us in as tourists and guide us. . . . My dad didn't go with us. I can definitely say that Miami makes one feel very comfortable because it's the place where so many of the Hispanics are located.

These transitions are not easy, and a counselor needs to be patient with the Hispanic immigrant because we come from different countries with different beliefs and customs and [counselors should] understand that the person is not going to readily adapt all the customs and the country from one day to the other depending at which age the immigrant comes, and that it's going to take a while, not so much for children though. My elder brother has more of an accent than me, and my mother took so many classes but you can still hear the accent. Both my parents can defend themselves, but my mom [is] embarrassed to express herself for fear of not expressing herself adequately, of not forming sentences correctly. She actually wanted me to get her one of these English courses for her birthday so she could learn to speak well! She's still struggling with that to this day, despite being able to understand everything that she hears. I didn't realize until I had children just how difficult it is to learn English as opposed to Spanish. I barely had to teach [my kids] Spanish since the pronunciations are so precise, but in English there are so many different ways to interpret and to speak and there are many exceptions to rules. A friend of mine, who's a pediatrician, learned that up to 10 years of age, the brain is able to soak up and grab languages much more so than later in life.

In facing all these situations I always remained thankful and I suggest that is something that the Hispanic or any other immigrant needs to focus on. It is important to be grateful, to thank God that this country gives all the opportunities that it gives to those who live in it, and that anyone who doesn't get ahead here just doesn't want to. There's the freedom to try, to experiment, with anything you want to do. Depending on the state [one lives in], that will vary, but here in Miami, being "the gateway to the Americas," you definitely feel more comfortable. It's easier in that respect. The freedoms are endless. The people who wash cars . . . even for them, the possibilities are endless. One thing I forgot to mention that I've never forgotten—I remember that when we came here, to Little Havana, it was very close to the Orange Bowl, and some people were throwing fireworks and I ran to hide under a table. I could only imagine it was one thing—bullets, *las bombas de nuevo* . . . [the bombs] again. But it was instinctual; I didn't even think about it. I remember they had to pull me from under the table, assuring me that it wasn't what I thought it was, that it was fireworks.

I'd like to think that I'm very strong, that I have a strong personality, and this incident only happened once. The only thing that scares me now is thinking of my kids not having me around whenever they're coming out of school, of them being alone and unprotected, especially after what I went through as a small child when we first came here, looking down those long hallways that seemed endless! I never said anything to my mom nor [sic] complained. My mom didn't have a choice!

Nubia's Losses

- Loss of homeland
- Loss owing to war
- Loss of a loved one (temporarily)
- Loss of security
- Loss of status
- Loss of self-identity
- Loss of appropriate care
- Loss of childhood
- Loss owing to moving

Nubia's story is similar to those of many other immigrants who need to flee their country owing to the political situation. In her overwhelming account, one can identify many losses, both from her time in Nicaragua as a little child and the losses she endured with her family as they moved to Miami. Nubia reconstructed her story, focusing on the good things she had, relying on her strengths, and transforming her life to give her children the life she didn't have as a little girl. However, because she experienced a civil war in her country and had to assume a mature role as a little girl, the counselor's task would be to work on any past issues that were not resolved, including trauma or painful memories. We can see how Nubia found gratitude to be an essential component of living a life with purpose. She also discovered that self-reliance and responsibility are qualities Hispanic immigrants need to acquire if they want to succeed here in the United States. The country already offers the opportunity, she says, but one needs to work for it. In a case such as Nubia's, the counselor must work with the client to dig into those qualities and resources and make the client aware of his or her own skills and abilities. You can work with your clients in writing a list of the strengths they have and identifying the circumstances that can bring a satisfactory change to their lives.

Illegal immigrants comprise a unique subgroup of U.S. Hispanics. A 2008 report by the Pew Hispanic Center estimated that 11.9 million unauthorized immigrants lived in the United States; it concluded that the undocumented immigrant population grew rapidly from 1990 to 2006 but has since stabilized (Passel & Cohn, 2009).

Illegal immigrants face challenges different from those of legal immigrants, because fear and insecurity are emotions they continually experience. Jorge, a Catholic coordinator in a detention center for immigrants, described the situation many immigrants face when they do not have their legal documents in order:

In this center there are two types of immigrants. One is the people who cross the border without documents. The other group are people who entered the country with a legal visa but once this expires they remain in the country. These people face many losses and grieve in these centers and women express their grief differently than men. Women openly cry and manifest their pain and manifest how they miss their family. Men are more reserved and express more anger. Some cry, but in private.

Lawyer Grisel Ibarra offered a clear picture of what this group of people experience on a regular basis:

> The situation with immigrants is divided into two categories: those who have documents and those who are here illegally. Those who have some form of documentation have the hope of moving forward with their lives and to resolve their situations. Those who don't have any documents live in a dark underworld, if you will, filled with terror. They fear being persecuted at the gas station, they drive without licenses or insurance and fear being pulled over, they fear calling 911 if their children get into accidents. It's a life of fear and terror and that's what affects them most because imagine that every morning you wake up, thinking that today might be the day the *migra* or immigration might find you, so without peace of mind, you don't have stability. What happens then, they fall into the hands of people who end up hurting them, particularly the women. They are offered residency through marriage, for example, among many other things, and they are in turn abused sexually or physically. They start working under the table with people who will hide their passports from them or make them sleep in closets and grossly underpay them for their work. That being said, the most important thing that counselors and mental professionals have to understand is what these people are going through and to be able to distinguish between these two distinct groups of immigrants.

Many immigrants face difficult situations in the United States. For example, Mario is a Colombian who has been living in the United States for 10 years. When he moved from Colombia and his visa expired, he hired a lawyer to solve his situation. To his astonishment one day someone knocked at his door: It was an immigration officer saying he was going to be deported because he was illegal. Moreover, they said he had married a Cuban woman who was an American citizen because he wanted to get the residency through her. He then realized that the lawyer had been a fraud and never processed any of his papers. He was taken to jail in front of his wife and two children. He felt like a criminal, like a murderer. For 10 years he had thought a lawyer was handling his case. During this time he worked *sin papeles* [with no legal documentation] with the expectation that his case would be solved. With the help of another lawyer, and after a long and arduous process, Mario was able to solve his case.

Most people who face a situation like this may experience an array of emotions, including fear, distrust, hopelessness, anger, frustration, anxiety, and stress. Their self-concepts may be damaged. In working with this population it is important you establish good rapport with clients so they will trust you and share how they are feeling. One way of establishing rapport is by being nonjudgmental and validating what the client is experiencing. It is important for the person to know that he or she is understood. Sometimes people feel relief just by telling their story, but I always stress the fact that they need to do some grief work (i.e., acknowledge the loss and work through their feelings) to transform their situation.

In the following story, Milagros shares how difficult it was to grow up in the United States as an illegal immigrant and describes how her situation influenced her potential to develop professionally.

Milagros, Age 29

I was 9 years old when my entire family (on my mother's side) moved to the United States from Perú. We came here due to economic reasons and also terrorism. During the 80s, Sendero Luminoso [a guerilla organization] was terrorizing the country, and most of all, business owners, and anyone who had any influence. My father worked alongside his family in the family's industrial factory, and during our last few years there he started to receive threats from the terrorists scrawled on the dusty driver side door of his truck. During that time, my mom's side of the family all decided to move to Miami, where a couple of my aunts were living already, and we were the last to arrive.

Leaving my house was a devastating moment and I felt like a part of me had broken off and stayed there with it, which probably explains why once in a while I will exclaim that I want my ashes to be scattered there when I pass away. Anyway, that was 20 years ago and I have fully integrated myself into this country's way of life, at least Miami's way of life. Deep down in my heart, however, I will always be Peruvian, with our food, our customs, our teachings, and our heritage.

Going through the immigrant experience as a child was tough. I would be sick much of the time [in] the first year I started going to school, which was not long after we arrived, and I had to take a private bus at four in the morning and then a regular school bus in order to get to the elementary school to which I had been assigned.

It was pretty far from the house we were renting, and my parents would end up coming to get me out of school on most days because I would be sick to my stomach. I was scared, despite having a basic . . . knowledge of the [English] language, and I didn't have my brother or sister around me. It was a completely different experience from private school in Perú. By the time I made it to fifth grade, however, I had immersed myself in the language and could easily communicate with others. I excelled in school because it was my nature, although I cannot say the same for my two siblings once they hit high school. What carried me through those first 10 years here were the friends I made along the way, particularly in high school. My home life was falling apart and there didn't seem to be any end in sight.

The money we had when we first arrived was getting used up fairly quickly since my father could not find a comparable career/position without a degree and he refused to do anything else. My father was a brilliant man but all he knew was in his head, unfortunately. That being said, my mother's resentment continued to grow at a steady pace as the money dwindled and my father's attempts at [starting] a business kept costing us what little we had. We lived without much furniture during that first decade in Miami, [with] only what was absolutely necessary. It certainly felt like a nightmare to me. Mom effectively made our lives miserable and acutely severed any feelings any of us could have had for one another as a family. Instead of "sticking together," we all just wanted to run away from the situation and pretend it had never happened. On top of that, my mother had cut all ties with her extended family a few years after we arrived, and thus cut us off from the few cousins we knew in this country. All the while, behind this ordeal that was our life, the problem of our legal status started to come up. We were only OK until we graduated high school . . . my father had a work visa; my mother didn't have anything. What truly saved us was the fact that my grandfather used much of the money he had when we arrived to get most of us Social Security, the children and the husbands. So we had papers, sort of.

Of all the places to live, Miami was definitely the safest bet, not only because it was "the place to be" if you were from South America and you wanted to live elsewhere, but it's where most Hispanics came to live in the States. I am grateful to have grown up here without the prejudice I fear I would have encountered in mostly white American states, despite my firm grasp of the language.

Once my sister and I were old enough to leave the nest, we did, and in a hurry. At this point, however, we were stuck in the inevitable hole that was being illegal and not having any money. My brother ran away from home one night when I was 15 and in high school in order to live as far away from our mother as he could get and also to get married and resolve his legality issue. It was devastating to me because I never once thought he could do something like that, to abandon us, no matter how crazy our mother got to be. The only way we could get out of that mess would be to get married to an American citizen . . . so in retrospect, I don't blame him for taking that route. And so we worked. I always feared that I would be asked to show a work permit, that if I told anyone about my situation that they would then betray me and turn me over to immigration to have me deported. I lived in terror at the thought of losing that precious driver's license most people didn't care to have replaced if lost or stolen. After a few years, I found out I couldn't renew my license without having to show identification papers at the [Department of Motor Vehicles], and so it began, my life filled with anxiety and worry and bouts of depression.

I was able to pull myself together as needed, but all my relationships suffered in some way due to the unstable environment I was living in, particularly with my very unstable mother lurking in the background. I knew that I had to do what was necessary in order to survive, and that was work, pay bills, and keep my mouth shut. I felt like a criminal, pretty much, confined to live only a little bit and to be grateful for the scraps of fun I enjoyed along the way because I had this terrible secret to hide. After a few years of being with the same boy I had met while in high school, I thought [I would marry him and that] my biggest problem would be resolved and I could finally start my life. I felt such bitterness whenever I would think of my friends moving on with their lives, going to college, and getting their careers. Out of my group of friends, I had the best grades, and I couldn't do a thing with them. As the years went by and I kept working as a secretary, I felt myself slowly slipping away into nothingness, into a shadow, insecure and trapped in a situation in which I had never asked to be, but I couldn't blame my parents—how could they have possibly known this would happen to their kids? I became more insecure, unsure of what would happen to me if I didn't cling onto this one person who was promising me roses and sunshine year in and year out, all the while accumulating more and more debt. I could have easily fallen into a lifestyle of drugs or alcoholism, but that's not how I was raised, and my father was an alcoholic until I was six, so I vowed never to do that to myself. Even having "some" documents to my name did not alleviate the background stress I felt, and the more this quasi-boyfriend of mine kept on ignoring my pleas [to get married], the more I started to feel like maybe I didn't deserve it, that perhaps I was being punished for something, and so my self-esteem took a dive, but I kept it to myself as much as possible. Instead, I manifested my feelings through vengeance and did things to him that I'm not proud of, but at least I was taking control of some part of my life. Not living in a normal state of being definitely made me overcompensate in other areas, and I wanted to take full control over whatever little things I could, such as my finances, to a meticulous degree.

Now that I have overcome this hurdle in my life, I can look back and see how much I was affected by the entire experience of moving to this country, both as a child who lost her youth far too early in life and as a woman who lost her soul in all her sorrow and had to teach herself how to be kind and not think the world was a scary place but to have courage to face it all.

Any mental professional dealing with a Hispanic immigrant needs to be kind, first and foremost, and listen to their story. Like any victim of forced or perceived danger . . . this individual will manifest symptoms of emotional trauma, first due to the separation from their homeland and second, from the alien environment in which they find themselves living, not to mention the hardships they are enduring. The immigrant needs to acquire the tools to manage their feelings in practical, simple ways in which to alleviate those feelings, and most definitely, words of reassurance and encouragement. Medication is not the way, in my opinion, unless there's a clinically diagnosed condition present. I took an antidepressant for less than a year and while it did help me to keep my grip on the situation, I knew that it was not a permanent fix and I had to pull myself together, one way or another, and so I did.

Milagros's Losses

- Loss of security in her country of origin
- Loss of homeland
- Loss of self-identity

- Loss of family connectedness
- Loss of opportunities

In the context of losses, Milagros suffered multiple ones, and many of them seem to be interrelated, including the grief that the divorce of her parents brought. In her case, writing separate letters to her father and her mother was suggested. In this letter she could express her feelings but also she could forgive both of her parents and find peace within herself.

Second-Generation Immigrants

Children of immigrants who were born in the United States face a unique situation. In many cases, they may not identify with their parents' homeland but at the same time may also feel different from the mainstream culture.

Our last story is that of Dolores, a Nicaraguan woman who was born in Managua and moved to Miami when she was just one year old. Although she was raised like a Latina, she does not identify with this culture. She is acculturated to the United States, according to Cafferty and Engstrom's (2002) definition: "[Acculturation is] the process of taking on the culture of another population or society at the expense of one's own culture" (p. 115). Now an adult, she speaks only English and does not engage in any Latin traditions.

Dolores, Age 30

I came to this country when I was just one year old, so it is like if I was born here. I remember, as a young child, how my mom wanted me to learn Spanish, and for this reason she spoke to me only in that language. At the beginning it was great. I spoke Spanish with her and my grandmother, who did not speak English at all, but would watch the cartoons in English. When I entered school, I had many Latin friends, mostly Cubans, but we spoke in English. Little by little I got used to speak[ing] only English, so the way of communicating with my mom was as follows: She talked to me in Spanish and I responded in English. Only with my grandmother and my nanny I spoke Spanish. I didn't like it. Besides, I didn't want people to think of me as a "Latina immigrant." At home my mom used to play Latin music all the time, and I hated it! The worst thing is that she wanted me to like it. When my friends from school visited me I was embarrassed they would hear this music. What is funny is that most of them were also Hispanics, from Cuba, Nicaragua, Colombia . . . but many of them also disliked the music or the language. As I grew up many things were imposed on me that I internally rejected. One of them [was] the constant reminder of my mom, as I moved away from home: "Remember to call your grandmother on a regular basis. In Nicaragua my grandmother lived with us." I know over there [it] is different with older adults, they are taken care of by their children and grandchildren, but here I also have a life. Although I love my grandmother, I cannot be attached to her like my mom wants me to. Another aspect that was not easy growing up was going back to my mom's homeland because I didn't feel I belonged there. I became acculturated to the United States, like most of my friends. Still, now that I am 30 years old I really wish I could have paid more attention. I am not able to cook any Nicaraguan dish, and I even call my mom asking for recipes. Now I want to go back to Nicaragua and discover all the beauty it has to offer.

Dolores's Losses

- Loss of tradition
- Loss of language
- Loss of self-identity
- Loss of family connectedness

In assessing Dolores's story one can find subtle losses. Although she identifies with the American culture, certain aspects of herself are now showing some nostalgia for her ethnic heritage. This is the case with many children of Hispanic parents who are born in the United States or who, like Dolores, came here at a very young age and became acculturated. The counselor's task is to help their clients discover who they are, how they feel about their heritage, and how they can integrate certain family traditions in their own lifestyle, especially if this is an important issue when they get together as a family. An exercise I like to do with my clients is to ask them to write an essay responding to the question, "Who am I?" We then explore each of the most salient issues and determine whether there are unprocessed losses that cause them grief at an unconscious level.

HELPFUL SUGGESTIONS

- Learn to identify the different groups of immigrants so that you can expand your understanding of individual situations. The members of each group present their own challenges and losses; therefore, the way they express and cope with their grief may be different. I suggest you do a history of losses (see Chapter 8, this volume) as part of your assessment with members of each group so that you can have a holistic approach to their situation.
- Engage your clients to focus on the good things they have in their lives now, instead of dwelling on what they are missing. If they have unresolved issues, help them explore their feelings and express them in ways that empower them.
- If you have a problem dealing with immigrants because of your personal convictions, refer a client to a colleague. If you experience negative feelings or question a client's right to live in this country, he or she will perceive it, and any rapport will be compromised.

PERSONAL REFLECTIONS FOR THE COUNSELOR

- Do you find yourself comfortable working with immigrants?
- Do you think immigrants have the same rights as natural-born U.S. citizens?
- Are you able to understand the losses an illegal immigrant may experience, regardless of whether you agree with his or her situation?

Conclusion: Assessing Your Understanding of Hispanics

First, I want to thank you for picking up this book because it shows that you care for your clients and want to connect at a meaningful level with people from my Hispanic culture. Although grieving is often associated with the death of a loved one, when we understand it as a response to any loss we gain a more comprehensive view. Furthermore, when we consider the many losses our clients may face, particularly those who come to a new country with a different language and customs, the need for heightened awareness and sensitivity is readily apparent.

In taking this journey together through the experiences many Hispanics face, we have established that, for many people, new realities can be filled with losses. Sometimes these losses are not even recognized. Counselors who are not aware of the multiple situations Hispanics experience that bring grief to their lives may not be able to recognize the problem or effectively help their clients. It is equally important to develop an understanding of salient factors in the Hispanic client's culture. Where do they draw strength from, what is meaningful to them, what hurts them?

I have written this book in a holistic manner because I consider that working with the inner self is a vital component of the healing process, especially when facing a tragedy. If our clients are given the necessary tools to live through their losses and process their grief from a place of serenity and inner peace, the therapeutic process will be more meaningful, growth will be possible, and they will be able to transform their losses and change their lives. It all has to do with accompanying clients through self-exploration—becoming aware of how they think about themselves, what they want, and the choices they have and will eventually make. I can say these words as both a professional and from my own personal experience.

As I have noted throughout this book, although Hispanics have common characteristics and values, it is crucial for health care professionals and counselors to always keep in mind that there is not a single prototype of a Hispanic person or family. Hispanics come from different countries, each of which has its traditions and customs. I am constantly learning of nuances from other Latin countries that are not part of my Nicaraguan traditions, and this expands my own understanding of the rich mosaic of traditions that exist in our Hispanic culture.

To facilitate an estimation of the client's cultural background, I have included the following self-evaluation to help you get a better understanding of your clients' worldview.

- What are Hispanics' most salient values and traditions?
- Do you think these values and traditions are kept in the United States?
- What are some of the challenges Hispanics living in the United States face?
- Are there any differences among the different groups of Latinos?
- What are the most important losses Hispanics face?
- Do you think that Latinos can lose their self-identity? Their self-esteem?
- What do you think could help them to keep it?
- What do you think are the best ways to help Hispanic clients grieve their losses?
- What are the essential elements of a counselor who works effectively with Hispanics?

Remember: The more you know, understand, and respect the cultural identity of your Hispanic clients, the better able you will be to use this knowledge to help them, with maximum efficacy, to transform their loss.

References

Abalos, D. T. (2002). *The Latino male: A radical redefinition*. Boulder, CO: Lynne Rienner.

Abbady, T. (2002, March 3). Venezuelans are flocking to South Florida. *The Miami Herald*.

Andrade, R. A. (1992). Machismo: A universal malady. *Journal of America Culture, 15,* 33–41.

Aponte, J. F., Rivers, R. Y., & Wohl, J. (1995). *Psychological interventions and cultural diversity*. Needham Heights, MA: Allyn & Bacon.

Arciniega, G. M., Anderson, T. C., Tovar-Blank, Z. G., & Tracey, T. J. G. (2008). Toward a fuller conception of machismo: Development of a traditional Machismo and Caballerismo scale. *Journal of Counseling Psychology, 55*(1), 19–33.

Atkinson, D. R. (2004). *Counseling American minorities* (6th ed.). New York, NY: McGraw-Hill.

Avila, E., & Parker, J. (2000). *Woman who glows in the dark*. New York, NY: Tarcher/Putnam.

Badillo, D. A. (2006). *Latinos and the new immigrant church*. Baltimore, MD: The Johns Hopkins University Press.

Barnett, T. L. (2004). *Immigration from South America*. Philadelphia, PA: Mason Crest Publishers.

Barrett, R. K. (1998). Sociocultural considerations for working with Blacks experiencing loss and grief. In K. J. Doka & D. D. Joyce (Eds.), *Living with grief: Who we are, how we grieve* (pp. 83–96). Philadelphia, PA: Hospice Foundation of America.

Barton, P. (2006). *Hispanic methodists, Presbyterians, and Baptists in Texas*. Austin, TX: University of Texas Press.

Bassett, R. L., Garrick, I., Fogarty, M., Giacalone, S., Kapuscinski, A., Olmstead, M., . . . Distaffen, R. (2008). Walking down the sunny side of the street: Three studies developing a spiritually nuanced measure of optimism. *International Journal for the Psychology of Religion, 18*, 330–352. doi: 10.1080/10508610802229171

Becker, L. T. (2009, October). Pushed to the limits of our fragility: Religion and rebuilding the shattered assumptive world. *ADEC Forum, 35*(4).

Benet-Martinez, V., Leu, J., Lee, F., & Morris, M. W. (2002). Negotiating biculturalism: Cultural frame switching in biculturals with oppositional versus compatible cultural identities. *Journal of Cross-Cultural Psychology, 33*(5), 492–516.

Bissler, J. V. (2005, July/August/September). Group counseling with bereaved parents. *The Forum, 31*(3), 4–5.

Bonanno, G. A. (2004, January). Loss, trauma, and human resilience: Have we underestimated the human capacity to thrive after extremely aversive events? *American Psychologist, 59*(1), 20–28.

Borges-Diaz, F. (2009, Summer). Santería. Research paper [World Religions]. Miami Dade College, Florida.

Boss, P. (1999). *Ambiguous loss: Learning to live with unresolved loss.* Harvard, MA: The President and Fellows of Harvard College.

Boss, P. (2006). *Loss, trauma, and resilience: Therapeutic work.* New York, NY: W. W. Norton & Company.

Bougere, M. H. (2008). *Culture, grief and bereavement: Applications for clinical practice.* Retrieved from http://www.minoritynurse.com/culture-grief-and-bereavement-applications-clinical-practice

Bowlby, J. (1993). *Attachment.* New York, NY: Basic Books.

Brammer, R. (2004). *Diversity in counseling.* Canada: Thomson, Brooks & Cole.

Brandes, S. (2006). *Skulls to the living, bread to the dead.* Malden, MA: Blackwell Publishing.

Breggin, P. R. (1997). *The heart of being helpful: Empathy and the creation of a healing presence.* New York, NY: Springer Publishing.

Bridges, W. (2004). *Transitions: Making sense of life's changes, revised 25th anniversary edition.* Cambridge, MA: Da Capo Press.

Brinkley-Rogers, P. (2001, June 6). Colombian exiles face uncertain U.S. future. *The Miami Herald.*

Burns, D. D. (1999). *The feeling good handbook.* New York, NY: Penguin Books.

Burr, J. A., Gerst, J., Kwan, N., & Mutchler, J. E. (2008). Economic well-being and welfare program participation among older immigrants in the United States. *Generations, 32*(4), 53–60.

Cafferty, P. S. J., & Engstrom, D. W. (2002). *Hispanics in the United States: An agenda for the twenty-first century.* New Brunswick, NJ: Transaction Publishers.

Caine, K. W., & Kaufman, B. P. (1999). *Prayer, faith and healing. Cure your body, heal your mind, and restore your soul* (1st ed.). Emmaus, PA: Rodale Press.

Calhoun, L. G., & Tedeschi, R. G. (Eds.). (1998). *Handbook of posttraumatic growth: Research and practice*. Mahwah, NJ: Lawrence Erlbaum Associates.

Carbajal, F., & Medina, H. (2008). *Building the Latino future*. New Jersey: John Wiley & Sons.

Cardenas, D., Garces, C., & Johnson, D. (2004). *End-of-life care: The Latino culture*. Culture Clues. University of Washington Medical Center.

Carillo, C. (1982). Changing norms of Hispanic families: Implications for treatment. In E. E. Jones & S. J. Sheldon (Eds.), *Minority mental health* (pp. 250–266). New York, NY: Praeger Scientific.

Carrillo, R., & Tello, J. (2008). *Family violence and men of color* (2nd ed.). New York, NY: Springer Publishing.

Centers for Disease Control and Prevention. (2010). HIV Among Hispanics/Latinos. Retrieved from http://www.cdc.gov/hiv/hispanics/index.htm

Chavez, L. (1991). *Out of the barrio: Toward a new politics of Hispanic assimilation*. New York, NY: Peseus Books Group.

Cherlin, A. J. & Furstenberg, F. F. Jr. (1992). *The new American grandparent: A place in the family, a life apart*. Cambridge, MA: Harvard University Press.

Chovan, W. (2005, January/February/March) The value of communicating with dying patients. *The Forum*, 9.

Clark, M. A. (2007). *Santeria: Correcting the myths and uncovering the realities of a growing religion*. Westport, CT: Praeger Publishers.

Clutter, A. D., & Nieto, R. D. (n.d.). *Understanding the Hispanic culture*. Ohio State University Fact Sheet Family and Consumer Science. Retrieved March 1, 2009, from http://ohioline.osu.edu/hyg-fact/5000/5237.html

Comas-Díaz, L., & Greene, B. (1994). *Women of color: Integrating ethnic and gender identities in psychotherapy*. New York, NY: The Guilford Press.

Conoley, C. W., & Conoley, J. C. (2009). *Positive psychology and family therapy: Creative techniques and practical tools for guiding change and enhancing growth*. Hoboken, NJ: John Wiley & Sons.

Corr, C. A., Nabe, C. M. & Corr, D. M. (2008). *Death and dying; Life and living* (6th ed.). Belmont, CA: Wadsworth Cengage Learning.

Cros Sandoval, M. (2006). *Worldview, the orichas, and santeria: Africa to Cuba and beyond*. Gainesville: University Press of Florida.

Cuadrado, M., & Lieberman, L. (2002). *Traditional family values and substance abuse (The Plenum series in culture and health)*. New York, NY: Kluwer Academic and Plenum Publishers.

Cuevas de Caissie, R. M. (2009). *Hispanic cultural values family*. Retrieved from http://www.bellaonline.com/articles/art31982.asp

Cullen, J. (2004). *The American dream: A short history of an idea that shaped a nation*. New York, NY: Oxford University Press.

Cutcliffe, J. R. (2004). *The inspiration of hope in bereavement counseling*. London, UK: Jessica Kingsley Publishers.

Davis, K. G. (2005, July 29). From Gomez to Gomez: Grief and joy in Hispanic ministry. *National Catholic Reporter*.

De la Torre, M. A. (2004). *Santeria: The beliefs and rituals of a growing religion in America*. Grand Rapids, MI: Wm. B. Eerdmans Publishing.

De Vries, B., Blieszner, R., & Blando, J. A. (2002). The many forms of intimacy, the many faces of grief in later life. In K. J. Doka (Ed.), *Living with grief: Loss in later life* (pp. 225–241). Washington, DC: Hospice Foundation of America.

Del Rosario, I. V. (2004). A journey into grief. *Journal of Religion and Health, 43*(1), 19–28.

Descilo, T. (2009). *Client-centered exposure treatment* (p. 6). Workshop Manual. Miami, FL: Victim Services Center.

DeSpelder, L. A., & Strickland, A. L. (2005). *The last dance: Encountering death and dying* (7th ed.). New York, NY: McGraw-Hill.

DeSpelder, L. A., & Strickland, A. L. (2007). Culture, socialization, and death education. In D. Balk (Ed.). *Handbook of thanatology: The essential body of knowledge for the study of death, dying, and bereavement* (pp. 213–226). Northbrook, IL: Association for Death Education and Counseling.

Diaz, R. M. (1998). *Latino gay men and HIV: Culture, sexuality, and risk behavior*. New York, NY: Routledge.

Didion, J. (1987). *Miami*. New York, NY: Simon & Schuster.

Doka, K. J. (Ed.). (2002). *Disenfranchised grief: New directions, challenges, and strategies for practice*. Champaign, IL: Research Press.

Dossey, L. (1993). *Healing words: The power of prayer and the practice of medicine*. New York, NY: HarperCollins Publishers.

Dossey, L. (1996). *Prayer is good medicine: How to reap the healing benefits of prayer*. New York. HarperCollins Publishers.

Duarte-Velez, Y. M., & Bernal, G. (2007). Suicide behavior among Latino and Latina adolescents: Conceptual and methodological issues. *Death Studies, 31*(5), 435–455.

Egan, G. (1994). *The skilled helper* (5th ed.). Belmont, CA: Brooks/Cole Publishing.

Eliot, T. S. (1948). *Notes towards the definition of culture*. London, UK: Faber and Faber Limited.

Elizondo, V. (2007). *Jesus De Galilea/Jesus of Galilee*: Chicago, IL: Loyola Press.

Empereur, J. (2005). Popular piety and the liturgy: Principles and guidelines. In P. C. Phan (Ed.), *The directory on popular piety and the liturgy: Principles and guidelines—A commentary* (pp. 1–18). Collegeville, MA: Liturgical Press.

Enos, R., & Southern, S. (1996). *Correctional case management*. Akron, OH: Anderson Publishing.

Erez, M., & Earley, P. C. (1993). *Culture, self-identity, and work*. New York, NY: Oxford University Press.

Erikson, E. H. (1963). *Childhood and society.* New York, NY: W. W. Norton & Company.

Erikson, E. H. (1968). *Identity, youth and crisis.* New York, NY: W. W. Norton & Company.

Espin, O. (1999). *Women crossing boundaries: A psychology of immigration and transformations of sexuality.* New York, NY: Routledge.

Espin, O. O., & Macy, G. (2006). *Futuring our past: Explorations in the theology of tradition.* Maryknoll, NY: Orbis Books.

Espinosa, G., & Garcia, M. T. (Eds.). (2008). *Mexican American religions: Spirituality.* Durham, NC: Duke University Press.

Fajardo, A. G. (2009, April). Accordions can cry: Music as healing for Latino bereavement. *The Forum, 35*(2), 11–12.

Falicov, C. J. (1998). *Latino families in therapy: A guide to multicultural practice.* New York, NY: The Guilford Press.

Fears, D. (2003, August 25). Latinos or Hispanics? A debate about identity. *Washington Post,* p. A01.

Figueredo, D. H. (2002). *The complete idiot's guide to Latino history and culture.* Indianapolis, IN: Alpha Books.

Flores, M. T., & Carey, G. (2000). *Family therapy with Hispanics.* Boston, MA: Allyn & Bacon.

Flores-Borquez, M. (1995). A journey to regain my identity. *Journal of Refugee Studies, 8*(1), 95–108. doi:10.1093/jrs/8.1.95

Fortaleciendo la Familia Hispana [Approaches to strengthening the Hispanic family]. (2009). The National Council of La Raza. Retrieved January 25, 2010, from www.nclr.org/files/58221_file_Best_Practices_Book_2009_FINAL.pdf

Foster, J. D., Kernis, M. H., & Goldman, B. M. (2007). Linking adult attachment to self-esteem stability. *Self and Identity, 6*(1), 64–73.

Fowler, J. W. (1981). *Stages of faith: The psychology of human development and the quest for meaning.* San Francisco, CA: Harper & Row.

Fox, G. (1997). *Hispanic nation culture, politics, and the constructing of identity.* Tucson, AZ: University of Arizona Press.

Frijda, N. H. (1994). Emotions are functional most of the time. In P. Ekman & R. J. Davidson (Eds.), *The nature of emotion: Fundamental questions.* Series in affective science. New York, NY: Oxford University Press.

Galanti, G.-A. (2008). *Caring for patients from different cultures.* Philadelphia, PA: University of Pennsylvania Press.

Garland, J., & Garland, C. (2001). *Life review in health and social care: A practitioner's guide.* Philadelphia, PA: Brunner-Routledge.

Giddens, S., & Giddens, O. (2003). *Coping with grieving and loss.* New York, NY: Rosen Publishing Group.

Giger, J. N., & Davidhizar, R. E. (2007). *Transcultural nursing: Assessment and intervention.* St. Louis, MO: Mosby.

Gilbert, P. (Ed.). (2005). *Compassion: Conceptualisations, research and use in psychotherapy*. New York, NY: Routledge.

Gloria, A. M. (2001). The cultural construction of Latinas: Practice implications of multiple realities and identities. In D. B. Pope-Davis & H. L. K. Coleman (Eds.), *The intersection of race, class, and gender in multicultural counseling* (pp. 3–24). Thousand Oaks, CA: Sage Publications.

Godfrey, R. V. (2006, January/February/March). Losing a sibling in adulthood. *The Forum, 7*.

Goizueta, R. (2004). The symbolic realism of U.S. Latino/a popular catholicism. *Theological Studies, 65*(2), 255–274.

Gomez, C. (2000). The continual significance of skin color: An exploratory study of Latinos in the Northeast. *Hispanic Journal of Behavioral Sciences, 22*(1), 94–104.

Gonzalez, R. (1996). *Muy macho: Latino men confront their manhood*. New York, NY: Anchor Books.

Gonzalez-Wippler, M. (1989). *Santería: The religion*. New York, NY: Crown Publishers.

Goodstein, L. (2007, April 25). Hispanics reshaping U.S. Catholic Church. *The New York Times*.

Gracia, J. J. E. (2008). *Latinos in America: Philosophy and social identity*. Malden, MA: Blackwell Publishing.

Gracia, J. J. E., & De Greiff, P. (Eds.). (2000). *Hispanics/Latinos in the United States*. New York, NY: Routledge.

Greenberg, L. S., Elliott, R., & Pos, A. (2007). Special topics: Emotion-focused therapy. *European Psychotherapy 2007: Scientific Journal for Psychotherapy Research and Practice, 7*(1), 19–39.

Gutmann, M. C. (1996). *The meanings of Macho: Being a man in Mexico City*. Berkeley: University of California Press.

Hablamos Juntos. *Latinos: The fastest growing consumer market*. Retrieved January 23, 2010, from http://www.hablamosjuntos.org/resourcecenter/pdf/00306272003.pdf

Hadlock, D. C. (2004, October/November/December). Hospice programs: Intensive care with a difference. *The Forum, 30*(4).

Hagan, J. M. (2008). *Migration miracle: Faith, hope, and meaning on the undocumented journey*. Cambridge, MA: Harvard University Press.

Hartley, L. (2004). *Somatic psychology: Body, mind and meaning*. Philadelphia, PA: Whurr Publishing.

Harvey, J. H., & Miller, E. D. (Eds.). (2000). *Loss and trauma: General and close relationship perspectives*. Philadelphia, PA: Brunner-Routledge.

Hays, P. A. (2001). *Addressing cultural complexities in practice: A framework for clinicians and counselors*. Washington, DC: American Psychological Association.

Hernandez, E. I., Peña, M., Davis, K., & Station, E. (2005). *Strengthening Hispanic ministry across denominations: A call to action.* Retrieved from http://faithandleadership.com/programs/spe/resources/ppr/latinoministry.pdf

Hill, C. E., & O'Brien, K. M. (1999). *Helping skills: Facilitating exploration, insight, and action.* Washington, DC: American Psychological Association.

His Holiness the Dalai Lama. (2002). *Advice on dying and living a better life* (J. Hopkins, Trans. & Ed.). New York, NY: Atria Books.

Hodgson, H., & Krahn, L. (2005). *Smiling through your tears: Anticipating grief.* North Charleston, SC: BookSurge Publishing.

Houben, L. M. (2009). *Transform your loss: Your guide to strength and hope.* Sevierville, TN: Insight Publishing.

Howard, G. R. (2006). *We can't teach what we don't know: White teachers, multiracial schools* (2nd ed.). New York, NY: Teachers College Press.

Humphrey, K. M. (2009). *Counseling strategies for loss and grief.* Alexandria, VA: American Counseling Association.

Hwang, P. O. (2000). *Other esteem: Meaningful life in a multicultural society (accelerated development).* Ann Arbor, MI: Sheridan Books.

Hynes, P. (2009). Contemporary compulsory dispersal and the absence of space for the restoration of trust. *Journal of Refugee Studies, 22*(1), 97–12. doi: 10.1093/jrs/fen049

Idler, E. L., Boulifard, D. A., Labouvie, E., Chen, Y. Y., Krause, T. J., & Contrada, R. J. (2009). Looking inside the black box of "Attendance at Services": New measures for exploring an old dimension in religion and health research. *The International Journal for the Psychology for religion, 19*(1), 1–20.

Inter-American Development Bank. (2007). *Survey of Mexican and Central American immigrants in the United States.* Retrieved August 8, 2007, from http://www.iadb.org/news/docs/remitmex.pdf

Jackson, L. A. (1995, January). *Stereotypes, emotions, behavior, and overall attitudes toward Hispanics by Anglos.* Retrieved January 24, 2010, from http://www.jsri.msu.edu/RandS/research/irr/rr10.pdf

James, B. (1994). *Handbook for treatment of attachment—Trauma problems in children.* New York, NY: The Free Press.

Janoff-Bulman, R. (2006). Schema-change perspectives on posttraumatic growth. In L. G. Calhoun & R. G. Tedeschi (Eds.), *Handbook of posttraumatic growth: Research and practice* (pp. 81–99). Mahwah, NJ: Lawrence Erlbaum Associates.

Jonas, S., Goldsteen, R., & Goldsteen, K. (Eds.). (2007). *An introduction to the U.S. health care system* (6th ed.). New York, NY: Springer Publishing.

Jones, E. E. (1985). Psychotherapy and counseling with Black clients. In P. B. Pedersen (Ed.), *Handbook of cross-cultural counseling and therapy* (pp. 173–179). Westport, CT: Greenwood.

Kabat-Zinn, J. (1990). *Full catastrophe living: Using the wisdom of your body and mind to face stress, pain, and illness.* New York, NY: Bantam Dell.

Kamel, H. K., Mouton, C. P., & McKee, D. R. (2002). Culture and loss. In K. J. Doka (Ed.), *Living with grief, loss in later life* (pp. 281–291). Washington, DC: Hospice Foundation of America.

Kardec, A. (1987). *The gospel according to spiritism.* Retrieved from http://www.sgny.org/main/Books/ESE.pdf

Kauffman, R. A. (Compiler). (2008). *Christianity Today, 52* no 2 F p. 70.

Kelly, U. A. (2009). *Migration and education in a multicultural world: Culture, loss, and identity.* New York, NY: Palgrave Macmillan.

Kemp, C., & Rasbridge, L. A. (2004). *Refugee and immigrant health: A handbook for health professionals.* New York, NY: Cambridge University Press.

Kessler, R. (2004). Grief as a gateway to love in teaching. In D. P. Liston & J. W. Garrison (Eds.), *Teaching, learning, and loving: Reclaiming passion in educational practice* (pp. 137–152). New York, NY: Routledge.

Klimo, J., & Heath, P. (2006). *Suicide: What really happens in the afterlife?* Berkeley, CA: North Atlantic Books.

Kochlar, R. (2009, February 12). *Unemployment rose sharply among Latino immigrants in 2008.* Pew Hispanic Center. Retrieved January 30, 2010, from http://pewhispanic.org/reports/report.php?ReportID=102

Koenig, H. G. (2007). *Spirituality in patient care: Why, how, when, and what.* Conshohocken, PA: Templeton Foundation Press.

Koenig, H. G. (2008). *Medicine, religion, and health: Where science and spirituality meet.* Conshohocken, PA: Templeton Foundation Press.

Koenig, H. G., & Cohen, H. J. (Eds.). (2002). *The link between religion and health: Psychoneuroimmunology and the faith factor.* New York, NY: Oxford University Press.

Koenig, H. G., McCullough, M. E., & Larson, D. B. (2001). *Handbook of religion and health.* New York, NY: Oxford University Press.

Korzenny, F. (1999). *Acculturation vs. assimilation among US Hispanics: E-mail self-reports.* Article ID 19991105. http://www.quirks.com/articles/a1999/19991105.aspx?searchID=19454982&sort=5&pg=1

Kumar, S. M. (2005). *Grieving mindfully.* Oakland, CA: New Harbinger Publications.

Lamers, W. J. (2001). Communicating with families during advanced illness. In K. J. Doka (Ed.), *Living with grief loss in later life* (pp. 71–81). Washington, DC: Hospice Foundation of America.

Lavrin, A. (1978). *Latin American women: Historical perspectives.* Westport, CT: Greenwood Press.

Leahy, R. L., & Holland, S. L. (2000). *Treatment plans and interventions for depression and anxiety disorders.* New York, NY: The Guilford Press.

Ledley, D. R., Marx, B. P., & Heimberg, R. G. (2005). *Making cognitive-behavioral therapy work: Clinical process for new practitioners.* New York, NY: The Guilford Press.

Lee, M. G. (2008, July–September). *Religious Education, 103*(4), 456–468.

Lee, M. Y., Ng, S.-M., Leung, P. P. Y., & Chan, C. L. W. (2009). *Integrative body–Mind–Spirit social work: An empirically based approach to assessment and treatment.* New York, NY: Oxford University Press.

Leick, N., & Davidsen-Nielsen, M. (1991). *Healing pain: Attachment, loss and grief therapy.* New York, NY: Routledge.

Leong, F. T. L., & Leach, M. M. (2008). *Suicide among racial and ethnic minority groups theory, research, and practice.* New York, NY: Routledge.

Levine, E. S., & Padilla, A. M. (1980). *Crossing cultures in therapy: Pluralistic counseling for the counseling.* Monterey, CA: Brooks & Cole Publishing.

Lew, A. A. (2005). *A US Commonwealth: Puerto Rico.* Retrieved from http://www.geog.nau.edu/courses/alew/ggr346/ft/overseas/index.html

Liston, D. P., & Garrison, J. W. (2003). *Teaching, learning, and loving: Reclaiming passion in educational practice.* New York, NY: Routledge.

Lochhead, C. (2006, May 21). Give and take across the border-1 in 7 Mexican workers migrates—Most send money home. *San Francisco Chronicle.*

Lopez, S. J., & Snyder, C. R. (2009). *Oxford handbook of positive psychology (Oxford library of psychology).* New York, NY: Oxford University Press.

Lopez-Ibor, J. J., Christodoulou, G., Maj, M., Sartorius, N., & Okasha, A. (Eds.). (2005). *Disasters and mental health.* Chichester, UK: John Wiley and Sons.

Maldonado Jorge, E. (2003). *Crisis, perdidas y consolacion en la familia.* Grand Rapids, MI: Libros Desafio.

Martinez-Houben, L. (2004). *La Virgen Maria y la Mujer Nicaraguense: Historia y Tradicion.* Managua, Nicaragua: Imprimatour.

Martz, E., & Livneh, H. (2007). *Coping with chronic illness and disability.* New York, NY: Springer Publishing.

Massey, D. S., Alarcon, R., Durand, J., & Gonzalez, H. (1987). *Return to Aztlan: The social process of international migration from Western Mexico.* Berkeley and Los Angeles: University of California Press.

Mayo, Y. Q., & Resnick, R. P. (1996). The impact of machismo on Hispanic women. *Affilia, 11*(3), 257–277.

McGoldrick, M., Gerson, R., & Petry, S. (2008). *Genograms: Assessment and intervention* (3rd ed.). New York, NY: W. W. Norton & Company.

McGoldrick, M., Giordano, J., & Garcia-Preto, N. (Eds.). (2005). *Ethnicity and family therapy* (3rd ed.). New York, NY: The Guilford Press.

McKay, M., Davis, M., & Fanning, P. (2007). *Thoughts and feelings: Taking control of your moods and your life.* Oakland, CA: New Harbinger Publications.

McKay, M., Wood, J. C., & Brantley, J. (2007). *The dialectical behavior therapy skills workbook*. Oakland, CA: New Harbinger Publications.

Medina, N. (2009). *Mesizaje: Remapping race, culture and faith in Latina/o Catholisicm*. Maryknoll, NY: Orbis Books.

Menard, V. (2004). *The Latino holiday book* (2nd ed.). New York, NY: Marlowe & Company.

Merluzzi, T. V., & Hedge, K. (2003). Implications of social and cultural influences for multicultural competencies in health psychology. In D. B. Pope-Davis et al. (Eds.), *Handbook of multicultural competencies in counseling & psychology*. Thousand Oaks, CA: Sage Publications.

Miranda, R. & Ratliff, W. (1992). *The civil war in Nicaragua*. Piscataway, NJ: Transaction Publishers.

Mishan, F. (2005). *Designing authenticity into language learning materials*. Bristol, UK: Intellect Books.

Montalban-Anderssen, R. A. (1998). *What is a Hispanic? Legal definition vs. racist definition*. Web of Culture. Retrieved 15, 2009, from http://homepages.wmich.edu/~ppastran/3170/3170what_is_hispanic.pdf

Mooney, J. (n.d.) Health in Latin America. *Women in world history*. Fairfax, VA: The Center for History and New Media (CHNM) at George Mason University. Available at http://chnm.gmu.edu/wwh/modules/lesson15/lesson15.php?s=0

Mujeres Latinas en Accion. *Domestic violence*. Retrieved from http://www.mujereslatinasenaccion.org/

Murphy, P. A., & Price, D. M. (2002). Dying and grieving in the inner city. In K. J. Doka (Ed.). *Living with grief, loss in later life* (pp. 113–120). Washington, DC: Hospice Foundation of America.

Nadeau, J. W. (2002). Family construction of meaning. In N. Thompson (Ed.), *Loss and grief: A guide for human services practitioners* (pp. 95–111). Basingstoke, UK: Palgrave Macmillan.

Neimeyer, R. A. (1998). *Lessons of loss: A guide to coping*. Memphis, TN: Center for the Study of Loss and Transition.

Neimeyer, R. A. (2001). *Meaning reconstruction and the experience of loss*. Washington, DC: American Psychological Association.

New World Encyclopedia. (2008). Social status. Retrieved January 29, 2010, from http://www.newworldencyclopedia.org/entry/Social_status

Noble, J., & Lacasa, J. (1991). *The Hispanic way*. Chicago, IL: Passport Books.

Nunez, L. M. (2006). *Santeria stories*. New York, NY: Spring Publications.

Nuñez-Molina, M. A. (2001). *Community healing among Puerto Ricans: Espiritismo as a therapy for the soul*. Retrieved July 2009 from http://www.uprm.edu/socialsciences/SOULHEAL.pdf

O'Connor, J. (2001). *NLP workbook: A practical guide to achieving the results you want*. London, U.K.: Harper Collins Publishing.

O'Connor, J., & Lages, A. (2004). *Coaching with NLP, how to be a master coach.* London, UK: Harper Collins Publishing.

O'Donohue, W. T., & Fisher, J. E. (Eds.). (2009). *General principles and empirically supported techniques of cognitive behavior therapy.* Hoboken, NJ: John Wiley & Sons.

Oklobdzija, S. (2006). *More Hispanics leaving Catholicism for evangelical Protestantism.* Retrieved from http://www.hispanic5.com/more_hispanics_leaving_catholicism_for_evangelical_protestantism.htm

Padilla, A. M., & Salgado De Snyder, N. (1985). Counseling Hispanics: Strategies for effective intervention. In P. B. Pedersen (Ed.), *Handbook of cross-cultural counseling and therapy* (pp. 157–171). Westport, CT: Greenwood.

Pantoja, S. (2005). *Religion and education among Latinos in New York City.* Leiden, Boston: Brill (online version, retracted from University of Miami on September 14, 2009).

Pargament, K. L. (1997). *The psychology of religion and coping. Theory, research, practice.* New York, NY: The Guilford Press.

Passel, J. A., & Cohn, D. (2009). *A portrait of unauthorized immigrants in the United States.* Retrieved from http://pewhispanic.org/reports/report.php?ReportID=107

Peterson, C., & Seligman, M. (2004). *Character strengths and virtues: A handbook and classification.* New York, NY: Oxford University Press.

Pew Forum on Religion & Public Life. (2007). *Changing faiths: Latinos and the transformation of American religion.* Retrieved from http://pewforum.org/Changing-Faiths-Latinos-and-the-Transformation-of-American-Religion.aspx

Pineda-Madrid, N. (2006). The formation of community, the transmission of faith. In O. O. Espin & G. Macy (Eds.), *Futuring our past: Explorations in the theology of tradition* (pp. 204–226). Maryknoll, NY: Orbis Books.

Poole, S. (1995). *Our Lady of Guadalupe: The origins and sources of a Mexican national symbol* (pp. 1531–1797). Tucson, AZ: The University of Arizona Press.

Pope-Davis, D. B., Coleman, H. L. K., William, M. L., & Toporek, R. (2003). *Handbook of multicultural competencies in counseling and psychology.* Thousand Oaks, CA: Sage Publications.

Rallying Points. (2002). *Improving community end-of-life care through coalitions.* Diversity Notes.

Ramsey, J. L., & Blieszner, R. (2000). Community, affect, and family relations: A cross-cultural study of spiritual resiliency in eight old Women. *Journal of Religious Gerontology, 11(1),* 39–64.

Rando, T. (Ed.). (2000). *Clinical dimensions of anticipatory mourning: Theory and practice in working with the dying, their loved ones, and their caregivers.* Champaign, IL: Research Press.

Ridley, C. R. (2005). *Overcoming unintentional racism in counseling and therapy: A practitioner's guide to intentional intervention* (2nd ed.). Thousand Oaks, CA: Sage Publications.

Rivera, F. (2007). Contextualizing the experience of young Latino adults: Acculturation, social support and depression. *Journal of Immigrant Minority Health, 9*(3), 237–244.

Rizzetto, D. E. (2005). *Waking up to what you do.* Boston, MA: Shambhala Publications.

Rodriguez, J. (1994). *Our Lady of Guadalupe: Faith and empowerment among Mexican-American women.* Austin, TX: University of Texas Press.

Rogers, T. G., & de Souza, M. B. (2003). Preaching cross-culturally to Spanish-speaking U.S. Hispanic Americans. *Homiletic, 28*(1), 1–10.

Rosenblatt, P. C. (2007). Culture, socialization, and loss, grief, and mourning. In D. Balk (Ed.), *Handbook of thanatology: The essential body of knowledge for the study of death, dying, and bereavement* (pp. 115–120). Northbrook, IL: Association for Death Education and Counseling.

Rosenblatt, P. C. (2009). *Shared obliviousness in family systems.* Albany, NY: State University of New York Press.

Rosner, R., & Powell, S. (2006). Posttraumatic growth after war. In L. G. Calhoun & R. G. Tedeschi (Eds.), *Handbook of posttraumatic growth* (pp. 197–213). Mahwah, NJ: Lawrence Erlbaum Associates.

Sagula, D., & Rice, K. G. (2004). The effectiveness of mindfulness training on the grieving process and emotional well-being of chronic pain patients. *Journal of Clinical Psychology in Medical Settings, 11*(4), 333–342.

Sam, D. L., & Berry, J. W. (2006). *The Cambridge handbook of acculturation psychology.* New York, NY: Cambridge University Press.

Sandoval, M. (2006). *On the move: A history of the Hispanic church in the United States.* Maryknoll, NY: Orbis Books.

Santiago-Rivera, A. L., Arrendondo, P., & Gallardo-Cooper, M. (2002). *Counseling Latinos and La Familia (Multicultural aspects of counseling and psychotherapy).* Thousand Oaks, CA: Sage Publications.

Saunders, D. C. (2002). The philosophy of hospice. In N. Thompson (Ed.), *Loss and grief: A guide for human services practitioners* (pp. 23–33). Basingstoke, Hampshire: Palgrave Macmillan.

Schaefer, J. A., & Moos, R. H. (2001). Bereavement experiences and personal growth. In M. S. Stroebe, W. Stroebe, R. O. Hansson, & H. Schut (Eds.), *Handbook of bereavement research: Consequences, coping, and care* (pp. 145–167). Washington, DC: American Psychological Association.

Scheper-Hughes, N. (1993). *Death without weeping: The violence of everyday life in Brazil.* Berkley, CA: University of California Press.

Schupp, L. (2007). *Grief: Normal, complicated, traumatic.* Eau Claire, WI: Pesi Healthcare.

Schutte, O. (2000). Negotiating Latina identities. In J. J. E. Gracia & P. De Greiff (Eds.), *Hispanics/Latinos in the United States: Ethnicity, race and rights*. New York, NY: Routledge.

Schwarzbaum, S., & Thomas, A. J. (2008). *Dimensions of multicultural counseling: A life story approach*. Los Angeles, CA: Sage Publications.

Shaver, P. R., & Tancredy, C. R. (2001). Emotion, attachment, and conceptual commentary. In M. S. Stroebe, W. Stroebe, R. O. Hansson, & H. Schut (Eds.), *Handbook of bereavement research: Consequences, coping, and care* (pp. 63–88). Washington, DC: American Psychological Association.

Sheldrake, P. (2001). *Spaces for the sacred: Place, memory, and identity*. Baltimore, MD: The Johns Hopkins University Press.

Shorris, E. (1992). *Latinos: A biography of the people*. New York, NY: W. W. Norton & Company.

Sims, A. (2007). The spiritual dimension in psychiatry. *Journal of Pakistan Psychiatrist Society, 4*(2).

Smith, D. C. (2006, April/May/June). Spiritual assessments: Keep them simple, but not too simple. *The Forum, 32*(2).

Smith, R. L., & Montilla, E. R. (Eds.). (2006). *Counseling and family therapy with Latino populations: Strategies that work (family therapy and counseling)*. New York, NY: Routledge.

Smith, T. B. (Ed.). (2004). *Practicing multiculturalism: Affirming diversity in counseling and psychology*. Boston, MA: Pearson.

Sosa, J. J. (1999). *Sectas, cultos y sincretismos*. Miami, FL: Ediciones Universal.

Spradlin, S. E. (2003). *Don't let your emotion run your life: How dialectical behavior therapy can put you in control*. Oakland, CA: New Harbinger Publications.

Sproul, R. C. (2009) Selective compassion: Social stigmatization and complicated parental grieving. *The Forum, 35*, 1.

Stalker, P. (2001). *The no-nonsense guide to international migration*. Oxford, UK: New Internationalist Publications.

Stavans, I. (Ed.). (2005). *Encyclopedia Latina: History, culture, and society in the United States* (Vol. 3). Danbury, CT: Grolier Academic Reference.

Stavans, I. (Ed.). (2007). *Collins Q&A, the ultimate question and answer book: Latino history and culture*. New York, NY: HarperCollins Publishers.

Stroebe, M. S., Stroebe, W., & Hansson, R. O. (Eds.). (1993). *Handbook of bereavement: Theory, research, and intervention*. Cambridge, UK: Cambridge University Press.

Stroebe, M. S., Stroebe, W., & Hansson, R. O. (Eds.). (2001). *Handbook of bereavement research: Consequences, coping, and care*. Washington DC: American Psychological Association.

Strong, S. R. (1969). Counseling: An interpersonal influence process. *Journal of Counseling Psychology, 15*, 31–35.

Suárez-Orozco, M. M., & Paez, M. M. (Eds.). (2002). *Latinos remaking America.* Berkeley, CA: University of California Press.

Sue, D. W., & Sue, D. (2003). *Counseling the culturally diverse: Theory and practice.* New York, NY: John Wiley & Sons.

Sullivan, T. A. (2002). A demographic portrait. In P. S. J. Cafferty & D. W. Engstrom (Eds.), *Hispanics in the United States: An agenda for the twenty-first century* (pp. 1–29). New Brunswick, NJ: Transaction Publishers.

Sulmasy, D. P. (2002). A biopsychosocial-spiritual model of the care of patients at the end of life. *The Gerontologist, 42*(Special Issue III), 24–33 (quoted in VonDras and White).

Thomas, R. M. (2000). *Multicultural counseling and human development theories: 25 theoretical perspectives.* Springfield, IL: C. C. Thomas.

Thornton, G., & Zanich, M. L. (2002). Empirical assessment of disenfranchised grief: 1989–2000. In K. J. Doka (Ed.), *Disenfranchised grief: New directions, challenges, and strategies for practice* (pp. 79–89). Champaign, IL: Research Press.

Torero, A. (1983). *La familia Linguistica Quechua, America Latina en Sus Lenguas Indígenas,* Caracas: Monte Avila.

Torres Rivera, E. (2005). Espiritismo: The flywheel of the Puerto Rican spiritual tradition. *Revista Interamericana de Psicologia/Interamerican Journal of Psychology, 39*(2), 295–300.

Trotter, R. T., & Chavira, J. A. (1997). *Curanderismo, Mexican American folk healing* (2nd ed.). Athens, GA: University Georgia Press.

Trusty, J., Looby, E. J., & Sandhu, D. S. (2002). Multicultural counseling: Context, theory and practice, and competence. Huntington, NY: Nova Science Publishers.

Tweed, T. A. (1997). *Our lady of the exile: Diasporic religion at a Cuban catholic shrine in Miami.* New York, NY: Oxford University Press.

U.S. Census Bureau. (2006). *Hispanic or Latino origin by specific origin.* American Community Service Survey. Retrieved February 20, 2009, from http://factfinder.census.gov/servlet/DTTable?_bm=y&-geo_id=01000US&-ds_name=ACS_2006_EST_G00_&-redoLog=false&mt_name=ACS_2006_EST_G2000_B03001

U.S. Census Bureau. (2007). Hispanic or Latino. Origin by race. American Community Survey. Retrieved from: http://factfinder.census.gov/servlet/DTTable?_bm=y&-ds_name=ACS_2007_1YR_G00_&- CONTEXT=dt&-mt_name=ACS_2007_1YR_G2000_B03002&-redoLog=true&-geo_id=01000US&-format=&-_lang=en&-SubjectID=15233308

U.S. Census Bureau. (2009). *Census bureau estimates nearly half of children under age 5 are minorities.* Retrieved from http://www.census.gov/newsroom/releases/archives/population/cb09–75.html

Updegraff, J. A., & Taylor, S. E. (2000). From vulnerability to growth: Positive and negative effects of stressful life events. In J. H. Harvey & E. D. Miller

(Eds.), *Loss and trauma: General and close relationship perspective* (pp. 3–21). Philadelphia, PA: Brunner-Routledge.

Van Heck, G. L., & De Ridder, D. T. (2001). Assessment of coping with loss: Dimensions and measurement. In M. S. Stroebe, W. Stroebe, R. O. Hansson, & H. Schut (Eds.), *Handbook of bereavement research: Consequences, coping, and care* (pp. 449–469). Washington, DC: American Psychological Association.

Van Hook, J., & Bean, F. D. (1999). The growth in noncitizen SSI caseloads 1979–1996: Aging versus new immigrant effects. *Journals of Gerontology-Series B: Psychological Sciences and Social Sciences, 54*(1), s16–s23.

Vázquez, R. L. (2004). *Hispanic or Latino?* Retrieved January 25, 2009, from http://www.lasculturas.com/aa/aa070501a.htm

Von Dras, D. D., & White, J. L. (2006, April/May/June). Spirituality has many different characterizations, of which each person has his or her own unique understanding. *The Forum, 32*(2), 1, 3–4.

Wainrib, B. R., & Bloch, E. L. (1998). Crisis intervention and trauma response: Theory and practice. New York, NY: Springer Publishing.

Waldinger, R. (2007). *Between Here and There: How Attached are Latino Immigrants to their Native Country?* Pew Hispanic Center. Retrieved from http://pewhispanic.org/reports/report.php?ReportID=80

Walter, C. A., & McCoyd, J. L. M. (2009). *Grief and loss across the lifespan: A biopsychosocial perspective*. New York, NY: Springer Publishing Company.

Weigel, G. (2001). *The truth of Catholicism: Ten controversies explored*. New York, NY: HarperCollins Publishers.

Welland, C., & Ribner, N. (2008). *Healing from violence. Latino men's journey to a new masculinity*. New York, NY: Springer Publishing.

Whittington, H. (2009, October). Living in the body: Using awareness of physical sensation to cope with loss. *The Forum, 50.*

Wingett, Y. (2006). Funeral homes tailoring services to Hispanics. *The Arizona Republic*. Retrieved July 15, 2009, from http://www.tucsoncitizen.com/ss/business_edge/30943

Wood, E.J. (2003). *Insurgent collective action and civil war in El Salvador*. Cambridge, UK: Cambridge University Press.

Worden, J. W. (2002). *Grief counseling and grief therapy* (3rd ed.). New York, NY: Springer Publishing.

Worden, J. W. (2008). *Grief counseling and grief therapy* (4th ed.). New York, NY: Springer Publishing.

Wunnenberg, K. (2000). *Grieving the loss of a loved one*. Grand Rapids, MI: Zondervan.

Zimmerman, T. S. (2001). *Integrating gender and culture in family therapy training*. Binghamton, NY: Routledge.

Index